Yesterday's News

Yesterday's News

The future of long-form journalism and archives

Marco Braghieri

Peter Lang

Oxford · Bern · Berlin · Bruxelles · New York · Wien

Bibliographic information published by Die Deutsche Nationalbibliothek
Die Deutsche Nationalbibliothek lists this publication in the Deutsche
Nationalbibliografie; detailed bibliographic data is available on the Internet at http://
dnb.d-nb.de.

A catalogue record for this book is available from the British Library.

Library of Congress Cataloging-in-Publication Data
Names: Braghieri, Marco, 1982- author.
Title: Yesterday's news : the future of long-form journalism and archives /
   Marco Braghieri.
Description: Oxford ; New York : Peter Lang, 2021. | Includes
   bibliographical references and index.
Identifiers: LCCN 2020035014 (print) | LCCN 2020035015 (ebook) | ISBN
   9781789979411 (paperback) | ISBN 9781789979428 (ebook) | ISBN
   9781789979435 (epub) | ISBN 9781789979442 (mobi)
Subjects: LCSH: Journalism--History--21st century. | Online journalism. |
   Archives--Administration--Data processing. | Information networks.
Classification: LCC PN4815.2 .B73 2021 (print) | LCC PN4815.2 (ebook) |
   DDC 070.4--dc23
LC record available at https://lccn.loc.gov/2020035014
LC ebook record available at https://lccn.loc.gov/2020035015

Cover design by Brian Melville for Peter Lang
Cover image: Courtesy of Associazione Archivio Storico Olivetti, Ivrea, Italy.

ISBN   978-1-78997-941-1 (print) • ISBN   978-1-78997-942-8 (ePDF)
ISBN   978-1-78997-943-5 (ePub) • ISBN   978-1-78997-944-2 (mobi)

© Peter Lang Group AG 2021
Published by Peter Lang Ltd, International Academic Publishers,
52 St Giles, Oxford, OX1 3LU, United Kingdom
oxford@peterlang.com, www.peterlang.com

'What haunts the digital cul-de-sacs of the twenty-first century is not so much the past as all the lost futures that the twentieth century taught us to anticipate'

(Fisher, 2012)

Table of Contents

Figures

Tables

Preface

This book is essentially about how journalism combines with the digital. As a student, journalist, editor and researcher, journalism has been a constant presence in many of my recent years. I have tried to remember and use all the different perspectives that I experienced to create *Yesterday's News*. However, this book does not begin by talking about journalism, rather by focusing on what currently defines and surrounds contemporary experience: the digital. Reflecting on and attempting to assess the landscape which has so profoundly changed journalism appeared to be an obligatory starting point. By describing long-form journalism and archives, their relation and development, this book tries to assess and explore the possibilities around the past, present and future narratives. By combining different methods, it suggests that a multidisciplinary approach is best suited to assess the nature of these two entities. Finally, it suggests a possible avenue for long-form journalism and archives, connected to digitisation, datafication and curation.

Acknowledgements

I would like to thank Tobias Blanke, without whom this book would not exist. I feel profoundly grateful and lucky to have met him and to have had the chance to work with him. He has not only led me through this work but has also been a constant reference at each and every turn. I owe my gratitude to Mark Coté, for all the confidence and support he has always expressed towards me. His help has come across in many ways and countless times over the years. I would like to thank Joe Sexton and Andy Rossback for agreeing to be interviewed and allowing me to use their words in this work.

There are many other individuals who have helped me to conceive, start and finish this book. I am indebted to every one of them.

List of Abbreviations

AMP	Accelerated Mobile Pages
API	Application Programming Interface
CAR	Computer-Assisted Reporting
CDN	Content Distribution Network
CMS	Content Management System
CSV	Comma-Separated Values
GB	Gigabyte
INI	initialization file format
JSON	JavaScript Object Notation
OCR	Optical Character Recognition
PDF	Portable Document Format
PNG	Portable Network Graphics
SaaS	Software as a Service
TIFF	Tagged Image File Format
URI	Universal Resource Identifier
URL	Uniform Resource Locators
XML	eXtensible Markup Language

Introduction

Long-form journalism and archives, the two entities that this book focuses on, sit at the intersection between journalistic production and the digital. Through a number of different methods, this book aims not only to establish a connection between these two entities but also to assess and describe how and why their nature is directly connected with the digital. This book starts with focusing on the digital itself, which we define as the 'digital landscape'. By investigating the nature of the digital landscape and its main actors – which we identify in individuals, crowds and platforms – this book builds an ad hoc framework to assess and examine long-form journalism and archives. Finally, we look at the possible future interactions of long-form journalism and archives with the digital landscape, identifying an ongoing process of digitisation, datafication and curation which potentially opens up future avenues for these two entities.

This book is framed within the digital humanities, conceived as 'an array of convergent practices that explore a universe in which print is no longer the primary medium in which knowledge is produced and disseminated' (Burdick et al., 2012: 122). Liu describes digital humanities as a method consisting 'in repeatedly coadjusting human concepts and machine technologies until [...] the two stabilize each other in temporary postures of truth that neither by itself could sustain' (Liu, 2013: 419). In order to assess the entities at the centre of this book, following the multidisciplinary nature of digital humanities (Burdick et al., 2012), numerous methods have been employed. Methods used in this book include text analysis (Philo, 2007) as part of critical discourse analysis (Fairclough, 2001), case-study (Feagin, Orum and Sjoberg, 1991), digital methods (Rogers, 2013), data profiling (Olson, 2003) and data cleaning (Verborgh and De Wilde, 2013) and semi-structured interviews (Galletta, 2013).

The main reason for this book to begin with the assessment of the digital is not only its direct and indirect influence over the entities at the centre of this book but also its pervasive nature which directly organises and modifies each individual's experience and thus also the creation and fruition of long-form journalism and archives. We define the digital land-scape as sets of interaction ecosystems, which comprise three entities: individuals, crowds and platforms, which interact in an apparently frictionless manner. The digital landscape is defined by two main features, its nature as constant flux and a disruption enhancer.

Within the relationship between the main actors in the contemporary digital landscape, we focus on the role of technological mediators, such as the ubiquitous nature of networks and devices (Lanier, 2011). The rise of entities such as crowds and platforms has altered the nature of the World Wide Web, originally intended as a non-hierarchical system (Berners-Lee, 2010) (Blanke, 2014). In the contemporary digital landscape, individuals cluster together crowds to interact with platforms. This interaction is characterised by two main features, which are the pervasiveness of for-profit clouds and the absence of friction between crowds and clouds. Individuals gathered in crowds tend to act within platforms as a flock of birds (Reynolds, 1987), clustering with their peers, hardly interacting with other clusters of individuals and keeping up with their peers mainly through the development of filters (Pariser, 2012).

This interaction eventually becomes a source of data and as platforms allow crowds to connect and perform tasks, enforcing a narrative based on the notion of flux. As crowds and clouds are bound together in order to exist, due to their collaborative nature (Blanke, 2014), within this narrative they can thrive if flux within the contemporary digital landscape is promoted and idealised. Within this frame, obstacles such as consent and regulation are opposed as sources of friction, which would be harmful to the flux and thus for the existence of platforms and, subsequently, for the existence of individuals clustered in crowds.

In the contemporary digital landscape, a further distinctive feature aside from flux is non-creative destruction. This feature derives from a classical economic theory based on creative destruction as a distinguishing feature of capitalism, resulting in its reinvention from within (Schumpeter, 2010). However, creative destruction has gained unprecedented traction due to the nature of distribution within the contemporary digital landscape

(Brynjolfsson and McAfee, 2014). Thus, due to the systemic strength of platforms rather promoting continuous growth of competitors, it has promoted monopolies (Lanier, 2011), thus leading to a form of what we have defined as non-creative destruction.

The concept of the contemporary digital landscape, its main actors and features are then used to frame the evolution of news production and, more specifically assess the nature of long-form journalism and archives. In the last decades, the news media industry – along with other sectors – has faced a process of deindustrialisation (Rowthorn, 1997), among a consistent decrease in circulation numbers and advertising revenues. The conception of advertising as the main revenue source for news media outlets (McLuhan, 1994), has led the news media industry to adopt strategies within the digital landscape aimed at increasing the number of readers (Bruns and Highfield, 2012). This aspect has proven to be especially relevant as the intermediary role between advertisers and the public, which was once performed mainly by the news media industry, in the contemporary digital landscape is performed more efficiently by platforms. Thus, distribution strategies aimed solely at increasing volume and the insurgence of new, more efficient intermediaries have determined a cycle of non-creative destruction.

Platforms such as Google, Apple and Facebook, which all have their own specificities, have all developed intermediation activities which have proven detrimental to the news media industry. These intermediation activities are based on the premises that, within the digital landscape, news media outlets are bound to fraction their production into single items and leave distribution to third-party entities, abdicating control over their content and its revenue streams. This process has to be framed within the nature of the digital landscape as dominated by for-profit platforms which are able to organise offer regardless of shelf space, thus proving more effective in meeting a demand that has spread to niche markets along what has been described as the long-tail model (Anderson, 2009b). Thus, within the news media field, the role of the intermediary has been interpreted by platforms rather than by news media outlets.

We identify the digital landscape as a digital public sphere (Gripsrud and Moe, 2010). However, the digital public sphere faces a number of challenges, deriving from the commodification and acceleration of the news cycle (Klinenberg, 2005). The latter has impacted production, as news media outlets are driven to produce increasing quantities of content, and consumption, shortening the lifespan of content. The acceleration of the news cycle has also affected past news media outlets production, highlighting its frailty in the digital landscape (McCain, 2015). Such frailty has impacted news media outlets digital archives and long-form journalism, as the content published on the World Wide Web has proven to be prone to deterioration (Lafrance, 2015). We understand the archive as 'everything currently existing in digital format anywhere' (Manoff, 2004: 10), feeding into the 'archive drive' (Mackenzie, 1997) which with 'real-time processing' informs the contemporary digital landscape.

We then shift our focus onto long-form journalism, having established a broad framework for the digital landscape and explored how the news media industry has failed to adapt to it. In order to formulate a definition for long-form journalism, we identify several features, such as its nature as an in-depth narrative and the development of elements based specifically on the possibilities provided by the digital landscape. Thus, we define long-form journalism as built with the participation of many different professionals aside from the sole journalist, uniting text, audio and visual content together with data visualisation tools and specifically built datasets. However, these elements can be combined differently, without any being compulsory. Long-form journalism is likewise defined by its capacity to attract reader time rather than the number of words.

After providing a possible definition for long-form journalism in the digital landscape, we assess the existence of common ground between long-form journalism and archives. The digital landscape has been identified as an impact factor on both long-form journalism production and preservation, as increasingly they are based on networked elements. Along with this factor, curation and distribution were defined as a possible common ground between long-form journalism and news media outlets digital archives. Moreover, within the frame of an accelerated news cycle, long-form journalism and archives are based on a more comprehensive production and consumption time frame. Thus, this different time frame can be identified as a common feature between these two entities, separating them from the broader news production.

We then proceed to focus on two separate long-form journalism stories. The first has been considered as a landmark production in this field (Dowling and Vogan, 2015), such as 'Snow Fall' by *The New York Times* (Branch, 2012). The second is a collaborative effort by two non-profit news organisations, 'An Unbelievable Story of Rape' by *ProPublica* and *The Marshall Project* (Miller and Armstrong, 2015), which has been adapted into a series on Netflix in 2019, highlighting a possible future route for the re-use of long-form journalism.

Coherently with our framing of the digital landscape, we develop a multi-method analysis of long-form journalism which we applied to both long-form journalism stories we aimed to assess. This multi-method analysis combines text analysis as part of a critical discourse analysis (Fairclough, 2001), followed by the assessment of the reception of each long-form journalism story (Philo, 2007), which was performed applying digital methods (Rogers, 2013). Moreover – in one of the two case-studies – we performed two semi-structured interviews (Galletta, 2013). with professionals involved in the creation of these two long-form journalism stories. This multi-method analysis proves to be an effective toolset to assess the different aspects of long-form journalism production in the digital landscape and provides a model for future analysis of this type of entity. By combing different methods, we aim to assess the multifaceted aspects that positioning long-form journalism within the digital lands we are able to assess the dev cape implies. This approach, which combines different methods, is meant to indicate a possible combination that aims to assess at multiple levels the complexities of digital affordances such as long-form journalism stories and archives.

We can assess the development of long-form journalism as a manner of establishing news media outlets within the digital landscape, thus creating environments which are attractive for advertisers (Franck, 2016). Thus, it is possible to establish a parallel between the nature of long-form journalism and what American writer David Foster Wallace described as the role of entertainment in his novel *Infinite Jest*. Foster Wallace stressed that in his work 'entertainment's chief job is to make you so riveted by it that you can't tear your eyes away, so the advertisers can advertise' (Lipsky, 2010: 79).

While the two case studies in exam exemplify the use of different structures and digital tools, both adopt narrative techniques with a significant tradition among text production, such as the use of in medias res leads followed by digressions, which is typical of classical epic structures (Genette, 1980). Both case studies highlight the use of different perspectives in the narration, which is one of the features of New Journalism (Murphy, 1974), enhanced by the implementation of tools in the digital landscape (Berning, 2011). Thus, it is possible to assume that long-form journalism in the digital landscape, while making extensive use of digital possibilities, considers past narrative forms as a reference for techniques developed to captivate readers. Such techniques are then adapted to the digital landscape, which provides new manners in which they can be enforced, thus enhancing their captivating force. Overall, while our case study analysis has highlighted connections and differences between long-form journalism in the digital landscape and prior narrative forms, both examples can be envisioned as a manner in which news media outlets establish their position, thus justifying the intense workload required to create this specific narrative form (Dowling and Vogan, 2015).

We then shift our focus to archives. In order to assess their role, we established a framework of the notion of time within the contemporary digital landscape. Thus, we referred to Mark Fisher's definition of 'continuous present' (Fisher, 2009: 58) to describe the progressive dissolution of the past and the future within the contemporary digital landscape. We used this conception of the present to identify a practice within the contemporary digital landscape, which we define as 'feed fruition', a specific practice where individuals browse autonomously updated and personalised lists. We identify 'feed fruition' as a constitutive element of platforms such as social networks, connecting it with the rise of ubiquitous technologies such as mobile devices and applications.

The relationship between 'feed fruition' and archiving practices was established by envisioning the digital landscape as a product of two dynamics, 'real-time processing' and 'the archive drive' (Mackenzie, 1997: 60).

Within the contemporary digital landscape, we assess how platforms rather than individuals define archiving practices and possibilities. Having established this general framework of 'feed fruition' and platform control over archiving practices, we focus on news media outlets digital archives. We identified three major types of digital news archives, such as digital archives originated only from the digitisation of hard-copy archives, digital archives originated by the collation of hard-copy archives and digital production, and digital archives generated by news media outlets which operate only in digital format.

The first type of news media outlets digital archive we identified originates from the digitisation of traditional hard-copy archives, often recurring to OCR technology. However, we also underlined how OCR technology has limitations, specifically regarding the precision of its digital conversion and the loss of the visual dimension of the source (Bingham, 2010; Mussell, 2012). This issue is shared by the second type of news media outlets digital archives we identified, which are archives deriving from news media outlets that have produced content both in hard-copy and digital format. We also underline the challenges brought by harmonising archived content between digital and hard-copy sources as computers started to be used within newsrooms. Thus, we established the central role of Content Management Systems as a gateway in production but also archival practices. We then focus on digital archives originated by news media outlets which operate only in digital format, underlining how this type of digital news archives is influenced by the frailty of content produced within the digital landscape.

Thus, in the following part of this work, we focus on the common features of long-form journalism and archives. Our findings indicate that long-form journalism and archives in the contemporary digital landscape share three main features such as their relevance over time, their nature as unstructured content which has been digitised but not yet datafied and, finally, possible aggregation and curation practices.

Regarding relevance over time, we establish that long-form journalism is capable of attracting interest for a more extended period if compared to standard news items (Smith, Connor and Stanton, 2015). News media outlets are inclined to publish older long-form journalism content, indicating not only that it is perceived as valuable but that it is sourced – regardless of its publishing date – from digital archives, thus establishing a further point of contact between long-form journalism and archives in the contemporary digital landscape.

Regarding their nature of unstructured content which has been digitised but not yet datafied, both long-form journalism and news media outlet archives originally comprise content which can be defined as unstructured and, as such, it constitutes an underused resource. While digitisation has been performed extensively on news media outlet archives, datafication (Mayer-Schönberger and Cukier, 2013) is yet to be fully undertaken. Regarding long-form journalism and archives, this process implies the transformation of content which is originally unstructured into a structured format, thus opening possibilities for its value extraction. While long-form journalism and archives have been digitised but not yet datafied, a number of tools based on datafication processes have been developed, such as person-centric mining (Coll Ardanuy et al., 2016) or geospatial organisation of content (Yzaguirre et al., 2016), thus establishing long-form journalism and archives as entities at the centre of possible future datafication processes.

Curation and distribution practices are the final common element between long-form journalism and archives. Within the contemporary digital landscape, this process is generally undertaken by platforms, as in the long-tail model envisioned by Anderson (2009b). Platforms act as aggregators which tend to perform an intermediary activity more efficiently if compared to traditional market operators. In the field of long-form journalism and archive curation and aggregation, we focused on a single intermediary service as case-study, named Longform.org. We provide a quantitative analysis of a full year of Longform.org's activity through data obtained using digital methods (Rogers, 2013), data profiling (Olson, 2003) and data cleaning (Verborgh and De Wilde, 2013) demonstrating that this aggregator, while tending to privilege more recent long-form journalism stories, also performs a selection on a very wide time frame. While legacy news media outlets play a significant role in news media outlet selection, Longform.org achieves a great variety focusing primarily on sourcing smaller, digital-only news media outlets.

While this work is based on a multi-method approach to assess the nature of long-form journalism and archives, it both draws upon and contributes to literature from a range of fields, the main being platform studies and digital journalism. While platform studies contribute to the assessment of the digital landscape and its main actors, digital journalism is the broader area in which our analysis of long-form journalism is positioned.

However, platform studies have proven to be essential not only in our assessment of the digital landscape per se but also in assessing how news production, distribution and consumption are structured within the digital landscape. Thus, platform studies provide a fundamental contribution to the understanding of how media is deeply connected and conditioned by the platform-driven nature of the digital landscape. we assessed how digital journalism production constitutes a relevant example of a platform-informed practice in itself, thus providing further insight into platform studies as a field of exploration within the contemporary digital landscape.

This book aims to establish common traits between long-form journalism and archives within the analysis of the digital landscape, envisioned as an environment in which individuals, crowds and platforms interact. By applying this framework to these two forms of media production, we were able to assess long-form journalism and archives as entities influenced by specific practices within the digital landscape, such as digitisation, datafication and curation. Thus, this book approaches long-form journalism and archives as entities open to new forms of aggregation and curation, which are based on the outcomes of an ongoing datafication process. By envisioning long-form journalism and archives as entities at the centre of datafication, our work establishes a specific perspective on the possible outcomes of this process. Moreover, it outlines the possible development of user-oriented tools, aimed at providing a diverse way of fruition of these forms of media production. Within this frame, both long-form journalism and archives are envisioned as sources of a diverse form of fruition of the information they contain, not only in their present form but also if envisioned as data-rich entities, which can be recombined developing new narrative forms. Hence, by imagining these artefacts as possible objects of a datafication-based recombination process, the approach envisioned in this work can also be applied to other forms of cultural production, opening new perspectives on aggregation, curation and recombination practices within the digital landscape.

PART I

The Digital Landscape and Journalism

CHAPTER I

The Digital Landscape

Defining the Digital Landscape

The Digital Landscape and Its Main Actors: Individuals, Crowds and Platforms

Long-form journalism and archives are positioned at the intersection of individuals, crowds and platforms, identified as the main actors within the contemporary, which we describe as a 'digital landscape'. We chose long-form journalism and archives as they represent, at the same time, the embodiment and the opposite of leading digital news production. Long-form journalism and archives incarnate digital production as their current practices are influenced and defined by the main features of the digital landscape. However, long-form journalism and archives, due to their nature as in-depth, time-consuming entities, are at the same time in conflict with the ephemeral nature of content production and the overwhelming role of the present within the contemporary digital landscape.

This work begins by depicting the digital landscape and its main actors – individuals, crowds and platforms – in order to build a framework where platform practices and platform studies become the source of insight into the production, distribution and consumption dynamics of digital journalism and, more specifically, long-form journalism. Long-form journalism and archives are envisioned as artefacts and practices influenced by the environment in which they are created, distributed and consumed. To analyse and assess long-form journalism and archives, we shall begin by providing a definition for the 'digital landscape'. We define the digital landscape as sets of interaction ecosystems, which comprise three entities: individuals, crowds and platforms, which interact in an apparently frictionless manner. The digital landscape is defined by two main features, its nature as constant flux and a disruption enhancer.

This framework will be established using a critical discourse analysis method. As defined by Norman Fairclough 'critical discourse analysis' is based on the premises that language has to be conceived as 'as discourse and as social practice' and should not be limited to text analysis or 'analysing the processes of production and interpretation'. Critical discourse analysis should extend to 'analysing the relationship between texts, processes and their social conditions, both the immediate conditions of the situational context and the more remote conditions of institutional and social structures' (Fairclough, 2001: 21).

To start providing a framework of the contemporary digital landscape, we shall begin from *Neuromancer*, a science fiction novel published in 1984 by William Gibson. In his novel, Gibson first used the term 'cyberspace' describing it as

> A consensual hallucination experienced daily by billions of legitimate operators, in every nation, by children being taught mathematical concepts ... A graphic representation of data abstracted from the banks of every computer in the human system. Unthinkable complexity. Lines of light ranged in the nonspace of the mind, clusters and constellations of data. Like city lights, receding ... (2000: 51)

The author's image of 'cyberspace' is useful to begin assessing the evolution that has taken place in the digital experience. While it is relevant to underline that *Neuromancer* is a work of fiction, Gibson's 'cyberspace' can be considered a 'proti arche' of the contemporary digital landscape. A 'proti arche' is a term first used in Pre-Socratic Greek philosophers such as Thales, Anaximander and Anaximenes and can be defined as 'a single, fundamental substratum, which also would be the primary source from which the universe originated' (Vamvacas, 2009: 24). Moreover, Vamvacas underlines that the 'proti arche' is 'not only the world's permanent constitution but also its capacity to change and evolve. The primary substratum is both self-moving and eternal' (Vamvacas, 2009: 24).

Thus, Gibson's image of 'cyberspace' is our starting point towards the definition of the contemporary digital landscape. Michael Benedikt provided a further definition of cyberspace as a 'a globally networked, computer-sustained, computer-accessed, and computer-generated, multidimensional, artificial, or "virtual" reality' (Benedikt, 1991: 122). Moreover, he underlined how his description of cyberspace was not to be intended as a portrait of reality: 'Now this fully developed kind of cyberspace does not yet exist outside of science fiction and the imagination of a few thousand people' (Benedikt, 1991: 122). As such, we can define the idea of cyberspace created by Gibson (2000) and developed by Benedikt (1991) as the 'proti arche' of the contemporary digital landscape. However, Jordan emphasises the distance between Gibson's original conception of cyberspace from reality as 'caution is needed because too enthusiastic a connection between such developments and Gibson's vision can misdirect us from the really existing matrix, within which cyberspace has emerged' (Jordan, 1999: 22). Moreover, he underlines: 'We do not have cyberspace as Gibson described it and we do have a computer network that can just about be described. Between the two has emerged a social, cultural, economic and political space of virtual human interaction – a real cyberspace' (Jordan, 1999: 55).

One of the features of the contemporary 'social, cultural, economic and political space of virtual human interaction' (Jordan, 1999: 55) is its ubiquitous nature. As Lessig underlines, 'the network is not going away […]. We are not going back to the twentieth century. In a decade, the majority of Americans will not even remember what that century was like' the network is not going away […]. We are not going back to the twentieth century. In a decade, the majority of Americans will not even remember what that century was like' (2009). Thus, Lessig establishes 'the network' as a permanent, non-reversible feature of the contemporary. The 'real cyberspace' (Jordan, 1999: 55) has evolved and rooted itself in the contemporary. Moreover, Lanier highlights how the digital experience is transforming the nature of the individual, as technologists

> make up extensions of your being, like remote eyes and ears (webcams and mobile phones) and expanded memory (the world of details you can search for online). These become structures by which you connect to the world and other people. These structures in turn can change how you conceive yourself and the world. (2011: 5–6)

Hence, the digital experience is not only a permanent feature of the contemporary (Lessig, 2009), but it also affects individuals' experiences, modifying bodies, perceptions and self-perception. In Lanier (2011), technology alters the relationship between the individual and the world, thus envisioning it as a non-neutral product. German sociologist Herbert Marcuse formalised this concept in his analysis of twentieth-century industrial society. For Marcuse, products 'indoctrinate and manipulate' (Marcuse, 2013: 14) and moreover so as technology becomes increasingly relevant in a growing number of individuals' life. Marcuse stresses how products also carry a form of indoctrination which 'becomes a way of life', as

> It is a good way of life – much better than before – and as a good way of life, it militates against qualitative change. Thus, emerges a pattern of *one-dimensional thought and behaviour* in which ideas, aspirations, and objectives that, by their content, transcend the established universe of discourse and action are either repelled or reduced to terms of this universe. (2013: 14)

Within the contemporary digital experience, the presence of physical products, such as devices and possibilities, such as networks, empower an implicit yet fundamental change in individual and collective behaviour. However, the current role of technology differs from the dynamic described by Marcuse (2013) in his analysis of products as artificial needs. As underlined by Eran Fisher, 'the discourse on technology is not simply a reflection of the centrality of technology in the operation of modern societies; rather, it plays a constitutive role in their operation and enables precisely that centrality' (Fisher, 2010: 17). Hence, technology is the element around which modern societies are built, imagined and narrated (Fisher, 2010).

We have chosen the term 'digital landscape' to define contemporary digital experience. Forman and Godron (1986, cited in Burel and Baudry, 2003: 43) define a landscape as 'a portion of heterogeneous territory composed of sets of interaction ecosystems that are repeated in a similar fashion in space'. Using Forman and Godron's insight, we can define the contemporary digital as a landscape resulting from a series of interaction ecosystems which, as we will see, are organised around the relationship between their main actors and within precise boundaries.

Going back to Gibson's vision of cyberspace, he described it as a 'consensual hallucination' regarding 'billions of legitimate operators, in every nation, by children being taught mathematical concepts' (Gibson, 2000: 51). Within the contemporary digital landscape, the number of 'operators' is constantly increasing: according to the International Telecommunication Union, the estimate of individuals 'using the Internet' has reached 4.1 billion, with an increase of the global penetration rate 'from nearly 17 per cent in 2005 to over 53 per cent in 2019' (International Communications Union, 2019: 1). However, it is relevant to underline that devices and networks, while ubiquitous by nature within the contemporary digital landscape, do not have even distribution over the globe and the world population. As the International Communications Union states: 'In developed countries, most people are online, with close to 87 per cent of individuals using the Internet. In the least developed countries (LDCs), on the other hand, only 19 per cent of individuals are online in 2019' (International Communications Union, 2019: 2). Moreover, the same report underlines an increasing digital gender gap in Internet usage, especially in developing and least-developed countries. Thus, the notion of sets of interacting – yet separated – ecosystems seems apt to be used in our definition of the digital landscape, which data describes as uneven in its presence around the world.

However, a sign of increasing pervasiveness and integration can be found in the rising presence of portable devices used by individuals to interact within the contemporary digital landscape. Lanier describes these devices as 'extensions of your being [...] structures by which you connect to the world and other people' (Lanier, 2011: 5–6). Aside from the increasing worldwide diffusion of smartphones in the last decade, there has been an equally significant growth of 'wearable' technology. This term is rather broad and refers to many different products, from medical devices to consumer goods, such as fitness trackers, glasses – for example, Google Glass which was retired from sale on 19 January 2015 (Wrobel, 2015) – or watches, such as the Apple Watch which, aside from other data, 'measures more than just the quantity of your movement, such as the number of steps you take. It measures the quality and quantity as well [...]. So you can live a better day and a healthier life' (Apple, 2015). A common and defining feature of these devices is their direct interaction with each individuals' body, as 'smartwatches have two strong advantages over other devices: their mount location, and (probably more important) the continual connection to the skin. Similar to augmented reality glasses, their interactions do not always require both hands' (Rawassizadeh, Price and Marian, 2015: 2). Hence, it is possible to identify a trend of miniaturisation and diversification of devices which are being designed to become increasingly present interfaces between individuals and networks in the digital landscape. As such, according to Castells, devices and networks are highly significant as 'technology is society, and society cannot be understood or represented without its technological tools' (Castells, 2010: 5). Moreover, as we shall see in Chapter 5 while assessing the role of archives within the contemporary digital landscape, these 'technological tools' (Castells, 2010: 5) are a decisive element in the diffusion of archiving practices among individuals.

However, 'operators' as imagined by Gibson, include but are not limited to individuals, as there is another entity within the contemporary digital landscape, machines. Within the interaction ecosystem described by Forman and Gordon (1986), humans utilise machines as 'structures by which you connect to the world and other people' (Lanier, 2011: 5–6). There are machines which operate different tasks, such as producing or aggregating content, organising information and extracting value from data. Together with devices and networks, data is becoming an increasingly central part of the contemporary due to the increase in computing power. Viktor Mayer-Schönberger and Kenneth Neil Cukier define data as 'a description of something that allows it to be recorded, analysed and reorganised' (Mayer-Schönberger and Cukier, 2013: 78). According to these two authors, data is at the centre of a process named 'datafication' and 'to datafy a phenomenon is to put it in a quantified format so it can be tabulated and analysed' (Mayer-Schönberger and Cukier, 2013: 78). However, the increasing relevance of data and the datafication process have a relevant impact on human interactions within the contemporary digital landscape, as underlined by Jose van Dijck (2014) in an article published by *Surveillance and Society*:

> With the advent of Web 2.0 and its proliferating social network sites, many aspects of social life were coded that had never been quantified before – friendships, interests, casual conversations, information searches, expressions of tastes, emotional

> responses, and so on. As tech companies started to specialize in one or several aspects of online communication, they convinced many people to move parts of their social interaction to web environments. (2014: 198)

Hence, within the contemporary digital landscape, alongside the ubiquitous nature of networks and the increasing relevance of devices as human extensions (Lanier, 2011), data quantification and exploitation has become possible at an extraordinary level, entering reals such as the individual experience with unprecedented force. Aside from the use of devices and the availability of networks, individual experience of the contemporary digital landscape is increasingly defined by the growing exploitation of data generated from interactions, mainly through platforms, of which social networks can be an example. Jordan describes social networks as functioning at the intersection of two different dynamics:

> first, social media networks are marked out as social by their creation of a space in which two dynamics of public and private inter-mix, and, second, they are marked by their enclosures that produce recursions from all the practices of sociality and identity that are contained within them. It is only the connection of these two practices that makes social media networks what they have become. (2015: 137)

As we have seen, since Gibson developed his vision of cyberspace, profound changes have taken place. The contemporary digital landscape has seen the rise of new actors and intermediaries which influence, shape and control how individuals interact. Moreover, profound alterations have taken place in the digital landscape, as digitally native technologies become increasingly relevant. Within the media industry, Dwyer defines this process as 'media convergence', as 'new technologies are accommodated by existing media and communication industries and cultures' (Dwyer, 2010: 2). New technologies as not only being accommodated within existing industries but have profoundly transformed the digital landscape, as underlined by Anderson and Wolff in an article published on *WIRED*: 'One of the most important shifts in the digital world has been the move from the wide-open Web to semi-closed platforms that use the Internet for transport but not the browser for display' (Anderson and Wolff, 2010). This transition, described by Anderson and Wolff (2010), has transformed the overall nature of the World Wide Web (Blanke,

2014). The World Wide Web has transformed 'into a digital platform for applications and content' (Blanke, 2014: 3). Blanke identifies a second actor within the contemporary digital landscape, 'crowds', which are defined as 'a collaboration of large number of humans on a common task' (Blanke, 2014: 3). Hence, the relevance of networks, devices and data has generated numerous changes within the digital landscape, also modifying its underlying technology and establishing new entities such as crowds and platforms.

As individuals cannot act in the digital landscape without a device or access to a network, their participation is possible only via what Bruno Latour (2005) defines as a 'mediator', an entity that can 'transform, translate, distort, and modify the meaning or the elements' (Latour, 2005: 37). Individual experience is mediated not only by devices and networks but likewise by consent and services. Both levels of mediation (devices and networks; consent and services) inherently involve various degrees of homologation as there are a limited number of device producers, networks to access and services to use. Thus, as individuals interact with the digital landscape, they become part of a crowd (Blanke, 2014). To access any network within the digital landscape, an individual needs a mediator, that in the majority of cases is not in her or his full control. Simply by opening a web browser or launching an application on a portable device, information instantly starts to be exchanged, beyond sight, control and consent. By entering a query on a search engine or sending an email through a webmail service, individuals become part of a particular crowd that interacts with a specific platform. However, due to the nature of the digital landscape, individuals can be part – at the same time – of different crowds. An individual can register on different social networks, multiple webmail services, use different web browsers or buy goods and services from multiple digital outlets. In each of these interactions, the individual becomes part of a crowd interacting with a specific platform. These interactions between crowds and platforms appear to take place in an environment where a conflict between individual and crowd and between crowd and platform is absent. As Blanke underlines 'the relationship between crowds and clouds […] is complementary and […] they must not be regarded as two separate forces' (Blanke, 2014: 3).

There are two fundamental aspects of crowd and platform interaction in the contemporary digital landscape which need to be assessed. The first is the pervasiveness of for-profit platforms within the digital landscape. According to Alexa Internet, a company owned by Amazon that provides data regarding global web traffic, the top ten most visited websites on the World Wide Web in September 2020 are all for-profit platforms (Alexa, 2020). The list comprises search engines and web service providers such as Google, Baidu, 360.cn, Qq.com, Sohu.com, Yahoo!, a video streaming platform owned by Google's parent company Alphabet (YouTube.com) and an online shopping platform (Tmall.com). The first non-profit platform is Wikipedia, which is ranked thirteenth. Hence, it is evident that individuals mainly aggregate in crowds that interact and sustain for-profit platforms.

The extreme commodification of the contemporary digital landscape entails a radical change in the role of the individual, which becomes a 'produser' as defined by Axel Bruns. Bruns describes produsers as 'users [that] are always already necessarily also producers of the shared knowledgebase, regardless of whether they are aware of this role – they have become a new, hybrid, *produser*' (Bruns, 2008: 2). Moreover, Fuchs (2010) envisions the notion of 'produser' as a fundamental element of the commodification of the digital landscape:

> Due to the permanent activity of the recipients and their status as produsers, we can say that in the case of the Internet the audience commodity is a produsage/prosumer commodity. The category of the produsage/prosumer commodity does not signify a democratization of the media toward a participatory or democratic system, but the total commodification of human creativity. (2010: 192)

As we have seen, the role of for-profit platforms is highly relevant, and moreover if we consider it as part of the crowd-platform dynamic described by Blanke (2014). This dynamic has also generated novel forms of consumption which we will define as 'feed fruition', a specific practice where individuals browse autonomously updated and personalised lists. We will focus on 'feed fruition' more in detail in Chapter 5 while assessing the role of time within the contemporary digital landscape. However, commodification within the digital landscape is not limited to platforms or the role of produsers. Coté and Pybus underline how 'communication and subjectivity – including the realm long considered "mere

consumption" – have become an active articulation of capitalist production' (Coté and Pybus, 2007: 97).

Aside from the pervasiveness of for-profit platforms, the second fundamental aspect of crowd-platform interaction is the apparent absence
of friction between these two entities. The absence of friction between
crowds and platforms is based on a narrative dating back to the beginning
of the digital landscape's evolution. In 1996, Treanor wrote an online article entitled *Internet as hyper-liberalism* where he underlined the absence
of friction as one of the main features of what he described as 'Net-ism'
(Treanor, 1996): 'Net-ism does not want a choice: it wants the Net, one
Net, one global Net, one Net everywhere, one universal cyberspace, and
nothing less. It seems that, as with the ideology of the free market [and
as with liberalism in general], no co-existence is possible with the Net'
(Treanor, 1996).

The crowd-platform dynamic has been perceived as frictionless mainly
through the proliferation of platforms and services where, according to
Lovink, 'we are forced to be "ourselves" [...]. We constantly login, create
profiles, and post status updates to present our Self on the global marketplace of employment, friendship and love' (Lovink, 2011: 13).

*Individuals, Crowds and Platforms Interactions within
the Digital Landscape*

After providing a general framework for the contemporary digital landscape, we shall now focus on its main actors – individuals, crowds and
platforms – and their interactions.

While it is not formally compulsory for individuals to participate in
crowds, it is de facto the only gateway to interact with other individuals
and with platforms. Hence, how can we define this form of crowd participation that organises interactions between individuals and regulates access
to services such as platforms? French philosopher Michel Foucault, while
analysing Jeremy Bentham's *Panopticon* prison model, underlined:

> The crowd, a compact mass, a locus of multiple exchanges, individualities merging
> together, a collective effect, is abolished and replaced by a collection of separated

individualities. From the point of view of the guardian, it is replaced by a multiplicity that can be numbered and supervised; from the point of view of the inmates, by a sequestered and observed solitude. (2012: 201)

Within the digital landscape, individuals are organised in crowds, yet not in a spontaneous or random manner. Hence, crowds within the digital landscape are the opposite of what Foucault described as crowds, which appear to be a 'collection of separated individualities' (Foucault, 2012: 201) as he defined prison inmates in Bentham's *Panopticon*. As we have seen in the previous section, individuals need to aggregate in crowds and participate in platforms (Lovink, 2011) constantly connected to networks using personal devices. This phenomenon is especially relevant for those whom Mark Prensky describes as 'digital natives' or 'native speakers of the digital language of computers, videogames and the Internet' (Prensky, 2001: 2). For individuals and increasingly so for digital natives, it feels mandatory to participate and be connected to platforms as part of crowds. However, within the digital landscape, crowds rather than being 'a compact mass, a locus of multiple exchanges, individualities merging together, a collective effect' (Foucault, 2012: 201) appear to be more similar to 'collections of separated individualities' (Foucault, 2012: 201). Hence, the participation dynamic is one of the fundamental aspects through which the digital landscape is imagined and challenged – or, more frequently – not challenged at all. Within the digital landscape, a narrative has developed around the role of individual and collective participation, stressing the irreplaceable role of contemporary platforms and networks, as underlined by Morozov (2013):

> The finality of 'the Internet' – the belief that it's the ultimate technology and the ultimate network – has been widely accepted. It's Silicon Valley own version of the end of history; just as capitalism-driven liberal democracy in Francis Fukuyama's controversial account remains the only game in town, so does the capitalism driven 'Internet'. (2013: 23)

The belief that 'capitalism driven "Internet"' represents 'the ultimate technology and the ultimate network' (Morozov, 2013: 23) appears to be in open contrast with the founding architecture of the World Wide Web, as envisioned by English computer scientist Tim Berners-Lee, which was at the basis of its success: 'Not only the open nature of the Web lend itself to a wide array of interactive, multimedia experiences, but by hewing to a non-hierarchical structure and open protocols, Berners-Lee's invention became enormously popular' (Burnett, Brunstrom and Nilsson, 2005: 7–8). Nevertheless, the leading conception of the digital landscape rather than being based on a 'non-hierarchical structure and open protocols' (Burnett, Brunstrom and Nilsson, 2005: 7–8) combines the 'finality of the Internet' (Morozov, 2013: 23) with the leading role of platforms, which organise crowds as 'collection of separated individualities' (Foucault, 2012: 201). Thus, how can we describe crowd movement in the digital landscape? A flying flock of birds might be a useful analogy to assess how crowds behave in the digital landscape. Reynolds describes a flock as 'a group of objects that exhibit this general class of polarized, non-colliding, aggregate motion' (Reynolds, 1987: 25). He underlines other features exhibited by the flock, as it

> is made of discrete birds yet overall motion seems fluid; it is simple in concept yet it so visually complex, it seems randomly arrayed and yet is magnificently synchronized. Perhaps most puzzling is the strong impression of intentional, centralized control. Yet all evidence indicates that flock motion must be merely the aggregate result of the actions of individual animals, each acting solely on the basis of its own local perception of the world. (1987: 25)

In his article, Reynolds (1987) describes the development of a computer-generated simulation of a flock of flying birds. In order to carry out his experiment,

> Reynolds introduced three heuristic rules that led to creation of the first computer animation of flocking [...]: 1) Flock Centering: attempt to stay close to nearby flockmates; 2) Collision Avoidance: avoid collisions with nearby flockmates; 3) Velocity Matching: attempt to match velocity with nearby flockmates. [...] These rules are also known as *cohesion*, *separation*, and *alignment* rules in the literature. (Olfati-Saber, 2006: 2)

All three rules developed by Reynolds (1987) described by Olfati-Saber (2006) can be applied to the interaction between crowds and platforms. Within the digital landscape, when individuals aggregate in crowds – for example, users of the same social network – they do so following other individuals and complying with environmental rules set by platforms, for example, by agreeing to mandatory terms of service. However, how do platforms manage to organise individuals in crowds, keeping them close to their peers (i.e. 'polarised'), hardly interacting with other clusters of individuals (i.e. 'non-colliding') and close to their cluster (i.e. 'aggregate')? According to Eli Pariser (2012), the mechanism is relatively uncomplicated and enhanced by the nature of the digital landscape. In Pariser, filter development is the central feature that enhances crowd formation within platforms thus enabling a flock-like behaviour, as

> the new generation of Internet filters looks at the things you seem to like – the actual things you've done, or the things people like you like – and tries to extrapolate. They are prediction engines, constantly creating and refining a theory of who you are and what you'll want to do next. Together, these engines create a unique universe of information for each of us – what I've come to call a filter bubble – which fundamentally alters the way we encounter ideas and information. (2012: 9)

Hence, within the contemporary digital landscape, individuals interact in environments where they relate with their peers in tailor-made 'filter bubbles' (Pariser, 2012: 9). Crowd behaviour produces data that can then be aggregated and eventually becomes predictable. Whereas crowds and platforms do interact on a complementary basis (Blanke, 2014), platforms usually harvest, exploit and strictly control data generated by crowds.

Platforms, being one of the main entities within the digital landscape, have drawn significant scholarly interest. Gillespie (2010) outlines the history of the term 'platform' and the evolution of its meaning within the digital landscape. A platform can indicate 'an infrastructure that supports the design and use of particular applications' (Gillespie, 2010: 349), but also 'online environments that allow users to design and deploy applications they design or that are offered by third parties' (Gillespie, 2010: 349). Gillespie underlines that 'Platforms are "platforms" not necessarily because they allow code to be written or run, but because they afford an opportunity to communicate, interact or sell' (2010: 351). Hence, the term 'platform' indicates a variety of infrastructures and services. According to Jordan (2015), there are three main types of platforms:

the first is cloud computing in which the materiality of devices and networks and protocols are obscured by the magic of mobility and flexibility in information management (Clouds). The second is securitisation in which nation-states seek to collect all information and then subject it to profiling to satisfy security agencies' desire to 'master the internet' (Securitisation of the Internet). The third is social media networks in which two different understandings of public and private relations interact within enclosures of data (Social Media Networks). (2015: 21)

Within our work, we are placing specific emphasis on the role of social media networks as this type of platform has heavily influenced the nature of news media content production and distribution. Social media networks have drawn significant scholarly interest (boyd and Ellison, 2007; Papacharissi, 2009). Regarding the role of social networks in information diffusion, Bakshy, Messing and Adamic (2015) – while focusing solely on Facebook – underline that 'the mass adoption of online social networking systems has the potential to dramatically alter an individual's exposure to new information' (Bakshy, Messing and Adamic, 2015: 8). Hence, the role of platforms (and more specifically, of social media networks) in information diffusion constitutes a significant element in our analysis of the dynamic between these entities and news production and distribution. More broadly, platforms have influenced both directly and indirectly the nature and form of the digital landscape, modifying behaviours at an individual and crowd level, while also exercising a form of direct and indirect influence on content creation and distribution performed by news media outlets. Thus, within this work, platform studies constitute a relevant field in the assessment of digital journalism as a practice within the digital landscape. Among platforms, social networks are a typical example of a power balance revolving around the ownership and accessibility of data, as

users (individually or collectively) are, usually, expressly forbidden from compiling even a (representative) sample of the data produced on that site. Of course, aggregate data (or statistics concerning these data) have the greatest value to marketers, and therefore, aggregate data are most profitable. (Rey, 2012: 411)

Hence, there is a complete asymmetry between crowds and platforms, as only the latter can access and profit from the data generated by the 'collection of separated individualities' (Foucault, 2012: 201) which interact within the digital landscape while exhibiting a flock-like behaviour (Reynolds, 1987). While crowds are the main force that drives platforms forward and allows them to thrive, in case of a sudden migration, they can also determine the end of their existence. However, as Rey (2012) underlines, platforms only succeed if individuals – clustered in crowds – produce a constant feed of data that platforms have learned not only to collect but also to exploit in order to create value. However, the exploitation of individuals' time and creativity is not framed within traditional boundaries, as

> In the physical confines of the factory, the worker was always directly aware of the objects of his or her labour and, ultimately, his or her separation from them. In the paradigm of digital information, users are often unaware of the full extent of the information that they are producing. (Rey, 2012: 410)

Such unawareness allows platforms to enforce a particular narrative. In the digital landscape, platforms formally allow crowds to perform tasks, reach goals, connect with peers and enrich experiences. Within this process, platforms present themselves using divine attributes with directly enforce this narrative. For example, Google and Facebook, in their mission statements claim that their objective is respectively 'to organise the world's information and make it universally accessible and useful' (Google, 2017) and to 'give people the power to share and make the world more open and connected' (Facebook, 2017). This self-narrative is accepted and enforced by crowds, who act as unquestioning actors rather than possibly conflicting forces within the digital landscape.

Main Features of the Contemporary Digital Landscape

The Digital Landscape as Constant Flux

After describing the digital landscape and the actor it comprises, we shall now focus on its most relevant features. We are concentrating on these two features in order to develop further a framework for the entities which will be at the centre of our work, such as long-form journalism and archives.

The digital landscape is not merely a pervasive feature of the contemporary, nor a sum of the entities that concur to its being, as its defining aspect are two distinct features, flux and digitally enhanced creative destruction. Thus, the main entities of the digital landscape – such as individuals clustered together in crowds and platforms and their interactions – must be assessed considering the influence of these two features.

We shall begin by describing the notion of flux, which underlines the transformative nature of the digital landscape, which – as we have seen in the previous section – is a defining aspect of the interactions between individuals, crowds and platforms. As these entities rely on each other in order to exist and operate, their connection through the exchange of information and data must be permanent. Hence, flux is envisioned here as a vital element for the digital landscape to operate and – in order to better function – its entities must be able to interact as freely as possible. However, the maximum amount of freedom can only be obtained in an environment which is void of any other rule other than the being itself of the network.

The absence of regulation as a critical element in the being of a network is rooted in the conception of the digital landscape as a perfect competition market. The American economist Milton Friedman, in an interview published on *New Perspectives Quarterly*, argued that the diffusion of the Internet had a major impact on markets, moving individuals closer to 'perfect information' (Friedman, 2006). However, this seems to be at odds with our depiction of the contemporary digital landscape, where platforms withhold and benefit from the data they collect, as we have seen in the previous section of this chapter. According to Friedman, 'the Internet is the most effective instrument we have for globalisation' (Friedman, 2006). Thus, within this ideological framework, any regulation which might constitute an obstacle to the notion of flux is opposed by platforms, who are also capable of organising crowds in vocal clusters within the digital public sphere that enforce the need for the Internet to be free from any form of regulation. Hence, regulation is often portrayed as a threat to the idealistic, native and 'open' World Wide Web. However, the original, non-hierarchical architecture of the World Wide Web (Burnett, Brunstrom and Nilsson, 2005) has been subverted by the leading conception of the digital landscape, organised around the prominent role of platforms. Moreover, there is another perspective from which to consider this phenomenon (MacKinnon, 2012):

> corporations and governments that build, operate, and govern cyberspace are not being held sufficiently accountable for their exercise of power over the lives and identities of people who use digital networks. They are sovereigns operating without the consent of the networked. (2012: xxi)

Internet freedom, as envisioned by platforms and institutions, is possible only without the consent of individuals clustered in crowds. Consent and understanding by individuals are viewed as both unnecessary and a possible source of friction. Moreover, flux within the digital landscape can gain traction only if a conflict is absent between crowds and platforms. As underlined by MacKinnon (2012), power within the digital landscape is distributed unevenly, as platforms act as monopolies (Lanier, 2011) and crowds' role is comparable to a contemporary version of serfdom. Thus, the 'collection of separated individualities' (Foucault, 2012: 201) acts as a de facto unconscious workforce, performing labour 'as if it were an absolute end in itself, a calling' (Weber, Parsons and Giddens, 2001: 25). While this description was developed by German sociologist Max Weber to describe the role of labour within Northern European and Protestant societies, it could also be applied to crowd input into platforms within the contemporary digital landscape. Whereas in the societies described by Weber 'work was regarded as a moral duty pursued for its own sake' (Norris and Inglehart, 2009: 578), in the digital landscape individuals clustered in crowds contribute to platforms, conceiving it as a way of affirming their very existence 'on the global marketplace of employment, friendship and love' (Lovink, 2011: 13).

The almost limitless power exercised by platforms and institutions within the digital landscape manifests itself in a seemingly frictionless environment: conflict appears to be absent between crowds and platforms, due to their complementary nature (Blanke, 2014). While this environment appears to void of conflict between the entities it comprises, it promotes disruption. As we have seen, conflict does not take place between entities, yet disruption resides in the very nature of the digital landscape, in its flux. What makes the flux profitable for platforms and exploitable for institutions is to be encouraged, and whatever constitutes an obstacle towards the leading conception of the contemporary digital landscape must be removed. Hence, consent requests and non-formalised spaces become less prominent. Crowds may exist and operate only if they do so within frames provided and exploited by platforms. Any possible deviation determines alteration of the flux, harming the network's functionality but also threatening an individual's existence. Thus, the contemporary digital landscape then becomes a product of 'a faith [...] that thrives when you can pretend that computers do everything and people do nothing' (Lanier, 2011: 14). The faith that Lanier refers to has its roots at the intersection between biology and technology. As such, this conception was first formulated by Kevin Kelly, founding executive editor of *WIRED* magazine. Lanier describes *WIRED* as 'the embassy in the old country' of what he depicts as 'cybernetic totalists' (Lanier, 2011: 14).

A year after *WIRED* started its publications in 1993, Kelly published a work, *Out of Control: The New Biology of Machines, Social Systems, and the Economic World*, focusing on the intersection between biology and technology. According to Kelly (1994), development and change are strictly interconnected, and hence the best environment is one of constant destruction and recreation. He underlines: 'If it's true that nature is fundamentally in constant flux, then instability may cause the richness of biological forms in nature' (Kelly, 1994: 86). This concept, originating in biology, is translated by Kelly within the digital landscape as follows: 'Every day authors all over the world add millions of words to an uncountable number of overlapping conversations. They daily build an immense distributed document, one that is under eternal construction, constant flux, and fleeting permanence' (1994: 389). This image describes what Lanier (2011) defines as the 'noosphere', an entity that combines every activity performed by individuals connected to the Internet. However, Lanier also underlines how

> digital network architectures naturally incubate monopolies. That is precisely why the idea of noosphere, or a collective brain formed by the sum of all the people connected to the internet, has to be resisted with more force than it is promoted. (2011: 19)

By introducing the parallel between nature and the Internet, Kelly (1994) contributed to promoting a biological conception of the network as it was a being. Moreover, Kelly regards disruption as a life-giving process, as a pure form of flux, thus implying a disregard for smaller actors such as individuals as it focuses on a different scale, in order to facilitate permanent change. However, in our definition of the digital landscape, we preferred to underline the diverse nature of 'sets of interacting ecosystems' which – while largely following Kelly's underlying ideology – are distinct from one another, with differences spurring from diverse cultural, geographical, economic and political backgrounds.

The Digital Landscape as a Disruption Enhancer

Having defined flux as the first main feature of the digital landscape, which influences the relationship between its actors, we shall now focus on the results of this interaction. The relationship between crowds and platforms, as described in the previous sections, can exist in the current form only if the flux is enhanced, promoted and idealised. Thus, the digital landscape does not need any rules other than the ones that grant its existence. However, its flux has profound effects on economic and cultural structures within society that are subject to laws and regulations. The digital landscape's flux is a destructive agent in their regard, and its ideological framework dates back to the notion of creative destruction in economics.

Austrian-American economic Joseph Alois Schumpeter defined creative destruction as 'the essential fact about capitalism' (Schumpeter, 2010: 83). In his work *Capitalism, Socialism and Democracy*, Schumpeter analyses both the capitalist and socialist models and provides a core definition of the 'fundamental impulse that sets and keeps the capitalist engine in motion', referring to a process that 'revolutionises the economic structure from within, incessantly destroying the old one, incessantly creating a new one' (2010: 83). As we apply this notion to the digital landscape, we can see how a process conceived originally within classic economics has gained new, unprecedented force and traction.

During the formation of the digital landscape and its subsequent rooting in the global economic process, we have experienced long cycles of 'creative destruction' (Schumpeter, 2010: 83). These cycles have first manifested themselves challenging musical media distribution practices, with the creation of peer to peer networks such as Napster, which started its operations in June 1999. Raymond Shih Ray Ku (2001) describes the profound impact of creative destruction in the digital landscape, under-lining how 'digital technology and the Internet strike at the foundation of copyright and the industries built upon copyright by eliminating the need for firms to distribute copyrighted works and for exclusive property rights to support creation' (Ku, 2001: 269). Since the end of the 1990s, starting from cultural production and distribution industries such as music, film and books, this impact has extended to other realms of consumption affecting numerous economic sectors and especially the news media production field, which we shall analyse in detail further on, in order to introduce the environment in which long-form journalism and archives shall be assessed.

However, the revolution of the economic structure 'from within' (Schumpeter, 2010: 83), has been greatly enhanced by the digital land-scape. Erik Brynjolfsson and Andrew McAfee, authors of multiple works on innovation and the role of technology, underline how

> Schumpeter's observation describes markets in software, media, and the Internet much better than traditional markets in manufacturing and services. But as more and more industries become increasingly digitized and networked, we can expect the Schumpeterian dynamic to spread. (2014: 205)

Hence, Brynjolfsson and McAfee view favourably the increasingly vital role played by technology in the working place. They envision a pro-cess that will allow production to be optimised by machines, requiring less human workforce, hence becoming more efficient and profitable. However, the result of the digitally enhanced creative destruction de-scribed by Brynjolfsson and McAfee (2014) should have been an accel-erated cycle of new incumbents in the market which develop disruptive products, services and companies. A critique of this idealisation is pro-vided by Lanier when he refers to the digital network architecture as an entity that tends to 'naturally incubates monopolies' (Lanier, 2011: 19).

Moreover, in the contemporary digital landscape, the economic and systemic strength of platforms is such that these entities absorb market innovators – often by merger and acquisitions – as soon as they become relevant. Hence, competition is increasingly sterilised, and incumbents face an increasingly hostile environment. However, according to Brynjolfsson and McAfee, the contemporary digital landscape is where a 'second machine age' (Brynjolfsson and McAfee, 2014: 205) is taking place. While during the Industrial Revolution machines became able to perform tasks better than humans

> computers and other digital advances are doing for mental power – the ability to use our brains to understand and shape our environments – what the steam engine and its descendants did for muscle power. [...] So a vast and unprecedented boost to mental power should be a great boost to humanity, just as the earlier boost to physical power so clearly was. (Brynjolfsson and McAfee, 2014: 205)

Moreover, according to the two authors, the creative destruction operated by digital technologies not only makes markets and business grow in efficiency but benefits 'all of us as consumers. As they increase government transparency and accountability and give us new ways to assemble and make our voices heard, they benefit us as citizens' (Brynjolfsson and McAfee, 2014: 205). Thus, Brynjolfsson and McAfee entail that the digital landscape's end goal is to enhance performance and productivity. The objective is to benefit a generic 'all' which is subsequently specified in 'consumers' (Brynjolfsson and McAfee, 2014: 205). Hence, according to the two authors, humans will be mentally enhanced by machines and will want to 'consume' a better government, which in the meantime has become more transparent and accountable. In this ideological framework, individuals do not promote change or conflict. Instead it is the digital technology which resolves all possible frictions within society and creates an environment with better markets and businesses and more transparent and accountable governments.

However, Brynjolfsson and McAfee's position is based on the precondition that each individual has the same access to the same resources, relying on their even distribution. Whereas digital distribution is indeed more efficient than traditional distribution – for example, an official document published on a government website is far more in reach than having to request a physical copy in an office – it does not automatically mean better for every individual, as this narrative would lead to believe. Thus, Brynjolfsson and McAfee promote top-down creative destruction: businesses and markets are the sole drives of digital creative destruction. This process is taking place in an environment with stronger and interconnected monopolies, and when it deviates from this path, fostering bottom-up disruption, it is immediately re-adapted into a more efficient business or market.

The original conception of creative destruction as a change of the economic structure 'from within' (Schumpeter, 2010: 83) is now being re-placed by a digitally enhanced form of what can be defined as 'non-creative' destruction. Moreover, there are other factors that are directly influenced by the nature of the contemporary digital landscape, such as distribution and price. According to Chris Anderson, contemporary creative destruction has taken place with 'near-zero "marginal costs of digital distribution"' (Anderson, 2009a: 3). For Anderson, price is the real gateway to further evolution within the digital landscape, as he underlines: 'Most of us depend on one or more Google services every day, but they never show up on our credit card. No meter ticks as you use Facebook. Wikipedia costs you nothing' (2009a: 3). Google and Facebook, aside from extracting value from data provided by individuals who use their services clustered in crowds, are the new gate-keepers of an increasingly disruptive economy. Moreover, as we shall see in the following chapter, this feature of the contemporary digital landscape has deeply affected the news industry and its production and distribution practices, including those regarding long-form journalism and archives.

We started this chapter with Gibson's vision of cyberspace in his novel *Neuromancer*, which we used as a starting point towards a definition of the contemporary digital landscape, defined as sets of interaction ecosystems, which comprise three entities: individuals, crowds and platforms, which interact in an apparently frictionless manner. The digital landscape is defined by two main features, its nature as constant flux and a disruption enhancer.

This overall framework provides us with a deeper insight of the contemporary which we will use in the following chapter to assess the nature of the digital news media industry and its evolution, focusing on long-form journalism and archives. In order to describe the nature of the digital news media industry in the contemporary digital landscape, we shall use elements which we have formalised in this chapter, such as the nature of platforms and their relationship with crowds. Moreover, we will identify what can be defined as a disrupting relationship between the news media industry and platforms, which we have assessed as a defining feature of the contemporary digital landscape.

The process that we have undertaken in this first chapter has led us from Gibson's initial intuition of cyberspace to the features of the contemporary digital landscape. Gibson himself, in an article originally published in *TIME* magazine in 2000, indicates how to frame his narration, underlining how

> the most memorable images of science fiction often have more to do with our anxieties in the past (the writer's present) than with those singular and ongoing scenarios that make up our life as a species: our real futures, our ongoing present. (2012: 213)

CHAPTER 2

The Media Industry and Archives in the Digital Landscape

Digital Media: A Non-creative Destruction

The Media Industry's Failed Adaptation to the Digital Landscape

In the first chapter, we have described the contemporary digital landscape, its main actors and their interactions and identified two of its defining features, flux and disruption. This analysis will be the framework for our assessment of the news media industry and its evolution. Moreover, we shall start focusing on a specific type of news media production, such as long-form journalism. In this chapter, we will provide a possible definition of long-form journalism in the digital landscape and explore its possible connections with digital news media archives. Using the framework developed in the first chapter, we shall analyse the strategies adopted by the news media industry in its approach with the digital landscape and see how they have contributed both to its shrinking economic relevance and its weakening role in the public sphere.

In the last decades, the news media industry is experiencing a process of deindustrialisation, which the International Monetary Fund describes as a dramatic fall of employment in manufacturing (Rowthorn and Ramaswamy, 1997), along with other sectors affected by this dynamic. While the transformative impact of distribution practices has enhanced deindustrialisation, the news media industry has experienced an even greater impact with the contemporary digital landscape, which has been partly enhanced by the industry's own choices, leading to what can be defined as a path of non-creative destruction.

Circulation, revenue from advertising and number of jobs in the news media industry have all declined heavily in the last decade. Data collected by the Pew Research Center indicates that 'estimated total U.S. daily newspaper circulation (print and digital combined) in 2018 was 28.6 million for weekday and 30.8 million for Sunday, down 8 per cent and 9 per cent, respectively, from the previous year' (Pew Research Center, 2019). Alongside a substantial decline in circulation, another major transformation has taken place, as 'the total estimated advertising revenue for the newspaper industry in 2018 was $14.3 billion [...] This is down 13 per cent from 2017. Total estimated circulation revenue was $11.0 billion, compared with $11.2 billion in 2017' (Pew Research Center, 2019). Moreover, newsroom employees have fallen from a peak of 74,410 in 2006 to 37,900 in 2018 (Pew Research Center, 2019), with a loss of almost half of the overall jobs (a 49 per cent decrease) between 'reporters, editors, photographers, or film and video editors' (Pew Research Center, 2019).

Within this frame, the vast majority of the current narrative on the decline of the news media industry is centred on the depiction of the digital landscape as a hostile environment for news media outlets, due to the deep fractures it has created within its revenue models which – as we have seen – have been profoundly affected by the evolution of the digital landscape. However, to better assess this phenomenon, we shall focus more specifically on the nature of the news media industry and its revenue model, assessing the influence of factors such as the presence of platforms and their relationship with crowds within the digital landscape, which we have described in the first chapter.

Canadian communication philosopher and author of *Understanding Media*, Marshall McLuhan wrote that 'our press is in the main a free entertainment service paid for advertisers who want to buy readers' (1994: 208). Decades after this definition was elaborated, news media outlets relying primarily on advertising revenue have experienced what can be defined as a wave of non-creative destruction in the contemporary digital landscape. As we assessed in the first chapter, the creative destruction envisioned as 'the essential fact about capitalism' (Schumpeter, 2010: 83) has been enhanced by the digital landscape's nature.

In order to fully understand the nature of the news media industry's crisis, it is useful to start from McLuhan's definition, as it envisions the media industry almost solely as a distribution intermediary between advertisers and the public. Hence, if we were to embrace fully this definition of the news media industry, we should likewise conclude that within the digital landscape, platforms are a more efficient mean of distribution and thus the role of the press as a vehicle to reach consumers has started to fade. As Chris Anderson wrote in his book *Free, the Future of a Radical Price*, with 'near-zero marginal costs of digital distribution' (2009a: 3), platforms offer 'free' services in exchange of data that can be mined and sold to the same advertisers which – in McLuhan's conception – were the true owners of the press. Moreover, as we have seen in the previous chapter, Brynjolfsson and McAfee (2014) stress that this process entails a new dimension of efficiency and an inherently 'Schumpeterian' destructive force that cannot be opposed as it is the very basis of capitalism. However, journalism's conception as a distribution intermediary for advertisers (McLuhan, 1994) is also fundamental in understanding a series of choices that the news media industry undertook when the digital landscape was in its early stages. The relation between the news media industry as a vehicle to deliver advertising to readers (McLuhan, 1994) and new entities in the digital landscape which perform the same task can be assessed using Clayton M. Christensen's description of 'disruptive technologies', as

> disruptive technologies bring to a market a very different value proposition than had been available previously. Generally, disruptive technologies underperform established products in mainstream markets. But they have other features that a few fringe (and generally new) customers value. Products based on disruptive technologies are typically cheaper, simpler, smaller, and, frequently, more convenient to use. (1997: 11)

Hence, we can assume that the actors who rose to prominence in the digital landscape, such as platforms, acted as a disruptive technology for those news media outlets which operated under the conception that the main scope of the press is to act as an intermediary between advertisers and consumers. To maximise their distribution capacity, many news media outlets adopted a very aggressive approach, essentially promoting the consumption of news media for free. As we have seen, this approach was based on the idea that the more efficient intermediary would prevail in connecting audience and advertisers. Moreover, as Georg Franck underlines

> Marketing information therefore need not mean selling it. It can also mean to market a medium that is capable of attracting the attention of the general public. Media attracting the attention of the general public is what the advertising industry is desperately seeking. (2019: 36)

Hence, in order to 'market a medium that is capable of attracting the attention of the general public' (Franck, 2019: 36), news media outlets have developed a number of strategies, which – as we will see in our case studies in the following chapters – also involve the production of long-form journalism as a way to 'put one's best product in the market in a way that participates in these trends in digital design and narrative while building and communicating an organization's brand' (Dowling and Vogan, 2015: 219). However, the primary strategy implemented by news media outlets to develop a medium capable of attracting the adverting industry is a practice based on digitally distributing content for free in order to maximise readers. This practice is named 'shovelware' and can be defined as follows:

> Digital platforms have been treated too often by traditional news organizations as just another opportunity to publish existing content. Many sites are filled with 'shovelware' – content that amounts to little more than electronic editions of words and pictures from traditional platforms. (Grueskin, Seave and Graves, 2011: 129)

Thus, the news media industry chose to rely even more on advertising rather than subscriptions as a revenue source, adopting a 'shovelware' approach. The adoption of this strategy was based on a number of reasons, which included a limited comprehension of the digital landscape (Bruns and Highfield, 2012). As underlined by Bruns and Highfield

> many early online news offerings by established news organizations simply replicated part of the content available in their corresponding newspapers (in formats ridiculed as 'shovelware'); even well into the 2000s and what is often (although not unproblematically) called the 'Web 2.0' era, few mainstream news Web sites sought to position their readers as anything other than largely passive audiences, or to directly engage and correspond with them. (2012: 2)

By adopting the strategy described by Bruns and Highfield (2012), the news media industry further paved the way for a wave of non-creative destruction, one of the two main features of the digital landscape which we described in the first chapter. The news media industry did not fully comprehend the transformative nature of digital distribution and the nature of the entities within the digital landscape, such as platforms. Hence, the news media industry placed itself in a downward spiral, devaluating its content without building distribution platforms that could in any way compete with the new, rising platforms, such as search engines and social networks. Only in 2009, *The New York Times* started its first paywall, partially limiting access to its content through payment. This first experiment was later dropped and since it has been replicated both by *The New York Times* itself and other news media outlets, with various degrees of intensity. Some news outlets, such as *The Times* and *The Sunday Times* 'adopted what might be called "radical" paywall, shutting users out of all content unless they pay, allowing no sharing, and blocking search engines' (Brock, 2013: 155). Other news media outlets, like *The New York Times*, have chosen a less radical approach, allowing readers to access a set number of news items before enforcing a paywall. As we shall see in Chapter 6, paywall implementation has a direct influence on the possibility of third-party aggregation and curation, which we shall prove as especially relevant for long-form journalism and archives.

Meanwhile, the news media industry has started to come to terms with the impact of platform-based distribution practices, which have profoundly changed news media consumption within the digital landscape. One of the first interactions with news media outlets and platforms was the launch of Google News in 2002. According to its creator, Krishna Bharat, the main idea behind Google News was presenting 'news clusters' or 'related articles in a group', the service would 'encourage readers to get a broader perspective by digging deeper into the news – reading ten articles instead of one, perhaps – and then gain a better understanding of the issues, which could ultimately benefit society' (Bharat, 2006). A few years earlier Bharat had provided a more detailed insight on Google News' inner mechanisms in a Q&A on the *Google Friends Blog*, which is now retrievable only via the Internet Archive's Wayback Machine (Google, 2003). In that instance, Bharat explained how Google News was employing many different metrics for determining the relative importance of web pages. PageRank is one of these factors, but the exact mix of determinants is part of our secret sauce and not something we're able to discuss in detail. We can say that Google News also integrates other attributes, such as the recency of the content, to help determine which stories get the most prominence. (Google, 2003)

Hence, we can see how Google exploited its nature as a search engine platform within the digital landscape to provide a service to its crowd. Google has undertaken other actions to become a gateway service between news media production and its crowd. In October 2015, Google started implementing a coding format to enhance content performance on mobile devices. This coding format, named Accelerated Mobile Pages (AMP), while open-source, is described on Google's website as a way to

improve the mobile web and enhance the distribution ecosystem. If content is fast, flexible and beautiful, including compelling and effective ads, we can preserve the open web publishing model as well as the revenue streams so important to the sustainability of quality publishing. (2015)

However, some issues arise with this type of approach, which can be enforced with such intensity only by a platform in a dominant position within the digital landscape. Google AMP does provide a number of advantages to its adopters, such as 'near-instantaneous loading, distribution on multiple platforms, and [critically] more prominent placement on Google properties' (Bohn, 2018). However, the main issue regards the fact that Google is effectively acting as a controlling force, promoting certain types of technology application while offsetting others, as underlined by Joshua Benton, director of the Nieman Journalism Lab at Harvard University. According to Benton, AMP tries to

change the way that the web is built, killing off some technologies and advantaging others. In a world of controlled platforms and walled app gardens, the web is the last open space standing, built over two decades, and there's something irksome about a few Google engineers deciding which parts to ban. (2015)

On 8 March 2018, in a blog post published by on the Accelerated Mobile Pages Project website, Malte Ubl, tech lead for Google AMP, described the future path of the project, stating:

we now feel ready to take the next step and work to support more instant-loading content not based on AMP technology in areas of Google Search designed for this, like the Top Stories carousel. This content will need to follow a set of future web standards and meet a set of objective performance and user experience criteria to be eligible. (2018)

Thus, Google's strategy aims to establish AMP as a standard, extending it to as much content published on the World Wide Web as possible. For Malte Ubl and David Besbris, vice president of search engineering at Google, Accelerated Mobile Pages are a part of the World Wide Web, as AMP 'do not need to use Google's servers or serve Google ads; they can be published and distributed completely independently of Google' (Bohn, 2018). However, it appears undeniable that Google is promoting this project from its platform perspective and is trying to influence web standards (Benton, 2015). Since Google itself is the first beneficiary of providing users with a smooth, fast and satisfactory mobile experience, its intervention on how standards are established in the World Wide Web comes inevitably from a position of major strength, moreover so if we consider that the bulk of content that should adopt Google's standards is produced by news media outlets which are experiencing a consistent economic pressure within the digital landscape, as we have seen in the first section of this chapter.

However, direct platform intervention in regulating and promoting news media content circulation among their crowds is not enforced only by Google. In June 2015, Apple launched its News application. Within Apple News, news media outlets are allowed to publish directly on the application which has become a standalone feature in all Apple products and, while 'content will be hosted and delivered on Apple's platform, the publishers will own the content and control the format of articles. Publishers will also be able to sell premium ads through the app and keep the revenue' (Gibbs, 2015). In 2011, Apple News application replaced Apple Newsstand. The choice Apple has made with its new application seems to replicate what it has done with iTunes as a distribution store for music. With Apple News, it is offering to news media outlets a closed environment and a percentage in advertising revenues to publishers in exchange for content. To build an efficient environment, Apple focused on the convenience for publishers is to have control over the propriety of content they choose to publish via Apple News but not on advertising nor the platform itself.

Another major platform in the contemporary digital landscape, Facebook, has started in 2015 to publish editorial content directly within its platform, sharing part of the advertising revenue with media outlets. The media critic at *The New York Times* David Carr wrote a year before Facebook's project was launched:

> That kind of wholesale transfer of content sends a cold, dark chill down the collective spine of publishers, both traditional and digital insurgents alike. If Facebook's mobile app hosted publishers' pages, the relationship with customers, most of the data about what they did and the reading experience would all belong to the platform. Media companies would essentially be serfs in a kingdom that Facebook owns. (2014)

The stance expressed by Carr (2014) was shared by other observers, such as Trevor Timm, who underlined 'the most crucial element of Facebook's new power: the right to choose between the free expression of ideas or to instead impose censorship when it deems content unworthy' (Timm, 2015). As Carr pointed out, this phase of digital publishing did constitute a turning point for the news media outlets and platforms alike, as the creation of entities that are not freely reachable represents a shift from what Tim Berners-Lee envisioned when he originally conceived the World Wide Web. In an article published in *Scientific American*, Berners-Lee described his original intent in creating the World Wide Web:

> The primary design principle underlying the Web's usefulness and growth is universality. When you make a link, you can link to anything. That means people must be able to put anything on the Web, no matter what computer they have, software they use or human language they speak and regardless of whether they have a wired or wireless Internet connection. (2010: 82)

Berners-Lee underlined the shift to websites and services that use the World Wide Web but keep the data from being universally available. The lack of data transferability from one context to the other, made Berners-Lee define these websites and services as 'a silo, walled off from the others' (Berners-Lee, 2010: 82). Thus, platforms are expanding walled-off silos, hosting and organising news media content without sharing production costs attached to it, while promoting crowd participation, following the dynamic we explored in the first chapter as we were describing the main actors of the digital landscape. The news industry, on the other side, has fractionated its production to the point it does not own the digital paper nor the digital printing press nor the digital distribution of its content. As we have seen, the path followed by the news media industry, based on its conception as an intermediary between advertisers and readers (McLuhan, 1994) has led to a pursuit of distribution practices that drove it into a wave of non-creative destruction.

However, this process has not been as frictionless as imagined by platforms which have opted to host news media content within their walled gardens. Whereas Facebook started its experiment with a limited number of publications in 2015, it subsequently made Instant Articles available to a more significant number of outlets. However, a research published on the *Columbia Journalism Review* in 2018 showed that over half of the news media outlets originally chosen to be Facebook partners have ceased to use this distribution practice (Brown, 2018). Among the news outlets which appear to have ceased to use Instant Articles are *The New York Times*, *The Guardian* and *The Washington Post*, whereas this tool has been embraced by other outlets, as stated by Facebook, which underlined that in June 2017 there were 10,000 publishers globally adopting Instant Articles (Brown, 2018). Hence, whereas the volume of publishers adopting Instant Articles has grown, their composition has evolved as some of the most relevant early adopters have ceased to embrace Facebook's standard. Emily Bell underlined what a complete adoption of these type of tools implies for news media outlets, as

> we will see news companies totally abandoning production capacity, technology capacity and even advertising departments and delegating it all to third-party platforms in an attempt to stay afloat. However, this is a high risk strategy: you lose control over your relationship with your readers and viewers, your revenue, and even the path your stories take to reach their destination. (2016)

Facebook has repeatedly addressed news media outlets' loss of control and revenue by underlining its nature as a distribution platform rather than a publisher. As we have seen in the first chapter, within the digital landscape, a platform aims to establish the most frictionless environment within the digital landscape and for Facebook qualifying itself as a distribution platform serves this purpose. Bell (2016) referred to an interview that Mark Zuckerberg did with Axel Springer CEO Mathias Döpfner where he expressed Facebook's point of view.

DÖPFNER: Is Facebook a distribution platform or a publisher?

ZUCKERBERG: Definitely a distribution platform.

DÖPFNER: Why don't you want to become a publisher?

ZUCKERBERG: Because we're a technology company. I think the platform is the core of our product that people use to share and consume media, but we ourselves are not a media company. [...] We want to remain a technology company. (Döpfner, 2016)

However, in 2018, Mark Zuckerberg announced a series of changes to the News Feed technology, the core of Facebook's operation, that indicate that there might have been a partial change in his stance. In a series of three updates published between January and February 2018 on his personal Facebook page, Zuckerberg outlined a new strategy that would regulate the relationship between the news media industry and Facebook. The first update announced a major overhaul in the News Feed's composition:

We're making a major change to how we build Facebook. [...] The first changes you'll see will be in News Feed, where you can expect to see more from your friends, family and groups. As we roll this out, you'll see less public content like posts from businesses, brands, and media. And the public content you see more will be held to the same standard – it should encourage meaningful interactions between people. (Zuckerberg, 2018a)

The second update, published on 19 January 2018, addressed two different matters, one concerning the quality of news content featured within Facebook's News Feed and the other concerning who should determine what sources are to be considered 'trustworthy':

Today I'm sharing our second major update this year: to make sure the news you see, while less overall, is high quality. I've asked our product teams to make sure we prioritize news that is trustworthy, informative, and local. And we're starting next week with trusted sources. [...] The hard question we've struggled with is how to decide what news sources are broadly trusted in a world with so much division. [...] We decided that having the community determine which sources are broadly trusted would be most objective. (Zuckerberg, 2018b)

In the third update, Zuckerberg underlined the intention of attributing further relevance to local news in the future composition of the social network's News Feed (Zuckerberg, 2018c). One of the most prominent critiques of Zuckerberg's position was published on *The Atlantic* by Franklin Foer, who defined the announced changes to the News Feed as 'a concession of defeat' (Foer, 2018), as Facebook transformed its self-identification from a distribution and technology platform into a publisher. According to the author, 'that description, which trumpeted Facebook's passivity and neutrality, could never really sustain close scrutiny. And after the election of Donald Trump, Facebook has received no end of that' (Foer, 2018). Moreover, according to Foer, this new evolution in Facebook's policy towards the news media will allow it to develop new strategies as 'digital advertising and ever-growing web traffic will never sustain the industry, especially if that traffic comes from monopolies like Facebook hoping to claim the entirety of digital-advertising dollars for themselves' (Foer, 2018). Other media sector observers, such as Mathew Ingram, underlined a different aspect that Facebook's decision might have, as

media companies are addicted to Facebook's algorithm-directed traffic, Facebook is the one who helped get them hooked. The company has spent years pushing media outlets to integrate themselves into its network, via video, Facebook Live, and Facebook's Instant Articles format for mobile. And in order to achieve the same kind of reach they had before, some are resorting to paying for their content to be promoted. That's a win for Facebook, and a loss for cash-strapped media companies. (2018)

Both authors – Foer (2018) and Ingram (2018) – seem to envision Facebook's policy evolution as a form of disengagement in its relationship with the news media industry. However, Facebook's new policy, outlined by Zuckerberg (2018a, 2018b) and the reactions it has provoked both reinforce the dominance that platforms have over the news media within the digital landscape. Moreover, rather than disengaging from the news media industry, Facebook's new policy appears to define more strict ground rules that publishers have to go by if they wish to interact – namely, receive traffic – with the platform's services. A long-form journalism story regarding Facebook published on *WIRED* in February 2018 (Thompson and Vogelstein, 2018), underlines how rather than being 'a defeat' (Foer, 2018), Facebook's new policy is 'is a retreat from "Anything goes if it works with our algorithm to drive up engagement"' (Thompson and Vogelstein, 2018). Moreover, this new evolution, according to the two *WIRED* writers, does not mean that Facebook will conceive itself as a publisher: 'The company has always answered that question defiantly – platform, platform, platform – for regulatory, financial, and maybe even emotional reasons. But now, gradually, Facebook has evolved' (Thompson and Vogelstein, 2018). However, it has evolved into a more controlling entity, thus not modifying the power balance in favour of the news media industry but rather strengthening its position as a gatekeeper.

In 2019, Facebook announced plans to move news outlet production into a dedicated space within the platform, named 'Facebook News' (Brown and Sarantakos 2019), claiming 'will feature a wide range of content across four categories of publishers: general, topical, diverse and local news'. This feature, at first available only for US users, has now expanded to the United Kingdom and other countries (Doub, 2020). Moreover, as underlined by Doub, 'We will pay publishers for content that is not already on the platform, help publishers reach new audiences and bring more advertising and subscription opportunities. The first group of publishers featured in Facebook News in the UK includes Archant, Conde Nast, The Economist, ESI Media, Guardian Media Group, Hearst, Iliffe, JPI Media, Midland News Association, Reach, STV and others' (Doub, 2020). The operation in the UK stems directly from the platform's experience in the us, as 'The UK launch in January will build on the success Facebook News has seen in the US, where we've found more than 95% of the traffic Facebook News delivers to publishers is new audiences that have not interacted with those news outlets in the past' (Doub, 2020). Monetizing content appears to be a consistent trend in more recent times. Google, as Facebook, as rolled out a plan to subsidize news media outlets: 'Google plans to pay $1 billion to publishers globally for their news over the next three years […] a step that could help it win over a powerful group amid heightened regulatory scrutiny worldwide' (Chee, 2020). The operation, named 'Google News Initiative' is set to allow 'publishers to pick and present their stories, will launch on Google News on Android devices and eventually on Apple devices' (Chee, 2020). The funding will be divided in three years and is aimed at some 200 publishers, and comes at a time when Google is under intense scrutiny over its practices, especially in Europe and Australia (Chee, 2020). However, as underlined in Chapter 1, both Facebook and Google's funding seems to be coherent with our definition of 'constant flux' as a distinguishing feature of the digital landscape, which has to be maintained in order to minimise conflict between individuals, crowds and platforms.

New Practices within the Digital Landscape: The Long-Tail Model and the Role of Filtering

As described in the previous section of this chapter, conceiving the media industry mainly as an intermediary between readers and advertisers (McLuhan, 1994) and a number of choices made within the industry have contributed to its current state within the digital landscape. Moreover, the digital landscape has developed specific consumption and distribution practices which have profoundly modified the manner in which goods, services and information are produced and distributed. One of the most prominent theories based on these practices is named the 'long-tail' (Anderson, 2009b).

Chris Anderson first published an article entitled 'The Long Tail' on *WIRED* magazine in 2004, later developing it into a book first published two years later. The author defines the long-tail as 'nothing more than infinite choice. Abundant, cheap distribution means abundant, cheap, and unlimited variety – and that means the audience tends to distribute as widely as the choice' (Anderson, 2009b: 180). Hence, for Anderson, 'in an era without the constraints of physical shelf space and other bottlenecks of distribution, narrowly targeted goods and services can be as economically attractive as mainstream fare' (Anderson, 2009b: 52). The main idea promoted by Anderson is that the digital landscape's nature has set the market free of physical constraints, thus redesigning the way supply and demand interact (Anderson, 2009b).

For Anderson, 'the Web is the ultimate marketplace of ideas, governed by the laws of big numbers' (Anderson, 2009b: 70). Hence, the long-tail creates a new, virtually limitless offer. The digital landscape is the 'perfect market' as it makes 'infinite choice' possible (Anderson, 2009a: 180), allowing the true shape of demand to emerge. However, the author underlines multiple times that the long-tail model only works under two conditions. The first regards shelf space, which has to be ample, while the second condition regards the sale price, which has to be lowered as much as possible. However, not all entities can do so, thus becoming what Anderson describes as 'entrenched industries' (Anderson, 2009b: 185), which fail to lower the cost of their goods, services or information and are thus incapable of adapting to the non-creative destruction we described in the previous section. Different actors within the digital landscape, such as crowds and platforms, exist only as marketplace actors: production, distribution and consumption of any type of good or service are possible only within the market frame. The more effective intermediation is, the bigger the profits will be for intermediaries, or 'aggregators' (Anderson, 2009b: 88). Thus, intermediation is the real value-generator in the long-tail (Anderson, 2009b). Hence, traditional producers, such as the news media industry, are disrupted by new subjects, aggregators, which are designed to aggregate multiple choices and create filters for individuals (which will be clustered in crowds) to use. To prove his point, Anderson refers to his news consumption, underlining

> I may not read any more words than I once did, but they're more likely to be meaningful to me, thanks to much better filters (better at suiting my own interests than, say, the editors of any newspaper) preselecting what I do read. (2009b: 137–138)

Individuals and crowds experience a new and enhanced filtering capacity due to the presence of aggregators, which perform this task at a more effective cost and operate without the need to compensate traditional intermediaries. For Anderson, the news media industry was

> the first industry to really feel the impact of the Internet. […] The decline of newspapers, which are down more than a third in circulation from their mid-Eighties

peak, is the most concrete evidence of the disruptive effect the Long Tail can have on entrenched industries. (2009b: 185)

However, this new filtering process will be more disruptive, and the market more effective only as far as the task it performs can be outsourced by aggregators from producers and traditional industries to consumers. As such, Anderson's long-tail theory is coherent with the framing described in Chapter 1, as we highlighted the role of filtering (Pariser, 2012) and produsers (Bruns, 2008) within the contemporary digital landscape.

The Digital Landscape as a Digital Public Sphere

As we have seen, the long-tail model developed by Anderson (2009b) complements our framing of the contemporary digital landscape, describing its features as a marketplace driven by infinite choice and lowering prices, where intermediaries have a leading role. However, further insights can be gained assessing if the digital landscape can also be defined as a public sphere. According to the European Organization for Nuclear Research (CERN), the World Wide Web has been available to public access since 6 August 1991, when Tim Berners-Lee 'posted a summary of the World Wide Web project on several internet newsgroups. [...] The move marked the debut of the web as a publicly available service on the internet' (CERN, 2012). However, as underlined by Papacharissi

> it should be clarified that a new public space is not synonymous with a new public sphere. As public space, the internet provides yet another forum for political deliberation. As public sphere, the internet could facilitate discussion that promotes a democratic exchange of ideas and opinions. (2002: 11)

In her analysis, Papacharissi focuses on three aspects, which are 'the ability of the internet to carry and transport information, its potential to bring people from diverse backgrounds together, and its future in a capitalist era' (2002: 12). The first aspect underlined by Papacharissi is that digital access is not granted to all individuals; the availability of devices and networks constitutes its preconditions. Moreover, once individuals gain access to further information, they might not be 'able or willing' to engage with it. The second aspect underlined by Papacharissi is the difference between the Internet and past spaces in which the public sphere developed, as 'the internet may actually enhance the public sphere, but it does so in a way that is not comparable to our past experiences of public discourse' (Papacharissi, 2002: 10). Finally, Papacharissi focuses on the risk that 'capitalist patterns of production may commodify these new technologies, transforming them into commercially oriented media that have little to do with promoting social welfare' (Papacharissi, 2002: 20).

Hence, according to Papacharissi (2002), whereas the World Wide Web has generated a new space which could enhance the public sphere, it is not by itself a guarantee of the birth of a digital public sphere. However, Jostein Gripsrud and Hallvard Moe, in describing the impact of digitisation on mass media 'which have always constituted the necessary infrastructure for the modern public sphere', conclude that

> by 2010, all media are fundamentally digital not only the by-now more-than-a-decade old World Wide Web. It also applies to television, radio and film, which have been digitized through and through. Even newspapers and books depend on digital technologies for their production and distribution, and they are also, as a rule, now produced in parallel digital editions. Consequently, the mediated public sphere is by now a digital public sphere. (2010: 9)

Gripsrud and Moe also define the three major challenges faced by the digital public sphere: 'First, by the processes of globalization in a broad sense; second, by a blurring of borders between media, which can be summed up as convergence; and third, by a thorough marketization of the media' (Gripsrud and Moe, 2010: 12). The impact of the three challenges outlined by Gripsrud and Moe has been so radical and profound that it has transformed the nature of entities in the digital landscape, as globally established, multi-sector for-profit platforms have prevailed, as we have seen in Chapter 1.

However, alternatives to this outcome were still thought as possible during the first years of the World Wide Web (McChesney, 1996). McChesney wondered how the non-profit, non-commercial sector would contribute to the new public sphere: 'In short, will this sector be able to create a twenty first century, Habermasian "public sphere", where informed interactive debate can flower independent of government or commercial control?' (McChesney, 1996: 108). Within the contemporary digital landscape, the commodification process of the news media industry has become increasingly related to the rise of ephemeral content production and consumption (Gripsrud and Moe, 2010). Hence, the hope for an enhanced role of a non-profit non-commercial sector of new media production (McChesney, 1996) has confronted itself with the increasing relevance of economic dynamics within the digital public sphere.

Within this process of commodification, the news consumption cycle in the digital public sphere has accelerated to a point it can be defined as 'a cyclone' (Klinenberg, 2005), spanning across twenty-four hours, seven days a week. Klinenberg underlines that 'the regular news cycle has spun into an erratic and unending pattern that I characterize as a *news cyclone.* [...] there is always breaking news to produce, consume, and – for reporters and their subjects – react against' (Klinenberg, 2005: 54). It is not just the news consumption cycle that has accelerated: the news production cycle in the digital public sphere has followed a similar path. However, this acceleration has also impacted news production quality, as underlined by Hachten and Scotton: 'The Internet and the twenty-four-hour cable news cycle can greatly accelerate a story, often to the detriment of traditional journalistic practices such as verifying sources and creating context' (Hachten and Scotton, 2016: 67).

As news consumption and production have both accelerated within the digital landscape, this dynamic has also had an impact on past digital production. In 1989, when Tim Berners-Lee proposed a system to manage information, one of his aims was to discuss 'the problems of loss of information about complex evolving systems' and offer solutions 'based on the distributed hypertext system' (Berners-Lee, 1989). However, in the contemporary digital landscape, the loss of information published on the World Wide Web is a constant and pressing issue. The United States Library of Congress program officer Abbey Potter focused on the matter, underlining 'We have clear data that if content is not captured from the web soon after its creation, it is at risk' (Potter, 2015).

The same conclusion has been reached by Andy Jackson, technical lead of the United Kingdom Web Archive. Jackson presented the following data while describing the Open UK Web Archive project during the 2015 General Assembly of the International Internet Preservation Consortium. In order to understand what happened to the archived collection over time and to better assess what Jackson defines as 'web's volatility' (Jackson, 2015), a random sample of 1000 URLs from each year of the archive was crawled in order to compare the URL and content status between the archived one and the present one. Results show that the amount of identical content is marginal if compared to the content which was rated either gone, error or missing. The URLs which appear to be the same or simply moved by redirects are more than half only if the search is limited to the last four years in exam (2013–2009), hence 'after just two years 40 per cent of the URLs are gone or missing' (Jackson, 2015). Moreover, among those URLs which were categorised as not moved or redirected, Jackson stresses that 'the vast majority have actually changed. Very few are binary identical, and while about half of the pages remain broadly similar after two years, that fraction tails off as we go back in time' (Jackson, 2015). In conclusion, '50 per cent of the content is lost after just one year, with more being lost each subsequent year' (Jackson, 2015).

The issue of deterioration on the World Wide Web is shared by all content, including news media production. This deterioration affects all types of news media production, including relevant long-form journalism stories. On *The Atlantic*, Adrienne Lafrance focused on the disappearance from the World Wide Web of a work published by American journalist Kevin Vaughan in 2007 (Lafrance, 2015). Vaughan's digital thirty-four-part series was a 2008 Pulitzer Prize finalist and disappeared from the World Wide Web as *The Rocky Mountain News*, the historic American outlet which published it, closed and its website went offline. According to Lafrance, the fate of Vaughan's long-form journalism production is highly relevant, as 'if a sprawling Pulitzer Prize-nominated feature in one of the nation's oldest newspapers can disappear from the web, anything can' (Lafrance, 2015). This issue, while certainly connected to the broader phenomenon of preservation of content in the digital landscape, is also connected to the accelerated production and consumption process of the news cycle.

Other factors are likewise emerging in the contemporary conservation of digital news production which can be subject to legal issues and economic pressure, as in the case of *Gawker*. *Gawker* was founded in 2003 and ceased operations in 2015, when 'the company fell victim to a barrage of lawsuits, filed by different plaintiffs but paid for by one person, the billionaire PayPal co-founder and Trump supporter Peter Thiel' (Bustillos, 2018). A partial response to the issue posed by news outlets disappearing has been the initiative led by the Freedom of the Press Foundation, which has launched an effort to store online archive collections. The Director of Special Projects Parker Higgins describes the decision to start from *Gawker*'s archive as a response to a possible acquisition of its archives by 'a hostile party' (Higgins, 2018). The Freedom of the Press Foundation's project will focus on outlets threatened by what is defined as the 'billionaire problem', meaning the influence that economically powerful individuals have over the fate of outlets which can either be bought and closed or hit by lawsuits against which they are not able to defend themselves.

Multiple factors, as we have seen, contribute to the precariousness of content published on the World Wide Web. These factors are moreover relevant for news media outlets which operate in the digital landscape, reinforcing the notion that the contemporary digital public sphere is increasingly based on the ephemeral content and an accelerated news cycle. Moreover, within this accelerated news production and consumption cycle, 'The Web dwells in a never-ending present. It is – elementally – ethereal, ephemeral, unstable, and unreliable' (Lepore, 2015).

In the first part of this chapter, we have analysed the evolution of the news media industry within the digital landscape, underlining how a revenue model based on advertising distribution has led to disruption by platforms, which operate as more effective intermediaries. Moreover, we have identified the digital landscape as a digital public sphere and underlined the issues it faces regarding content preservation. We have added our analysis of the news media industry evolution to the framework we provided in the first chapter, which focused on the main actors (individuals, crowds, platforms) and features (flux and non-creative destruction) of the contemporary digital landscape. Hence, we shall now narrow our focus to long-form journalism and archives, which are the two specific forms of news media production in the contemporary digital landscape at the centre of this work.

Long-Form Journalism and Archives

A Functional Definition of Long-Form Journalism

Having assessed the nature of the contemporary digital landscape as a digital public sphere and focused on the challenges that content preservation faces within the contemporary digital landscape, we shall now focus on the type of news media production which is at the centre of this work, long-form journalism.

However, before providing a definition of long-form journalism in the digital landscape, useful insights can be found in establishing its relationship with previous forms of journalistic production, such as 'New Journalism'. This relationship is established by Berning, who underlines: 'Online literary reportages become landmarks of the intertextual system that New Journalists used to spell out and according to which readers and texts become partners in the interpretative process' (2011: 2). The 'intertextual system' (Berning, 2011: 2) of New Journalism, was described by Tom Wolfe, one of its major interpreters and theorisers, as a discovery

> [...] modest at first, humble, in fact, deferential, you might say, was that it just might be possible to write journalism that would ... read like a novel. *Like a novel*, if you get the picture. This was the sincerest form of homage to The Novel and to those greats, the novelists, of course. (1973: 9)

According to Murphy (1974), Wolfe's approach to a new style of narration

> detailed the points of similarity and contrast between the New Journalism and the novel. The four techniques of realism that he and the other New Journalists employ, he wrote, had been the sole province of novelists and other *literati*. They are scene-by-scene construction, full record of dialogue, third-person point of view and the manifold incidental details to round out a character (i.e. descriptive incidentals). (1974: 6).

Murphy provides his own definition of New Journalism as 'an artistic, creative, literary reporting form with three basic traits: dramatic literary techniques; intensive reporting; and reporting of generally acknowledged subjectivity' (Murphy, 1974: 16). As we can see, both authors – Wolfe

(1973) and Murphy (1974) – describe New Journalism as utilising techniques that originate in different narrative spheres in order to obtain a very specific effect. Within the contemporary digital landscape, 'New Journalism' proved to be a significant source of effective tools, as emphasised by Berning (2011):

> Similar to the process of immersion, dramatic devices employed by New Journalists almost half a century ago are being transformed into participatory activities on the Internet. Moreover, the features of the Internet allow for new forms of multiperspectival narration. Taken together electronic properties can lead to an increase in authenticity and credibility for online narrative journalism. (2011: 4)

Our case studies analysis of two different long-form journalism stories, in Chapters 3 and 4, will demonstrate how 'the features of the Internet allow for new forms of multiperspectival narration' (Berning, 2011: 4), ideally connecting 'New Journalism' with contemporary long-form journalism in the digital landscape.

In order to provide a definition of long-form journalism in the digital landscape, it is relevant to focus on digital journalism as a scholarly field. Since the turn of the century, digital journalism has established itself as a significant field within journalism production. However, its definition has proven challenging, 'a moving target' (Kawamoto, 2003: 4). Yet, starting from the early 2000s, authors such as Pavlik identified a combination of 'economic, regulatory and cultural forces, driven by technological change' bound to produce 'a massive shift in the nature of journalism' (Pavlik, 2001: xi). Kawamoto defined digital journalism as 'the use of digital technologies to research, produce, and deliver (or make accessible) news and information to an increasingly computer-literate audience' (2003: 4).

Aside from the focus on a possible definition of digital journalism, a lot of attention has been devoted to long-form journalism, 'multimedia narratives that function as cognitive containers' (Dowling and Vogan, 2015: 212), aimed at captivating readers for a prolonged period of time. Tullloch and Ramon (2017), while focusing their analysis on long-form sports journalism, identify a series of traits specific to long-form journalism production in the digital landscape. These include a departure from hyper-accelerated news production (Le Masurier, 2016); the value placed into writing standards

and research (Le Masurier, 2015); the search for originality in content elaboration (Belt and South, 2016); the deployment quality-driven production
techniques (Greenberg, 2012); 'the transparency and self-reflexivity of
journalists' (Tulloch and Ramon, 2017: 653). Moreover, Hiippala underlines the importance of multimedia within digital long-form journalism,
defining it as 'the heart of its narrative structure' (2017: 421). Thus, Hiippala
underlines how multimedia has been at the centre of multimodal research,
a field that 'studies how language, images, typography, layout and other
modes of communication interact and co-operate in different contexts'
(Hiippala, 2017: 421). In his view, the defining aspects of long-form journalism 'appear to arise from the underlying materiality of screen and its
capability to render dynamic content' (Hiippala, 2017: 436).

In parallel, research on digital journalism has evolved, as described by
Domingo (2008) through a series of phases, focusing on the normative,
empirical and constructivist aspect. Moreover, Steensen and Ahva describe the emergence of 'a "fourth wave" of research on digital journalism'
(Steensen and Ahva, 2015: 1), focusing on a news environment profoundly
influenced by 'practices predominantly related to social media' (Steensen
and Ahva, 2015: 1). These practices are envisioned by Hermida as 'part of a
range of Internet technologies enabling the disintermediation of news and
undermining the gatekeeping function of journalists' (Hermida, 2010: 300).
More specifically, according to Pavlik, innovation in the field of digital
journalism and news media in general

> lies along at least four dimensions […] (1) creating, delivering and presenting
> quality news content, (2) engaging the public in an interactive news discourse,
> (3) employing new methods of reporting optimized for the digital, networked age,
> and (4) developing new management and organizational strategies for a digital,
> networked and mobile environment. (2001: 183)

Thus, as we can see, both digital journalism and studies focusing on long-
form journalism have been influenced by the digital landscape. While
this part of our work focuses specifically on the influence of platforms on
journalistic production, such influence has also been analysed from complementary perspectives such as those developed by Lasorsa, Lewis and
Holton (2012) which focus on how journalists use platforms – specifically

Twitter – and how 'they are normalizing it to fit their existing professional norms and practices, and how it is changing those norms and practices' (Lasorsa, Lewis and Holton, 2012: 32). The influence of platforms in the production process at an individual level is likewise described by Hermida as a decisive factor in the emergence of 'ambient journalism' which is defined as 'an awareness system that offers diverse means to collect, communicate, share and display news and information, serving diverse purposes' (Hermida, 2010: 301).

Hence, digital journalism can be envisioned at the intersection of what we have described as the main actors of the digital landscape such as individuals, crowds and platforms and appears to affect all entities in the digital landscape, influencing production, distribution and consumption among individuals, crowds and platforms. Thus, this work positions itself within the framework developed by Usher in her work *Interactive Journalism*, as she stresses both the novelty of digital long-form journalism as 'a new subspecialty of the journalism profession' (Usher, 2016: 15) and, more vitally, how 'interactive journalism is essential to understanding news production in the digital age' (Usher, 2016: 16).

Having established the connection between long-form journalism and New Journalism and provided an outlook on digital journalism, we shall now attempt to provide a comprehensive definition of long-form journalism in the contemporary digital landscape. As underlined by Johanna Vehkoo, this process can be challenging, since 'there are no universal quality criteria carved in stone. Judgments of quality are often culture-specific, or related to one's socio-economic background, level of education and so on' (Vehkoo, 2010: 4). However, long-form journalism seems to share a general objective that should be at the basis of journalistic activity, according to Bill Kovach and Tom Rosenstiel (2003). In their view, the purpose of journalism should be 'to provide people with the information they need to be free and self-governing' (Kovach and Rosenstiel, 2003: 35).

Long-form journalism in the digital landscape does appear to reflect this specific journalistic function, which is to develop in-depth narratives. Moreover, the creation of such in-depth narratives is based on a series of elements, some of which are specific to the digital landscape and concur to its creation. One of these specific elements is the involvement of different professionals that contribute to the creation of long-form journalism. Aside from reporters, editors and photo editors, all of which have been long present in the traditional journalistic production process, within the digital landscape they are joined by programmers, video and audio editors and content management system experts. However, it is important to underline that long-form journalism in the digital landscape is not defined by the number of words, which in the past reflected the importance attributed to a given journalistic production as space was limited and expensive, both in print newspapers and magazines.

Thus, we can provide the following definition for long-form journalism in the digital landscape:

> Long-form journalism in the digital landscape is built with the participation of many different professionals aside from the sole journalist, uniting text, audio and visual content together with data visualisation tools and specifically built datasets. However, these elements can be combined differently, without any being compulsory. Long-form journalism is likewise defined by its capacity to attract reader time rather than the number of words.

The Common Ground between Long-Form Journalism and News Archives

After defining long-form journalism in the digital landscape, we aim to explore if there is a possible common ground between this specific form of journalistic practice and the role of news archives within media outlets. Before assessing if this connection exists, it is relevant to underline the challenges in news production and distribution faced within the digital landscape as a digital public sphere. This aspect is especially relevant as we can identify long-form journalism as a provider of information individuals 'need to be free and self-governing' (Kovach and Rosenstiel, 2003: 35). Thus, news media outlet production within the digital landscape can be framed within the notion of information developed by Charlotte Hess and Elinor Ostrom (2003). Hess and Ostrom define information as a human artefact ('a discreet, observable, nameable representation of an idea or a set of ideas') with 'an important cultural component as well as intellectual, economic, and political function'; moreover, they describe it as a 'flow resource, that must be passed from one individual to another to have any public value' (Hess and Ostrom, 2003: 129–132).

In the digital landscape, as we analysed in the first section of this chapter, control over publishing forms has been shifting from news media outlets to platforms, which can also be defined as 'aggregators' within the long-tail model (Anderson, 2009b: 88). This shift is native to the digital landscape and is rooted in the better market-based distribution efficiency performed by these entities if compared to traditional news media outlets (Anderson, 2009b). This shift in distribution practices has direct consequences on the news industry capacity to produce and distribute content autonomously.

The influence of the digital landscape on news media outlets has not regarded only content creation and distribution practices but has had an impact on the role of news media archives and their maintenance and distribution practices. Thus, the effects of the shift between news media outlets and platforms are affecting both news production, consumption and news archival practices. As underlined by Kramer: 'Publishers must also think about workflows for archiving their original content published on these platforms […] for the benefit of future audiences, journalists, and historians' (Kramer, 2015).

Moreover, it relevant to underline how the task of archiving has begun to shift from the open market to secular democratic states 'charged with the duty of conservation, although not necessary selection' (Assmann, 2011: 342). Archiving practices performed by public entities are challenged by the insurgence of new operators such as platforms and are not limited to news outlets production, (Potter, 2015). Potter emphasises that

> news content that's available for purchase and printed in a newspaper is a small subset of the content that's created and available online. Videos, interactive graphs, comments and other user-generated data are almost exclusively available online. The absence of an acquisition stream for this content puts it at risk of being lost to future library and archives users. (2015)

Within this frame, long-form journalism and news archives share common challenges regarding preservation in the contemporary digital landscape, as both are increasingly based on networked elements. We have seen how multiple elements concur in the definition we have provided of long-form journalism, hence archiving these new digitalised productions requires new storage and repository schemes.

Together with new approaches to the challenges posed by the networked nature of the digital landscape, long-form journalism and archives share new distribution and curation possibilities, which we will analyse in detail in Chapter 6. As we will see, these possibilities have been exploited more widely by third-party aggregators rather than directly by news media outlets themselves. According to Anna Hiatt, as she describes in the second part of *Tales from the Great Disruption*, third-party aggregators such as LongReads or Longform.org constitute an answer to the long-tail model (Shapiro, Hiatt and Hoyt, 2015). These third-party aggregators' activity, better suited to adapt to the contemporary environment, have indicated that there is a possible new, prolonged life arc for long-form journalism in the digital landscape. In Chapter 6, we shall provide a case-study of one of these aggregators, Longform.org, which operates at the intersection between long-form journalism and archives. As we shall see, by curating digital anthologies, working on stories based on archives, long-form journalism re-enters the consumption cycle and is capable of doing so because it differs substantially from the vast mass of ephemeral content produced in the accelerated production cycle of the digital public sphere, which is created and consumed in a very short lapse of time.

Sharing both networking complexity and new distribution possibilities in the digital landscape, long-form journalism and news media archives are based on a time frame that differs radically from what is defined as production based 'on Internet time' (MacCormack, Verganti and Iansiti, 2001). MacCormack, Verganti and Iansiti (2001) describe flexibility as the main characteristic of this type of product development and underline

> constructs which support a more flexible development process are associated with better-performing projects in a highly uncertain and dynamic environment. This flexible process is characterized by the ability to generate and respond to new information for a longer proportion of a development cycle. (2001: 146).

However, as news media outlets transfer this type of flexibility into the production process, the by-product is a more productive yet profoundly homogeneous market, where speed is increasingly the main production factor. The increase in media and information production is not directly proportional to its usefulness as underlined by Nate Silver in his book *The Signal and the Noise*. As volumes in production increase, the signal (the original output) and the noise (the echo chamber effect in replicative iterations) become increasingly entangled (Silver, 2013). Silver underlines

> if the quantity of information is increasing by 2.5 quintillion bytes per day, the amount of *useful* information almost certainly isn't. Most of it is just noise, and the noise is increasing faster than the signal. There are so many hypotheses to test, so many data sets to mine – but a relatively constant amount of objective truth. (2013: 13)

Within the news media field, the entangling effect between the signal and the noise (Silver, 2013) becomes overwhelming very rapidly, as underlined by Shapiro, Hiatt and Hoyt:

> With access to every magazine published this week, not to mention the growing archives of every magazine on the stand, and more content being published by the day, it can feel to the eager reader a little like standing under a dam, watching the cement begin to crack and waiting for the water to sweep you away. The flood of content is overwhelming. (2015: 174)

Both long-form journalism and news media archives share the need for a different, wider time frame, both production and consumption wise. This shared time frame is also the factor that makes long-form journalism writing and news archive aggregation and curation stand out compared to the majority of the contemporary, intensive media production and indicate a common ground between these two entities within the digital landscape.

PART II

Long-Form Journalism, Two Case Studies

CHAPTER 3

'Snow Fall': A Landmark in Long-Form Journalism

The New York Times 'Snow Fall', a Turning Point

An Introduction to 'Snow Fall'

After assessing a framework of the digital landscape and focusing on the news media industry and providing a definition of long-form journalism, a case-study analysis of a single of long-form journalism story is one of the primary tools at our disposal to investigate in-depth the nature of this form of journalistic production.

We chose the case-study method as it allows in-depth analysis to be performed and the use of several data sources (Feagin, Orum and Sjoberg, 1991). Within our case-study analysis, we shall apply other methods, such as textual analysis and digital methods. We have chosen to adopt a text analysis method to formulate a 'strategic selection and presentation of analysed text as the evidence for the overall argument' (Fürsich, 2009: 240). However, we implemented text analysis as 'just one part of discourse analysis' (Fairclough, 2001: 91) in order to also provide an '*interpretation* of the relationship between text and interaction, and *explanation* of the relationship between interaction and social context' (Fairclough, 2001: 91). As described by Philo (2007), we aim to investigate 'mass communications as a totality in which meanings were circulated through the key dimensions of production, content and reception' (Philo, 2007: 194). Additionally, we shall apply digital methods (Rogers, 2013) as they are a useful tool to assess the production process and reception of this type of journalistic production within the digital landscape. This chapter and the following will focus on two case studies, to which we shall apply the methods described above in a cohesive manner, to produce comparable results between the two analyses.

The first long-form journalism story case-study is entitled 'Snow Fall: The Avalanche at Tunnel Creek' (Branch, 2012) and was published online by *The New York Times* on 20 December 2012. We have chosen this specific long-form journalism story as it has been defined as a landmark production in digital long-form journalism production (Martínez, 2013; Johnson, 2013; Dowling and Vogan, 2015; Hernandez and Rue, 2016). Moreover, within the news media industry, the title of this story has eventually become a proxy for a specific practice regarding long-form journalism production: 'To "snowfall" a work, then, means to put one's best product in the market in a way that participates in these trends in digital design and narrative while building and communicating an organization's brand' (Dowling and Vogan, 2015: 219).

'Snow Fall' comprises a six-chapter 17,000-word story, multiple videos and audio segments, a documentary, animations and photo galleries in an ad hoc created suite. John Branch, the 'Snow Fall' writer, has received a Pulitzer Prize in the Feature Writing category 'for his evocative narrative about skiers killed in an avalanche and the science that explains such disasters, a project enhanced by its deft integration of multimedia elements' (Pulitzer Prizes, 2013). 'Snow Fall' has also been awarded a Peabody Prize for its 'lucid, enveloping multi-media experience' (Peabody Awards, 2013) and a Webby Award for 'Best Use of Interactive Video' in the Online Film and Video category (Webby Awards, 2013).

The event at the centre of 'Snow Fall' is an avalanche that took place on 19 February 2012 at Tunnel Creek in the proximity of Stevens Pass, Washington, United States during a backcountry ski expedition, leaving three people dead and one injured. 'Snow Fall' (Branch, 2012) narrates what happened before, during and after the avalanche and its functional elements adhere to the ones provided in our definition of a long-form journalism story. 'Snow Fall' has been produced in three different formats. Aside from the digital version which was published online on *The New York Times* website on 20 December 2012, the story was also published in the print version of *The New York Times* on 23 December 2012. In that instance, the story was repackaged as a fourteen-page special section of the newspaper. Moreover, 'Snow Fall' was published two years later, in 2014, as an eBook by digital publisher *Byliner* featuring an additional chapter entitled 'The

Backcountry, Reconsidered' (Branch, 2014). Hence, while 'Snow Fall' exists in three different formats, we shall focus our analysis on the digital version published online on 20 December 2012 on *The New York Times* website.

The Production Process and Reception of 'Snow Fall'

Due to the relevance of this long-form story and the resources *The New York Times* devoted to its creation, it is relevant to describe 'Snow Fall's' production process. Assessing the number and role of professionals involved in the project is useful to better understand this production's outcome. Furthermore, 'Snow Fall' has also stimulated the birth of tools and services that aim to recreate what can be defined as a 'Snow Fall' experience. Moreover, 'Snow Fall' has evolved into a verb, as emphasised by the former *The New York Times* executive editor Jill Abramson: 'To "snowfall" means to tell a story with fantastic graphics and video and every kind of multimedia, and that is absolutely organic to the storytelling itself' (Martínez, 2013). Moreover, 'to snowfall', according to Dowling and Vogan, 'means to put one's best product in the market' (Dowling and Vogan, 2015: 219). While we shall analyse 'Snow Fall's' legacy later in this chapter, our first step shall be to reconstruct the production process as it has been described in *The New York Times* and elsewhere by both writer John Branch and the development team.

After the avalanche that took place at Tunnel Creek on 18 February 2012, *The New York Times* ran two separate stories. The first article was a chronicle of the events and was published online on 19 February 2012. The second article was a feature on the front page of the paper edition of *The New York Times*, published on 21 February 2012. After these two articles were published, John Branch was given the task to write an in-depth story by the Sports Editor at *The New York Times*, Joe Sexton. According to Branch

> a couple of days after the avalanche in February, *The Times* had a front-page article about the recent spate of avalanche deaths, particularly among expert skiers. To most editors, that would have been more than enough. But Joe saw the potential for telling the story in a more powerful, yet narrower, way. And he assigned me the task. (*The New York Times*, 2012)

'Snow Fall's' production process begun in a traditional work assessment fashion within news media outlets. An editor – Sexton – assigned the task to a journalist – Branch – who worked on it for six months. Branch described in detail his work on the story, which included 'interviews with every survivor, the families of the deceased, first responders at Tunnel Creek, officials at Stevens Pass and snow-science experts' (*The New York Times*, 2012). Branch also analysed 'reports by the police, the medical examiner and the Stevens Pass Ski Patrol, as well as 40 calls to 911 made in the aftermath of the avalanche' (*The New York Times*, 2012). Branch's approach 'was a classic application of the DOT methodology' (Maguire, 2014: 190). Maguire describes DOT acronym as the result of 'Documentary analysis and Observation made in the field [...] completed by substituting the word "talking" for "interviewing"' (Maguire, 2014: 5). Moreover, Branch also stated that, as he started writing his story, '*The New York Times* had committed to telling this story through multimedia' (*The New York Times*, 2012) and underlined that since the beginning of his reporting work, he teamed up with a photographer and a video journalist.

The 'Snow Fall' project also involved eleven among graphics and designers, a photographer, three video makers and one researcher ('Graphics and design by Hannah Fairfield, Xaquín G.V., Jon Huang, Wayne Kamidoi, Sam Manchester, Alan McLean, Jacky Myint, Graham Roberts, Joe Ward, Jeremy White and Josh Williams. Photography by Ruth Fremson. Video by Catherine Spangler. Additional video by Eric Miller and Shane Wilder. Kristen Millares Young contributed research' (Branch, 2012). As we shall see in detail in this section, the involvement of a diverse team of professionals is a fundamental element in the development of long-form journalism in the contemporary digital landscape. Long-form journalism, as we defined it in Chapter 2, is the result of the combination of diverse elements which require the work of different professionals, such as graphics, web designers, which typically operate in the contemporary digital landscape.

In an article published in *Source*, *The New York Times* team described the production process in further detail (Duenes et al., 2013). According to *The New York Times* graphics director Steve Duenes

> the multimedia group agreed that we didn't want to create a bunch of different overlapping pieces and hang them all off the text. We wanted to make a single-story

out of all the assets, including the text. So, the larger project wasn't a typical design effort. (Duenes et al., 2013)

Duenes also emphasised how the 'Snow Fall' project diverged from standard projects: rather than focusing solely on design, the team began to think in terms of 'an editing project that required us to weave things together so that text, video, photography and graphics could all be consumed in a way that was similar to reading – a different kind of reading' (Duenes et al., 2013) Duenes further stresses that the work by the team and the journalist and editors progressed in a parallel manner, 'exchanging files and reviewing process together' (Duenes et al., 2013). It is also important to underline that the team at work on 'Snow Fall' was also involved at the same time in other projects such as the 2012 London Olympic Games, Hurricane Sandy, the Presidential Elections in the United States and the Sandy Hook Elementary School Shooting in Newtown, Connecticut, United States.

It is important to highlight how the 'Snow Fall' project, while beginning in a traditional manner with an assignment from an editor to a journalist, morphed into a different type of production, aimed at creating a coherent suite that would feature text and elements developed by a large team of professionals, which all worked on the story as a unit. The relationship between the developing team and the editorial staff is further described by Branch, which acknowledges both the role of editors and developers: 'As for the multimedia, editors recognised during my reporting that the videos and audio clips we collected along with photographs and video interviews, would aid the telling of the story online' (*The New York Times*, 2012). Branch gives specific relevance to the role played by Jacky Myint, describing her as the 'the brainchild' of 'Snow Fall's' web design. Myint is a multimedia producer at *The New York Times* and is credited with developing the overall web design of 'Snow Fall'. She started her work imagining a framework design and then the team

went into the prototyping phase and collaborated on how best to integrate the graphics and video into the narrative experience. There was a lot of trial and error and experimenting. […] As we were getting closer to launch, we were able to step back and review the various elements to see how they fit editorially, and we made design revisions and tweaks. (Duenes et al., 2013)

In 2012, Myint also participated to a TED Conference and underlined how the development team 'chose which elements told the story at the right moment in the text, so that each media was doing what it's best at' (Lillie, 2013). After the publication of 'Snow Fall', a number of analysts dedicated attention to the project and how it was created. Media strategist Brook Ellingwood focused on how 'Snow Fall' was built from a technical point of view, identifying the variety of tools used by the development team (Ellingwood, 2012). While Jacky Myint underlined that some custom components were also used in other projects, tools used 'Snow Fall' 'include jQuery, underscore, jPlayer, HTML5 video, jQuery Reel, and jQuery addresses. In triggering scroll-based events, I took inspiration from Remy Sharp's inview jQuery plugin' (Duenes et al., 2013). Ellingwood, using the webpage source code, broke down in detail the combination of tools used by *The New York Times* team. Moreover, he focused on what can be considered as one of the distinguishing features of 'Snow Fall's' overall design, the interaction between video and text.

> When the page is loaded, a simple animation of the CSS 'opacity' property quickly fades in the video cover and title/byline text. This effect, which is certainly accomplished with jQuery, contributes to the cinematic feel and the sleight of hand which draws the viewer's attention to the video first, only realizing there's text after being mesmerized by the blowing snow. (Ellingwood, 2012)

Reconstructing the production process within *The New York Times* has allowed us to outline specific elements that contributed to shaping 'Snow Fall' as a unique piece of work. While the traditional reporting by John Branch was enhanced from the start by the presence of a photographer and a video journalist, it began months before the development team got involved in the project. However, as his editors sensed from the start that ad hoc multimedia components could be featured with the traditional writing, 'Snow Fall's' decisive difference is the fact that the development team was involved in every step of the suite construction, which resulted in a specific blend of words, multimedia elements and development tools. As such, 'Snow Fall' serves as an example of news production that places itself at the intersection between human input, with the different professionals involved and platform usage, with the different digital tools that have been exploited in order to create the end product.

'Snow Fall's' Structure and Writing

Having assessed the production process that led to the creation of 'Snow Fall', we shall now provide a text analysis of *The New York Times*' long-form journalism story, focusing on its structure and writing. We have chosen to apply a text analysis as part of a critical discourse analysis method (Fairclough, 2001) and to complement it with 'the study of key production factors in journalism' and 'the analysis of audience under-standing' (Philo, 2007: 175). However, before concentrating on 'Snow Fall's' features, it is relevant to explore the different structures that digital long-form journalism stories may have in the digital landscape. To do so, we shall utilise a taxonomy developed in an article by Paul Grabowicz, Richard Hernandez and Jeremy Rue published on the Berkeley Advanced Media Institute website (Grabowicz, Hernandez and Rue, 2014).

Grabowicz, Hernandez and Rue define 'online story packages' fol-lowing three major coordinates: 'narrative (linear, non-linear); multimedia (outside, embedded) and media forms (dominant, secondary)' (Grabowicz, Hernandez and Rue, 2014). As far as the 'narrative' coordinate is concerned, 'some stories are presented in a linear fashion similar to narratives in trad-itional media like TV or radio. Alternatively, non-linear stories are sliced into topical segments and it's up to the user to decide how to navigate the package' (Grabowicz, Hernandez and Rue, 2014). The position and role of multimedia in long-form journalism stories are highly relevant as it en-hances different types of consumption:

> sometimes text drives the story and multimedia components like video, graphics or photo slideshows are placed put off to the side. In other cases, multimedia is embedded inside a text story (or even embedded in a video story as interactive elements in the video) or are part of an immersive experience. (Grabowicz, Hernandez and Rue, 2014)

Grabowicz, Hernandez and Rue remark that while among 'online story packages' there is usually one type of media that can be defined as 'dominant', there are other examples that 'draw on many different media forms equally, with different parts of the story told in the type of media most appropriate to that kind of content' (Grabowicz, Hernandez and Rue, 2014). Hence, it is possible to utilise the taxonomy proposed by Grabowicz, Hernandez and Rue to analyse *The New York Times* 'Snow Fall'. From a narrative point of view, 'Snow Fall' is a linear story where multimedia is embedded, and text is the dominant media form. The three authors focus on 'Snow Fall' describing it as

> widely praised for how carefully it blended the multimedia into the text narrative. The multimedia was designed to be viewed while reading the main story [...]. Thus, animations and other graphics would slowly appear at relevant points in the text as you scrolled through. In some cases, the background colour of the text story would gradually change to match the colour of a graphic that would load as you scrolled down through the narrative. (Grabowicz, Hernandez and Rue, 2014)

This classification model was further developed by Hernandez and Rue (2016) in their book *The Principles of Multimedia Journalism: Packaging Digital News*. Hernandez and Rue imagined a triangle identifying three major poles: continuous, comprehensive and immersive, allowing the collocation of stories that featured intersections and contaminations between the different story models (Hernandez and Rue, 2016). According to Hernandez and Rue's new model, 'Snow Fall' can be defined as a 'comprehensive-continuous' story, as

> The continuous nature of the story is apparent in the fact it's a singular 16,000-word linear narrative text story. The story is separated into six chapters, which are designed to be read one after the other, but each is separate, with a title page and a unique topic of the story. The narrative is informational at parts, giving background information, including about avalanches and some of the tools used by skiers to mitigate getting trapped under the snow. The piece is designed with several media forms, including a short-form documentary at the end. When applied to our triangle diagram, we found 'Snow Fall' fit closer to a Continuous narrative, but may qualities fell under the Comprehensive rubric. (2016: 107).

Upon visiting <http://www.nytimes.com/projects/2012/snow-fall>, we are presented with a video header, looping in full-screen, with wind moving snow over a mountaintop. Soon, the title appears on the right side of the screen, reading 'Snow Fall The Avalanche at Tunnel Creek by John Branch'. As soon as the reader prompts any action via keyboard, mouse or trackpad, two lines of text appear at the bottom of the screen: 'The snow burst through the trees with no warning but a last-second whoosh of sound, a two-story wall of white and Chris Rudolph's piercing cry: "Avalanche! Elyse!"' (Branch, 2012).

As the first two lines of the article appear, so do chapter titles at the top of the screen, above the video header. Branch begins his article recurring to an specific lead writing technique, utilised in Homer's *Iliad* and *Odyssey* which 'start not at the beginning but plunge the reader or listener "in medias res", or into the middle of the action' (O'Nolan, 1969: 125). Hence, Branch's objective with his lead choice in 'Snow Fall' is to captivate the reader from the very beginning. The looping video complements Branch's choice, creating a visual frame which reinforces the importance of the first two lines of the text. In the first chapter, as the narration proceeds, Branch alternates parts focused on single victims of the Tunnel Creek avalanche with parts regarding backcountry skiing from a broader perspective.

The first chapter features three sections: the first is centred on one of the victim's first-person account of the avalanche, while the following section, entitled 'Tunnel Creek', focuses on historical elements on the area of the avalanche and backcountry skiing. This specific alternation of narrative elements, such as 'beginning *in medias res,* followed by an expository return to an earlier period, will become one of the formal topoi of the epic' (Genette, 1980: 30). Thus, Branch applies the narrative structure described by Genette (1980) to 'Snow Fall's' beginning, and this choice appears to be particularly effective. The victim's first-person narration provides an intense, compelling account of the event, which is then halted in order to provide background information, setting the pace for his narration of the whole event.

The same technique is used in the second chapter, in the sections 'Predicting Avalanches' and 'The Backcountry Beckons'. However, not all chapters utilise the same structure and are of the same length: out of the six that constitute 'Snow Fall', the first and second chapters are the longest ('Tunnel Creek' 3,000 words; 'To the Peak' 4,500 words) but starting from the third, chapters become shorter ('Descent Begins' 2,800 words; 'Blur of

White' 2,200 words; 'Discovery' 2,200 words; 'Word Spreads' 1,750 words) while animations provide not only technical details – such as the victims' positions on the mountain or how avalanches form – but become a narrative tool. The last three chapters, just as the first, feature a looping video header, making it one of the stylistic choices that constitute a trademark and a guide for the reader between the different chapters.

Moreover, one of the primary and identifying characteristics of 'Snow Fall' is the combined use of parallax scrolling and the curtain effect, 'which creates the sense of revealing or concealing panels of content as the user scrolls' (Rue, 2013). Parallax scrolling is used to make elements in webpage load at different times, move at different speeds, altering the perception of depth by the reader. When parallax scrolling is used jointly with a curtain effect, it produces a captivating outcome for readers (Dowling and Vogan, 2015). Dowling and Vogan underline how text 'gives way to a full-screen video. But when the clip ends, the screen automatically returns to the text. Along these lines, design elements including scrolling via the "curtain effect" create an immersive environment' (Dowling and Vogan, 2015: 211). The two authors compare this curtain effect to 'the drama of the rising curtain in live theatre, and the use of light to alternatively darken and illuminate the stage, constitute the old media converging into this technique' (Dowling and Vogan, 2015: 214). Hence, 'Snow Fall' constitutes a peculiar, innovative interpretation of how long-form journalism can be developed in the digital landscape. Moreover, it does so by utilising different techniques that the reader is accustomed to, such as the in medias res beginning of the narrative of a specific event, such as the avalanche at Tunnel Creek, to shed light into a more general phenomenon such as backcountry skiing and its perils. Aside from known techniques such as in medias res beginning (O'Nolan, 1969) followed by narrative digressions (Genette, 1980), the contamination between writing and multimedia elements has a specific aim. As underlined by Rue

> all of these components together create a more immersive experience for the viewer, like that found in traditional media like documentaries or long-form narratives. In a digital world, creating this experience needs to include design conventions and leveraging new technological innovations to engage readers. (2013)

What is relevant in 'Snow Fall' is not only the end result but also the narrative constructs created to exploit all the possibilities of the digital landscape. Moreover, all the techniques used in 'Snow Fall', aside from a narrative scope, are also built to enhance reader fruition and captivate their attention.

Long-Form Journalism Production in the Digital Landscape

'Snow Fall's' Legacy in the Development of Long-Form Journalism

After our analysis of the production process and the structure and writing of 'Snow Fall', we shall now focus on the developments that took place after the publication of the story on the World Wide Web on 20 December 2012. We shall begin by focusing on the available data on readers to assess the nature of 'Snow Fall's' fruition.

Journalist Jim Romenesko published on his blog an internal memo written shortly after the publication of 'Snow Fall' by *The New York Times* executive editor Jill Abramson. Abramson's memo describes the 'Snow Fall' project at length and provides some numbers on the story's readership, six days after it was published online. She emphasises how

> the project received around 2.9 million visits – some users coming back more than once – for more than 3.5 million page views. A huge portion of the traffic was from social media, and many of those visits came before the project was featured on the nytimes.com home page. (Romenesko, 2012)

Moreover, Abramson's memo reveals that

> 'users spent around 12 minutes, often more, engaged with the project', and that 'more than half a million visits went directly to "Snow Fall"', and more than half of those direct visits were from new *Times* users (or readers who hadn't visited the site in a long while) lured to our journalism by this feature. (Romenesko, 2012)

The reader data contained in the internal memo published by Romenesko (2012) is the only publicly available data on 'Snow Fall's' readership. Social network data regarding 'Snow Fall' are available and not limited to the first week after *The New York Times* long-form was published online. An API [Application Programming Interface] can be used to determine the relevance of a single URI [Universal Resource Identifier]. A URI is defined on the World Wide Web Consortium website as 'short strings that identify resources in the web: documents, images, downloadable files, services, electronic mailboxes, and other resources' (Berners-Lee, 1997). Hence, it is possible to determine the relevance of 'Snow Fall' within a social network such as Facebook. In order to do so, we shall use the Graph API, 'the primary way to get data in and out of Facebook's platform. It's a low-level <HTTP-based> API that you can use to query data, post new stories, manage ads, upload photos and a variety of other tasks that an app might need to do' (Facebook, 2015) according to Facebook.

This specific use of the Facebook Graph API is relevant in our assessment regarding the relevance of 'Snow Fall' on Facebook. As such, it constitutes an example of digital methods (Rogers, 2013; Venturini et al., 2018). The Graph API URL version, according to the social network's website, 'represents an external URL as it relates to the Facebook social graph – shares and comments from the URL on Facebook' (Facebook, 2016) Hence, we are able to determine how many times a specific URL, in our case <http://www.nytimes.com/projects/2012/snow-fall/>, has been present in interactions on Facebook, how many comments users have submitted and how many times it has been shared across the social network.

As of 4 March 2016, 'Snow Fall' has a 'share count' of 92,673 which comprises all types of interactions on Facebook. Gerlitz and Helmond describe the evolution of interaction tools that Facebook has introduced, adopting 'social buttons, also referred to as social bookmarking icons, which allow users to share, recommend, like or bookmark content, posts and pages across various social media platforms' (Gerlitz and Helmond, 2013: 1351). Specifically, Facebook first implemented the use of social buttons 'with the launch of the share icon in October 2006 as an easy way of sharing web content with one's contacts in order to invoke further social activities on the platform' (Gerlitz and Helmond, 2013: 1351). In 2009, Facebook added another type of social button, the 'like button' and according to Gerlitz and Helmond, 'liking was put forward as a social activity that can be performed on most shared objects within Facebook, such as status updates, photos, links or comments' (2013: 1352). Hence, within Facebook, users have different social buttons at their disposal. However, as we can see in Table 3.1, the Facebook Graph API provides only a generic 'share count'. A website service such as Like Explorer (Bailey, 2014). can help assess in detail the results provided by the Facebook URL API, dividing the share count among the different actions performed by 'users to share, recommend, like or bookmark content, posts and pages across various social media platforms' (Gerlitz and Helmond, 2013: 1351). According to Like Explorer (Bailey, 2014) the total share count of 92,673 is the result of 22,445 Facebook comments, 30,304 Facebook 'Likes', 39,924 Facebook 'Shares'. Hence, it can be concluded that 'Snow Fall' has been at the centre of multiple interactions on Facebook over a prolonged period and moreover that it has stimulated an intense debate within the Facebook platform,

Table 3.1 Facebook Graph URL API results for 'Snow Fall's' URL <http://www.nytimes.com/projects/2012/snow-fall/> obtained on 4 March 2016

```
{
"og_object": {
"id": "509181645782762",
"description": "Fresh powder beckoned 16 expert skiers and snowboarders into the back-country. Then the snow gave way.",
"title": "Snow Fall: The Avalanche at Tunnel Creek",
"type": "article",
"updated_time": "2016-03-04T19:52:11+0000",
"url": "<http://www.nytimes.com/projects/2012/snow-fall/>"
},
"share": {
"comment_count": 0,
"share_count": 92673
},
"id": "<http://www.nytimes.com/projects/2012/snow-fall/>"
}
```

with almost a quarter (24 per cent) of all interactions being comments written directly by users.

After analysing 'Snow Fall's' public readership data and available data on social networks, we shall now focus on the legacy that it has produced. Dowling and Vogan have summed up the different reactions to what they define as 'a watershed moment in digital journalism designed for the tablet' (Dowling and Vogan, 2015: 209). They identify two major fields, one praising 'Snow Fall' as a template for the development of journalism's future, the other critic towards its graphics complexity and the use of multiple resources, such as production time and individuals involved in the project. In line with this criticism, Bobbie Johnson, founder of the digital magazine *Matter*, wrote a highly negative essay on 'Snow Fall' published on the Medium platform. However, while Johnson stressed how 'Snow Fall' was not the first example 'of this new wave of online storytelling', he also underlined that it had 'become the canonical example' (Johnson, 2013). Thus, whatever the position on 'Snow Fall' itself, both those who praise and criticise 'Snow Fall' recognise it as a landmark production. This role has been attributed to *The New York Times* story due to a number of factors, ranging from the importance of the news media outlet to the number of individuals involved in the project and to the fact that it created, within the digital landscape, a compelling narrative environment that was reminiscent of long-form stories published traditionally on paper magazines, eventually becoming a synonym of producing a news media outlet 'best product in the market in a way that participates in these trends in digital design and narrative while building and communicating an organization's brand' (Dowling and Vogan, 2015: 219).

As a number of years have passed since its publication, it is possible to say that 'Snow Fall' has maintained its influence in long-form journalism in the digital landscape. The production process and technical efforts behind 'Snow Fall' are fundamental elements to assess the continuing influence of this single long-form journalism story. As of 2014, *The New York Times* produced an internal 'Innovation Report' (*The New York Times*, 2014a), which was subsequently leaked and published online by on *BuzzFeed* (Tanzer, 2014). The report was trying to address the challenges that *The New York Times* was facing in the digital landscape, from audience strengthening to newsroom organisation. In the 'Innovation Report' (*The New York Times*, 2014a), it is still possible to identify some of the issues raised by 'Snow Fall' within *The New York Times*, such as the time-consuming nature of its production and its non-replicable, non-scalable nature. In elaborating the report, *The New York Times* interviewed many competitors, one being Kevin Delaney, editor of *Quartz*, a digitally native publication. Delaney stressed that his publication was focused on 'building tools to create Snowfalls every day, and getting them as close to reporters as possible', adding that he would rather have 'a Snowfall builder than a Snowfall' (*The New York Times*, 2014a: 33).

Thus, in the contemporary digital landscape, 'Snow Fall's' legacy has become a template, despite its time and resource-consuming production process. It has become part of the canon that online services and news media outlets consider when they aim to produce long-form journalism capable of producing the same immersive effect. Hence, by becoming an aesthetic and functional model, 'Snow Fall's' legacy has reached a place that goes well beyond that of a single long-form journalism story, becoming a point of reference in production, readership and relevance in the digital landscape.

The Influence of the Digital Landscape in the Evolution of Long-Form Journalism

Having focused on 'Snow Fall' by *The New York Times*, we shall now concentrate on the relationship between this type of news production, long-form journalism and the digital landscape. The analysis of 'Snow Fall's' production process has highlighted a number of key elements such as the number of different professionals involved and the time devoted to the project. In reviewing 'Snow Fall', some critics (Lacy, 2012; McKenzie, 2013) underlined that only a legacy news organisation such as *The New York Times* could afford an effort that involved over a dozen people over a six-month period on a non-scalable project. Moreover, *The New York Times* deputy director of digital design Andrew Kueneman underlined that the story 'was not produced in our normal CMS (Content Management System), which is probably pretty obvious' (Greenfield, 2012). This aspect is one of the central elements of the critiques that 'Snow Fall' has faced. A CMS or Content Management System 'is the process of collecting, managing and publishing content' (Boiko, 2005: 68). Among news media outlets in the digital landscape, content management systems are commonly intended as

> the software systems that allow journalists to do a lot of the work on assembly, head-lines, pictures, layout and so on that used to involve separate specialists; and new CMSs also make it easier to publish and distribute content across multiple digital as well as the traditional print formats. (Doyle, Oakley and O'Connor, 2015: 112).

Hence, it is clear why in a phase of intense pressure on the news media industry, such as the one it is facing and that we have described in Chapter 2, 'Snow Fall' critiques focused heavily on this aspect. As we underlined before, while quoting *Quartz* editor Kevin Delaney from *The New York Times* 'Innovation Report', the main issue in his perspective was the ability to develop a CMS capable of replicating 'Snow Fall' endless times, becoming an integral part of software systems used by journalists (Doyle, Oakley and O'Connor, 2015).

Such a strong focus on scalability and content management systems is a direct consequence of a specific conception of the digital landscape that news media outlets have. According to Anderson's long-tail model which we analysed in Chapter 2, 'the Web is the ultimate marketplace of ideas, governed by the laws of big numbers' (Anderson, 2009: 70) and, as its shelf-space is virtually limitless, the sale price has to be lowered as much as possible. However, a price reduction is viable only if the production costs experience a consistent compression and, within the media production field, this seems to signal the need for scalable tools, capable of reducing the workforce behind the production of a single item, generally concen-trating multiple specialists' work into a single contributor (Doyle, Oakley and O'Connor, 2015).

The long-tail model, as envisioned by Anderson (2009b), might offer a key into understanding the development of numerous tools, plugins and ser-vices that aim to make long-form journalism production more scalable and cheaper to produce. In 2013, a start-up company named Scroll Kit claimed that while *The New York Times* 'spent hundreds of hours' hand-coding "Snow

Fall", using their software they 'made a replica in one hour' (Brown, 2013). A video, uploaded on YouTube, recorded the production process by Scroll Kit founder Cody Brown but *The New York Times*, with a cease and desist letter, demanded to put the video offline. Brown stressed how 'Snow Fall' had been both time and resource consuming to produce, and how 'most news orgs don't have anywhere near these kinds of resources, and this is why we've spent the past year creating a tool that opens the ability to produce these stories to significantly more people' (Brown, 2013).

What is relevant is that, even within the news media industry, streamlined, scalable processes are depicted as the only force capable of resisting and adapting to the digital landscape habitat. Long-form journalistic production before and after the publication of 'Snow Fall' has been driven not only by legacy media outlets developing single projects but likewise by the birth and growth of third-party services such as Atavist and Ceros, website and blog platforms and content management services such as Drupal and WordPress, with plugins like the Aesop story engine and Scroll Kit, which has been acquired by WordPress developer Automattic in 2014.

Hence, the digital landscape is a factor of influence the development of long-form journalism stories, affecting both the production process and final products. Moreover, the need to adapt this form of production to the challenges that the digital landscape poses appears to be at the centre of efforts by third-party entities, which increases the pressure on news media outlets. However, while there is a quantitatively significant number of long-form journalism stories, it is possible that adapting to the digital landscape might foster a further standardisation in the field. While platforms and content management systems are increasingly at the centre of this process, projects such as 'Snow Fall' with their 'hand-coded' nature appear to be a reference point for other entities within the digital landscape, as the end product of the most relevant long-form journalism stories in the digital landscape is the creation of immersive experiences aimed 'to allow the participant to actually enter a virtually recreated scenario representing the news story' (de la Peña et al., 2010: 292).

To gain readers, captivating experiences such as long-form journalism in the digital landscape have to function as a form of entertainment. As such, these environments are built on premises that – to fulfil their role – they must captivate the reader's attention, her or his time. As Franco 'Bifo' Berardi underlines, 'cyberspace overloads cybertime, because cyberspace is an unbounded sphere whose speed can accelerate without limits, while cybertime (the organic time of attention, memory, imagination) cannot be sped up beyond a certain point – or it cracks' (Berardi, 2012). Hence, one of the key objectives of news media outlets in the digital landscape is to captivate digital crowds 'cybertime' (Berardi, 2012), and to do so, seamless and entertaining environments must be created.

American writer David Foster Wallace described the function of entertainment similarly in his novel *Infinite Jest*. During an interview with David Lipsky, Foster Wallace underlined that in his novel 'entertainment's chief job is to make you so riveted by it that you can't tear your eyes away, so the advertisers can advertise' (Lipsky, 2010: 79). Thus, we can envisage news media outlets' tendency to build long-form journalism stories as a form of entertainment. In order to attract users and their valuable 'cybertime' (Berardi, 2012), these environments are generally as immersive and seamless as possible. They require full attention by the user and captivate him or her generally using technical tools to an aesthetic and narrative effect, as we have seen in 'Snow Fall'. Long-form journalism stories are not just tools to expose users to an advertisement, as was entertainment's role in Foster Wallace (Lipsky, 2010), yet this is one of their partial objectives, as underlined by Dowling and Vogan, which also identify other goals, such as

> building prestige for a media outlet's brand, which then reflects similar status on readers who share its works through social media. The business model is premised on crafting a signature product that communicates the best articulation of the company's brand identity and draws traffic to its pay site as it passes through social media. (2015: 210)

Hence, is it possible to understand the logic behind the creation by news media outlets of single, non-scalable projects such as 'Snow Fall'. In our definition of long-form journalism in the digital landscape, which we provided in Chapter 2, one of the common traits between the elements we singled out (text, audio and visual content, data visualisation tools and specifically built data sets) was their time-consuming nature for the audience, which ultimately defines their nature as long-form journalism.

Hence, the notion of continuum is a useful tool to analyse long-form journalism stories as environments built to demand user's cybertime due to their in-depth narratives, aesthetic appeal and information on a topic or a story.

The development of environments capable of attracting attention and 'cybertime' (Berardi, 2012) appears to not only strategic but a direct field of competition between news media outlets within the contemporary digital landscape, as it is 'the fight for attention which dominates (its) everyday culture' (Franck, 1998: 3). Within this frame, the development of 'Snow Fall' by *The New York Times* is to be seen as a successful example of 'building and communicating an organization's brand' (Dowling and Vogan, 2015: 219). This activity is to be considered within a wider strategy operated by news media outlets, which we have analysed in Chapter 2, based on marketing 'a medium that is capable of attracting the attention of the general public. Media attracting the attention of the general public is what the advertising industry is desperately seeking' (Franck, 1998: 4). As such, the creation of signature long-form journalism stories such as 'Snow Fall' by *The New York Times* answers to a typical production dynamic within the contemporary digital landscape.

The Future of Long-Form Journalism: 'An Unbelievable Story of Rape'

ProPublica and *The Marshall Project*'s 'An Unbelievable Story of Rape'

An Introduction to 'An Unbelievable Story of Rape'

We shall now focus on a second long-form story after analysing 'Snow Fall' by *The New York Times* (Branch, 2012). We have chosen as a case-study 'An Unbelievable Story of Rape' by T. Christian Miller and Ken Armstrong, which was published on 16 December 2015 by two non-profit media outlets, *ProPublica* and *The Marshall Project* (Miller and Armstrong, 2015). We have selected 'An Unbelievable Story of Rape' as it was published three years later than 'Snow Fall' in a collaborative form between two non-profit news outlets rather than a legacy publication such as *The New York Times*.

We will combine our case-study, an in-depth analysis based on different data sources (Feagin, Orum and Sjoberg, 1991), with other methods, as we did in Chapter 3 while analysing 'Snow Fall' by *The New York Times*. Similarly to the previous chapter, we shall apply a text analysis method (Fürsich, 2009) as 'part of discourse analysis' (Fairclough, 2001: 91), aiming to assess 'the key dimension of production, content and reception' (Philo, 2007: 194). Moreover, we shall apply the same digital methods (Rogers, 2013) used in Chapter 3 to assess readership and the production process. However, to gain further insight into both these aspects, we shall also rely on semi-structured interviews with two professionals directly involved with the production process of 'An Unbelievable Story of Rape'. We have chosen this type of interview as it allows to include

> both open-ended and more theoretically driven questions, eliciting data grounded in the experience of the participant as well as data guided by existing constructs in the particular discipline within which one is conducting research. (Galletta, 2013: 46)

As we underlined at the beginning of Chapter 3, we consider the broader environment of news media production as a decisive factor in analysing a single piece of long-form journalism production. However, by choosing a different time frame and news media outlet while implementing the same methods, we aim to compare findings in order to evaluate factors that determine differences in long-form journalism production within the digital landscape. Thus, by selecting 'An Unbelievable Story of Rape', we aim to assess long-form journalism's evolution over time.

ProPublica and *The Marshall Project* published on their respective websites 'An Unbelievable Story of Rape' on 16 December 2015. The long-form story was written by two journalists, one from each news media outlet: T. Christian Miller from *ProPublica* and Ken Armstrong from *The Marshall Project*. 'An Unbelievable Story of Rape' comprises a 12,000-word story divided into eight chapters with an introduction and an epilogue, multiple illustrations, photographs and one audio file. Among a number of prizes and nominations – American Society of News Editors Awards for non-deadline Reporting, winner 2015; Taylor Family Award for Fairness in Journalism administered by Harvard University Nieman Foundation, finalists 2015, Meyer 'Mike' Berger Award, winner 2015; Al Nakkula Award for Police Reporting, winner 2015; Dart Center for Journalism and Trauma, Excellence in Coverage Trauma finalist 2015; John Barlow Martin Award for Public Interest Magazine Journalism administered by Northwestern University Medill School of Journalism, winner 2015; Deadline Club Award, newspaper or digital feature reporting, winner 2015 (*ProPublica*, 2009b) – in 2016 the story won a Pulitzer Prize in the Explanatory Reporting category. The Pulitzer Prize motivation reads: 'for a distinguished example of explanatory reporting that illuminates a significant and complex subject, demonstrating mastery of the subject, lucid writing and clear presentation, using any available journalistic tool' (Pulitzer Prizes, 2016).

The two non-profit outlets which published 'An Unbelievable Story of Rape' are *ProPublica* and *The Marshall Project*. *ProPublica* describes itself as 'an independent, non-profit newsroom that produces investigative journalism in the public interest' (*ProPublica*, 2009a). It was founded in 2007 by Paul Steiger, former managing editor at *The Wall Street Journal*, and is led by editor-in-chief Stephen Engelberg and president Richard Tofel. *ProPublica* started publications in 2008 and two years later was the first digital news outlet ever to receive a Pulitzer Prize. While publishing most of its content on the World Wide Web, *ProPublica* collaborates on specific projects with other outlets, which include newspapers and magazines. *ProPublica*'s production is centred around 'Series', which are defined as 'special investigations and ongoing stories' (*ProPublica*, 2009c), which generally comprise one or more long-form journalism stories, additional content such as integrations and specifically built datasets. Moreover, *ProPublica* has developed a 'Data Store', which provides both free and premium access to data which has been at the centre of the news outlet's reporting. One of *ProPublica*'s first long-form journalism stories was entitled 'Dollars for Docs', a database-centred series first published in 2010 and still ongoing, which created an index of payments made by seventeen drug companies to doctors across the United States.

The Marshall Project is a non-profit news media outlet and started its digital publications in 2014. Its founding editor-in-chief is Bill Keller, former executive director at *The New York Times* from 2003 to 2011. Keller was succeeded by Susan Chira in March 2019 as editor-in-chief of the news outlet. *The Marshall Project* is a single-focus publication as it concentrates on the United States criminal justice system on which 'seeks to create and sustain a sense of national urgency' (*The Marshall Project*, 2014). Like *ProPublica*, *The Marshall Project* collaborates with other news media outlets, both digital and paper format. In 2016, *The Marshall Project* was awarded a prize – jointly with *Quartz*, another digital news outlet – for 'World's Best Designed Website' by the Society for News Design.

'An Unbelievable Story of Rape' was a collaborative effort between *ProPublica* and *The Marshall Project*. Each outlet contributed to the story by providing writers, editors, designers and staff. The story was published on the same day on both websites and uses all multimedia content, with slight variations due to the specifications of each outlet's website. However, it is relevant to underline that 'An Unbelievable Story of Rape' exists in two versions, one featured on *ProPublica*'s website and one featured on *The Marshall Project*'s website.

As we have underlined previously in this section, *ProPublica*'s main productions are organised around 'Series' that group together different contributions to a single topic that the outlet has chosen to pursue with as a long-term project. The construction of 'An Unbelievable Story of Rape' follows the same production pattern. Alongside the main long-form journalism story, all other connected contributions that *ProPublica* has developed are grouped in a single landing page of its website. As such, *ProPublica*'s 'Series' pages constitute a relevant example of convergence between long-form journalism and archives in the digital landscape as they represent both an archiving tool for long-form stories but also allow curation practices that group together content on a single topic.

Moreover, a 'Series' page as the one on *ProPublica*, provides users with a reference page that can be continuously updated with further entries, following an ordered path within the website. This type of content organisation places the series page in a leading position rather than the long-form story page itself, allowing for the original long-form journalism story to be preserved but likewise allowing further updates to be grouped in a single environment. This type of organisational modus operandi is highly relevant as it reflects the nature of long-form journalism in the digital landscape which, as we have seen in Chapter 2, is the combination of different elements (writing, visual and audio content, datasets). In this case, however, the relevant factor is that these elements are not necessarily part of the main long-form journalism story but are instead grouped in the main reference page. In October 2019, *The Marshall Project* also developed its own digital space devoted to 'An Unbelievable Story of Rape', named 'The Record' (*The Marshall Project*, 2019). The page includes a link to the original story and all the content developed by the news outlet, together with outside links, acting as an evolving repository of both the internal production and outside references.

Within our case-study analysis of 'An Unbelievable Story of Rape', two semi-structured interviews (Galletta, 2013) were carried out to better investigate the production process behind this specific long-form journalism story. We chose two different professionals, one from each news media outlets involved. Hence, we interviewed Joe Sexton, senior editor at *ProPublica*, and Andy Rossback, formerly an editorial designer at *The Marshall Project*.[1] When we asked about the 'Series' structure on *ProPublica*'s website, Sexton underlined that 'the subject matters, not the names on the bylines. Our reporting on rape happened accidentally, organically, with a powerful kind of momentum. Offering readers as much of it as possible seems the obvious and right thing' (J. Sexton, personal communication, 2017). By describing *ProPublica*'s reporting on the subject as happening 'accidentally, organically', Sexton underlines the flexible nature of an environment such as the 'Series' page. Allowing a growth that is both spontaneous yet manageable, this organisational practice permits the news media outlet to develop its production on a subject without limiting its potential growth in the future or any direction. The organic nature of reporting described by Sexton allows complex narrative structures to grow for years, as in the case of 'Dollars for Docs'.

Moreover, a structure such as *ProPublica*'s 'Series' allows different types of contribution to be added over time, which were not necessarily planned at the time of the inception of the long-form journalism story but are related to the first original contribution. While the non-hierarchical structure typical of *ProPublica*'s 'Series' pages allows fruition that does not necessarily start with the main long-form journalism story, it is always clear that all the material contained in the 'Series' page is developed as an environment, organised around a single main contribution. As such, environments as *ProPublica*'s 'Series' appear to assess some of the challenges that the digital landscape poses to news media outlets, organising content in flexible environments, allowing growth, modifications and alterations over time.

The Production Process and Reception of 'An Unbelievable Story of Rape'

After introducing the news media outlets that developed and published 'An Unbelievable Story of Rape', we shall now focus on its production process and reception, following a similar path as the one used for analysing 'Snow Fall' in Chapter 3.

---

1 The two interview transcripts are readable in Appendix A and Appendix B, respectively.

'An Unbelievable Story of Rape' was not conceived originally as a collaborative project between *ProPublica* and *The Marshall Project*. Both news media outlets had been working on the same story, without any prior knowledge of the other outlet's involvement. Stephen Engelberg, *ProPublica*'s editor-in-chief, described how the collaboration 'arose entirely by chance, months after both news organisations had begun work on different facets of what turned out to be the same story' (Engelberg, 2015). Both *ProPublica* and *The Marshall Project*, have developed a similar practice as they both routinely collaborate with other news media outlets as 'such collaborations are increasingly common in the economically devastated landscape of twenty first century journalism' (Engelberg, 2015). *ProPublica*'s then editor-in-chief underlines how, in the past, competition would have influenced what route to take, either abandoning the story or trying to outrun other news outlets. The decision to collaborate, according to Engelberg, is rooted in the nature of the two news media outlets, as 'our two organisations are dedicated to the idea that journalistic success is about more than advertising revenue and page views' (Engelberg, 2015). In his interview, Sexton likewise describes the nature of non-profit news media outlets as a contributing factor in the decision to collaborate given the circumstances that led to both *ProPublica* and *The Marshall Project* to work on the same story. According to Sexton, this choice was made 'not because non-profits are more virtuous. They just have developed fewer habits in their young lives' (J. Sexton, personal communication, 2017). The senior editor at *ProPublica*, who worked for twenty-five years at *The New York Times*, underlines that previously his idea 'would have been to race the competitor to publish or bail entirely on the story. (And) the reasons for that, if they sound ignoble, are pretty reasonable in the end. Newspapers are businesses. Competitive businesses, fighting for readers and economic models and survival. Of course, non-profits compete for things – attentions, awards, funding, brand extension' (J. Sexton, personal communication, 2017). In this specific instance, the non-profit nature of both *ProPublica* and *The Marshall Project* seems to have facilitated an outcome that neutralises some of the stress factors news outlets are subject to in the contemporary digital landscape.

As we have seen in Chapter 2, while economic pressure on news media outlets is increasing, numbers in newsrooms and revenue streams are shrinking. As long-form journalism is a labour-intensive form of journalism, it appears that the nature of non-profit news media outlets can be an asset in producing this specific form of journalism, as shown by the growth of non-profit news media outlets which engage in investigative journalism in the digital landscape (Kaplan, 2013). The 'Global Investigative Journalism: Strategies for Support' is keeping track of the number of non-profit news media outlets engaging in this specific type of long-form journalism. In 2007, the first edition of the report tracked thirty-nine news media outlets in twenty-six different countries, whereas the second edition in 2012 'shows that this rapid growth has continued, with 106 nonprofits in 47 countries' (Kaplan, 2013: 27). This growth is moreover significant as it has taken place within an industry where 'few journalistic organizations can afford to engage in much long-form, resource-intensive, investigative journalism' (Bruns and Highfield, 2012: 2). Within the digital landscape, non-profit news organisations, while not exempt from issues, retain some advantages, as underlined Picard: 'The primary advantages of the forms seem to result from reducing influences of commercial aspects of news business on content and improving the sustainability of news enterprises and providing means for preserving core journalistic values' (2011: 25).

ProPublica and *The Marshall Project* are both non-profit media outlets that, in our case-study, collaborated on a single, long-form journalism story. While, as we have seen, the collaboration was not decided at the beginning of the two outlets' work on the story, the two non-profit news media outlets managed to merge efforts, despite the fact that, due to their nature, both compete for 'attentions, awards, funding, brand extension' (J. Sexton, personal communication, 2017). Sexton in his interview underlined that 'the imperatives aren't as hard and fast' (J. Sexton, personal communication, 2017) if compared to traditional news media outlets.

The process that led to the creation of the story's structure and its development was also a joint effort between the two news media outlets. Sexton describes the process as 'a full collaboration. We agreed on an outline for the story before anyone started writing. We talked as a group after each draft. We jointly solicited outside feedback when we were close and uncertain about some things' (Personal communication, 2017). During an interview both Miller and Armstrong credit Sexton for developing the story's structure, while also underlining the role of Bill Keller as the lead editor for *The Marshall Project* as well as 'numerous other editors [that] contributed at different points in the process' (Fitzgerald, 2016). Gender was considered as an important factor, being both writers and lead editors male, there was an effort made to achieve gender balance in the editing process and, as Sexton underlines 'some women were naturally part of the process. [...] But we widened the circle of women, gave them the story cold and invited feedback' (J. Sexton, personal communication, 2017).

The two journalists involved in writing 'An Unbelievable Story of Rape', T. Christian Miller and Ken Armstrong, described in detail how they worked together in developing the story during a podcast (Gordy, 2015). A podcast as 'audio file containing information and music, which is available for downloading through the internet on media players or devices' (Bockarova, 2013: 520). Armstrong during the podcast specified that

> T. [Christian Miller] created a Google Drive site, and we decided we'd both dump all our documents in it. And I remember seeing all the records that T. [Christian Miller] had gathered in Colorado, and then I dumped all the records I had gathered [in the state of] Washington, and it was like each of us had half of a phenomenal story. And in one day, by dumping our notes into a common file, we suddenly had a whole story. (Gordy, 2015)

It is worth noting that in this case, an element of the contemporary digital landscape, such as file sharing environments, has allowed the collaboration to take place seamlessly, allowing full integration between the work of two journalists from two different news media outlets.

Having analysed the development of the production process within the two news media outlets that published 'An Unbelievable Story of Rape', we shall now focus on its structure, specifically its design and graphic features, following the same method we used to assess the features of 'Snow Fall' by *The New York Times* in Chapter 3. As 'An Unbelievable Story of Rape' was produced by both *ProPublica* and *The Marshall Project*, it had to adapt to each outlet's website and graphic style. Hence, there are very slight differences between the two versions of the story, which are currently online on the two news media outlets' websites. The differences are mainly in text font, layout and image selection and size choices.

In order to investigate the design process behind 'An Unbelievable Story of Rape', we interviewed Andy Rossback, who at the time was the editorial designer at *The Marshall Project* who worked on the story. Regarding the design, Rossback states that his work started from 'the early stages of design to create something that could work on either site and that we agreed upon conceptually' (A. Rossback, personal communication, 2017). Rossback explains in detail the choices that were made and that regard both page layouts and font usage. As for *The Marshall Project* design, Rossback clarifies that there is extensive use of different levels of 'typographic hierarchy' and enlarged lead paragraph fonts 'meant to signal to the reader that they are entering a new chapter of the story' (A. Rossback, personal communication, 2017). This feature is especially relevant as the suite design which was chosen for 'An Unbelievable Story of Rape' differs radically from the one chosen for 'Snow Fall', which we analysed in Chapter 3. While 'Snow Fall's' chapters are each on a different page which the reader has to click on, the design of 'An Unbelievable Story of Rape' is featured on a single webpage, despite being a 12,000-word story, which is published along with a number of illustrations, photographs and an audio file. Rossback underlines that choosing to split the story into different pages would have meant 'would introduce nine more mouse clicks into the project. A general principle of my job is to reduce the friction between the user and the content, removing pain points, like the need to click, which would likely get annoying after a chapter or two' (A. Rossback, personal communication, 2017). Moreover, there is another reason that led the design team to choose a single page layout. 'It's also of benefit to users who arrive from search engines. They are invited to read the story from the start instead of becoming confused when they have arrived on a specific chapter in the middle of the story, from their search query' (A. Rossback, personal communication, 2017).

As we have seen in Chapter 3, while describing the 'online story package' taxonomy (Grabowicz, Hernandez and Rue, 2014), while some stories adopt a traditional presentation, similar to other mediums, such as television or radio, other narratives are developed around non-linear models, leaving the user free to navigate the different pages. In 'An Unbelievable Story of Rape', the main issue underlined by Rossback was avoiding elements that would alter the perception of the story as a single, seamless environment. In 'An Unbelievable Story of Rape', the main driver behind the design appears to be the creation of an environment focused on the text. This focus is enhanced, in the version published by *The Marshall Project*, by the use of a parallax header, which makes the text fade out after each scroll, the use of different font sizes and relatively few images.

While 'An Unbelievable Story of Rape' has been built by focusing its design on the role of text, one of its most defining features is the use of illustrations. Both *ProPublica* and *The Marshall Project*'s version have five different illustrations which have been made by illustrator Wesley Allsbrook. As Sexton explains 'for all its gripping narrative, it was a historical piece on a brutal and nuanced topic, and not, actually, all that photographically vital. Illustrations allow readers to use their imagination more, I think. And they can, oddly, make the story more human, more universal' (J. Sexton, personal communication, 2017). Andy Rossback describes how the two news media outlets chose Allsbrook as the illustrator. 'Former *The Marshall Project* art director Lisa Iaboni worked with an illustrator from early on, because we knew since the main character is an anonymous source – it would be difficult to find a photography to lead the piece' (A. Rossback, personal communication, 2017). Illustrations, along with text hierarchy and a limited number of photographs, all contribute to creating an environment which is not as multimedia-based if compared to 'Snow Fall', with one exception. At the end of the last chapter of 'An Unbelievable Story of Rape', just before the epilogue, there is a small audio player placed at the centre of the page. It is a recording of the victim's voice that goes through her account of the attack, in a one minute and twenty-second audio clip. The narrative impact is very strong as being the whole long-form story built mainly around the text, inserting a single audio file amplifies its importance. Moreover, as Rossback recalls, '(the audio player) is labelled directly with a note saying that she wanted her story to be heard. It was important to me that this type was not played up or meant to feel like it payed any disrespect to her story or her request to hear it' (A. Rossback, personal communication 2017).

While the design of 'An Unbelievable Story of Rape', as we have de-scribed above, is very much text-focused, it utilises other media formats (namely visual and audio). However, the use of different media formats does not imply a balance between writing, visual and audio elements, which are still very relevant from a narrative point of view. This design choice seems close to what is defined as a minimalist design (Gardner, 2011). According to Gardner, this type of design 'often relies primarily on typography and spacing, not images, to enhance readability' (Gardner, 2011: 19). Hence, 'An Unbelievable Story of Rape', incorporates some minimalist design principles while using visual and audio elements to provide a seamless, yet captivating, reader experience.

Having assessed the production process of 'An Unbelievable Story of Rape', we shall now focus on the reception this long-form journalism story has had since its publication, on 16 December 2015. In order to do so, we shall present reader data, provided directly by *ProPublica*, detailing page views and reader time for 'An Unbelievable Story of Rape' as of 9 August 2016.

The reader data regarding the complete 'An Unbelievable Story of Rape' series from *ProPublica*'s website is particularly relevant as it allows us to measure the reader response to a long-form journalism story and, in *ProPublica*'s case, the impact of the connected content published in its 'Series' page. The data provided directly by *ProPublica* via email re-gards the period between 16 December 2015 and 9 August 2016. The data does not only provide the average time spent on each page but likewise details page views, unique page views, entrances, bounce rate and exit rate. To assess each term, we shall refer to Google Analytics Help Center (Google, 2011) as a source as *ProPublica* utilises Google Analytics. In order to better understand the terms, in Table 4.2 we will provide definitions for each term.

Hence, the data in Table 4.1 shows how the 'An Unbelievable Story of Rape' page has been loaded or reloaded 968,281 times in a little over nine months. Out of all the times the page was loaded or reloaded, the average time spent on the page is seventeen minutes and ten seconds, with a very high number of visitors which have interacted with this page alone, setting the bounce rate at 91,44 per cent.

Table 4.1 Engagement data on 'An Unbelievable Story of Rape' series (source: *ProPublica*)

Page	Page Views	Unique Page Views	Average Time Spent on Pages	Entrance	Bounce Rate	% Exit
\<www.propublica.org/article/false-rape-accusations-an-unbelievable-story\>	968,281	895,646	0:17:10	857,219	91.44%	90.35%
\<www.propublica.org/article/about-propublica-marshall-project-rape-story-collaboration\>	8,861	8,175	0:03:02	5,121	77.76%	60.47%
\<www.propublica.org/article/listen-to-our-collaboration-with-this-american-life\>	7,603	6,794	0:03:41	4,456	71.14%	60.52%
\<www.propublica.org/article/how-we-reported-an-unbelievable-story-of-rape\>	6,751	6,224	0:04:01	3,642	75.10%	58.82%
\<www.propublica.org/article/flawed-rape-statistics-hamper-understanding-and-preventing-the-crime\>	4,774	4,381	0:03:04	2,650	79.25%	62.99%
\<www.propublica.org/article/a-brutal-crime-often-terribly-investigated\>	2,772	2,555	0:02:30	1,068	71.32%	46.83%
\<www.propublica.org/podcast/item/how-almost-getting-scooped-brought-two-competing-reporters-together\>	2,127	1,953	0:03:35	904	70.99%	50.59%

Table 4.2 Definitions from Google Analytics Help Center

Pageview	An instance of a page being loaded [or reloaded] in a browser. Pageviews is a metric defined as the total number of pages viewed.
Unique Pageview	A unique pageview, as seen in the Content Overview report, aggregates pageviews that are generated by the same user during the same session. A unique pageview represents the number of sessions during which that page was viewed one or more times.
Entrance	Sessions are incremented with the first hit of a session, whereas entrances are incremented with the first pageview hit of a session. If the first hit of the session is not a pageview, you may see a difference between the number of sessions and the number of entrances.
Bounce Rate	Bounce Rate is the percentage of single-page sessions (i.e. sessions in which the person left your site from the entrance page without interacting with the page).
Exit Percentage	For all pageviews to the page, Exit Rate is the percentage that was the last in the session.

In order to better assess the data provided by *ProPublica*, we shall compare it to data provided in the 'State of the News Media 2016' report (Pew Research Center, 2016b). The report which underlines how 'audiences are continuing to turn to digital sources for their news, and the momentum is driven by users on their mobile devices rather than desktops' (Pew Research Center, 2016b: 44). Moreover, The Pew Research Center analysed the role of long-form journalism consumption on mobile devices in a different report which was published in 2016, emphasising how 'one particular area of uncertainty has been the fate of long, in-depth news reports that have been a staple of the mainstream print media in its previous forms' (Pew Research Center, 2016a: 5). However, the report stresses that 'when it comes to the relative time consumers spend with this content, long-form journalism does have a place in today's mobile-centric society' (Pew Research Center, 2016a: 5). Researchers found that reader engagement is influenced by a number of factors, which include the length of the story but also the topic. In particular, out of all different topics, crime stories both under and over the 5,000 words mark have the highest average reading time, with stories longer than 5,000 words clocking up to 490 seconds (or eight minutes and ten seconds) of average reading time on mobile devices (Pew Research Center, 2016a). The specific data provided by the Pew Research Centre regarding crime stories over the 5,000 words mark can be used as a comparable data point with the average time spent on 'An Unbelievable Story of Rape', as it is classifiable as a crime story over 5,000 words. In the data provided by *ProPublica*, the average reader time spent on the story is of seventeen minutes and ten seconds. While this data does not take into account the different devices accessing the story, it does signal a consistent engagement by readers. In Chapter 3, we referred to a memo by the then editor-in-chief of *The New York Times* Jill Abramson regarding the traffic generated by 'Snow Fall'. Whereas Abramson referred to data regarding the first six days since publication, she underlined 'users spent around 12 minutes, often more, engaged with the project' (Romenesko, 2012). While this type of reference to user engagement cannot be directly compared to the data provided by *ProPublica*, it does design a general trend where, within the contemporary digital landscape, long-form journalism can attract readers in considerable numbers and engage them for very long periods of time.

All the other web pages part of the 'An Unbelievable Story of Rape' series, totalled 33,888 visits with an average of three minutes and nineteen seconds. Whereas there are different types of content, it does appear that while the readers chose to behave in a substantially different manner, they did somehow appreciate the contents part of the *ProPublica* series, which in this case were centred on providing a complementary scenario to the main long-form journalism piece with stories such as 'How We Reported "An Unbelievable Story of Rape"' (Armstrong T. Christian, 2015), 'About That Unbelievable Story' (Engelberg, 2015) and 'How Almost Getting Scooped Brought Two Competing Reporters Together' (Gordy, 2015) rather than providing additional information on the subject of the long-form story, which was still present in stories such as 'A Brutal Crime, Often Terribly Investigated' (Miller, 2015a) and 'Rape is Rape, Isn't It?' (Miller, 2015b).

In order to better understand the engagement levels that 'An Unbelievable Story of Rape' has had among readers, some insight can come from data gathered on social network activity. As done in Chapter 3 with 'Snow Fall' by *The New York Times*, we will be using an API (Application Programming Interface) to determine how a single URL has been featured within a specific social network, Facebook. Thus, we are applying digital methods (Rogers, 2013) to exploit 'information made available by Internet platforms' (Venturini et al., 2018: 2). Using Facebook Graph API, we can gather insight on what type of interaction 'An Unbelievable Story of Rape' has generated, between 'likes', 'shares' and comments. We shall be applying the Facebook Graph API to both versions of the story, the one published on *ProPublica*'s website (Table 4.3) and the one published on *The Marshall Project*'s website (Table 4.4).

Data gathered on both versions of the story was collected within twenty-four hours. Hence, it is possible to sum interactions from both URLs as the two news media outlets published the story at the same time and with the same level of relevance and involvement. The total figure of interactions on Facebook recorded between 15 December 2015 and 3 October 2016 by the two URLs combined is 84,050.

Table 4.3 Facebook Graph URL API results for *ProPublica*'s version of 'An Unbelievable Story of Rape' as of 3 October 2016

```
{
"og_object": {
"id": "877876385643358",
"description": "An 18-year-old said she was attacked at knifepoint. Then she said she made it up. That's where our story begins.",
"title": 'An Unbelievable Story of Rape',
"type": "article",
"updated_time": "2016-10-03T13:30:31+0000"
},
"share": {
"comment_count": 0,
"share_count": 45365
},
"id": "<http://propublica.org/article/
false-rape-accusations-an-unbelievable-story>"
}
```

Table 4.4 Facebook Graph URL API results for *The Marshall Project*'s version
of 'An Unbelievable Story of Rape' as of 2 October 2016

```
{
"og_object": {
"id": "1051280811w558944",
"description": "An 18-year-old said she was attacked at knifepoint. Then she said she
made it up. That's where our story begins.",
"title": 'An Unbelievable Story of Rape',
"type": "article",
"updated_time": "2016-10-02T20:41:56+0000"
},
"share": {
"comment_count": 0,
"share_count": 38685
},
"id": "<https://www.themarshallproject.org/2015/12/16/
an-unbelievable-story-of-rape>"
}
```

To provide a meaningful comparison, we can compare this figure with
engagement figures on Facebook for a similar outlet and for stories which
have been online for a comparable amount of time. According to Newswhip,
a company that tracks engagement on different social networks, one of
the top three news media outlets on Facebook in 2015 was *The New York
Times* (Concoran, 2015). In February 2016, the same author published a
list of the twenty most shared stories published by *The New York Times* in
2015, which range from 177,541 shares totalled for 'In Zimbabwe, We Don't
Cry for Lions' to 45,278 shares for 'A New Way to Tackle Gun Deaths'
(Concoran, 2016). Our data regarding 'An Unbelievable Story of Rape'
would place it sixth among most shared stories in 2015 by *The New York
Times*. This placement by 'An Unbelievable Story of Rape' has been accom-
plished in under a year, as our data refers to 293 days since publication and
from two Facebook pages which have a smaller reach if compared to *The
New York Times* page. *ProPublica*'s page had 146,766 users on Facebook
as of 3 October 2016, and *The Marshall Project*'s Facebook page had 41,581
users, whereas *The New York Times* page had over twelve million users. One

further data point can be obtained by comparing the average number of interactions per day between 'Snow Fall' and 'An Unbelievable Story of Rape'. As of 3 October 2016, 'Snow Fall' had been online for 1,171 days, totalling 92,673 interactions on Facebook, with an average of 79,1 interactions per day. As of 3 October 2016, 'An Unbelievable Story of Rape' had been online for 293 days, totalling 84,050 interactions, with an average of 293 interactions per day. Whereas other factors such as the growth in Facebook users between 2012 – when 'Snow Fall' was first published – and 2016 is certainly to be taken into account, it appears clear that 'An Unbelievable Story of Rape' has had a significant capacity to stimulate interactions among Facebook users, exceeding the reach of the two publications involved. Moreover, according to the data provided by *ProPublica*, the story kept readers engaged for an average of seventeen minutes, thus proving to be a very significant example of long-form journalism in the digital landscape.

'An Unbelievable Story of Rape's' Structure and Writing

We shall now focus on 'An Unbelievable Story of Rape' structure and writing after we analysed its production process and reception in the previous section. As we have noted in the previous section, 'An Unbelievable Story of Rape' is a 12,000-word long long-form journalism story, accompanied by a number of visual elements, such as photographs and illustrations and a single audio file. In Chapter 3, while analysing 'Snow Fall' by *The New York Times*, we opted to use a 'critical discourse analysis' method which incorporates text analysis in a broader method (Fairclough, 2001), thus including further elements in order to achieve an examination that explores the 'dimensions of production, content and reception' (Philo, 2007: 194).

As we will see, the two authors – T. Christian Miller from *ProPublica* and Ken Armstrong from *The Marshall Project* – have worked on specific sections of the story. Miller and Armstrong described their work which comprised multiple interviews, document gathering through public records requests, court documents, consultation of police training guidelines and recovering a significant body of statistic data (Fitzgerald, 2016).

'An Unbelievable Story of Rape' begins with a short introduction and is divided into eight chapters and an epilogue. There are two different storylines, one set in Lynnwood, in the state of Washington, United States and the other set in Colorado, United States. Ken Armstrong from *The Marshall Project* worked on the storyline set in Lynnwood, Washington whereas T. Christian Miller from *ProPublica* worked on the second storyline set in Colorado. Armstrong describes in detail how the two conducted their reporting, defining the work as 'almost organic. I had done the bulk of the reporting on Washington and he had done the bulk of the reporting on Colorado. It made sense for us to take the lead on those different parts of the story' (Fitzgerald, 2016). Moreover, Armstrong stresses how the two worked to ensure there were 'no continuity errors' and on 'what to reveal where, in order to help the narrative build' (Fitzgerald, 2016). What Armstrong describes as 'the narrative build' is defined by Ettema and Glasser, in their analysis of crime-based investigative journalism, as 'the development, selection, and assembly of facts into a story serves the moral task at hand' (Ettema and Glasser, 1988: 24). The two authors identify the objective of this type of narrative as 'the evocation of righteous indignation – indignation at the plight of victims [...] and also indignation at the demeanor of officials who are, if not guilty of criminal behavior, at least guilty of indifference and hypocrisy' (Ettema and Glasser, 1988: 24).

Thus, 'the development, selection, and assembly of facts' (Ettema and Glasser, 1988: 24) which constitutes the 'narrative build' described by Armstrong (Fitzgerald, 2016) is one of the main features of 'An Unbelievable Story of Rape'. Such result is obtained not only by developing two parallel storylines but likewise by using the story's structure to enhance this result. Joe Sexton, senior editor at *ProPublica*, is credited by both writers as the individual who developed the structure. Sexton underlines that 'there were two great, propulsive narratives. The idea to braid them was hardly rocket science. For me, the daring part was to save the brutal rape scene for the end. And to begin with a scene of muted modesty and mystery' (J. Sexton, personal communication, 2017). The combined storylines dynamic accompanies the reader in a 'crescendo', one chapter after the other. A 'crescendo' is a musical term, which can be defined as 'a word intimating a gradual increase in loudness' (Busby and Hamilton, 1840: 49). The loudness in the story is represented by the victim's account of the violence which, as Sexton underlined in his interview, is the final part of one of the two narrative lines. The second narrative line, set in Colorado, reinforces the crescendo by describing the investigation on the perpetrator from the start, hence creating a sense of suspense which lasts until the epilogue, where both storylines converge. As noted by Rossback in the previous section, the choice of providing a single audio file with the victim's voice at the end of the narrative sequence reinforces the impact of the contribution. The whole narrative is built around the finale, which is constantly hinted in both storylines but never in an explicit way.

We shall now perform a text analysis of 'An Unbelievable Story of Rape' to assess its narrative dynamic as one of its main features. 'An Unbelievable Story of Rape' based on the story of Marie, who was coerced by the Lynnwood, Washington, United States police department to confess that she lied about being raped. In 1999, after retracting her account of events, the victim was then sued for making a false statement. She was forced to cover court costs and undergo counselling. In 2011, a serial rapist was arrested in Colorado during an investigation on four different rapes. The evidence the perpetrator kept on his victims led the Colorado detectives back to Marie, who was told her rapist had been arrested. 'An Unbelievable Story of Rape' narrates in parallel Marie's story, whose account was not believed by law enforcement officials, and the investigation that took place four years later, eventually convicting the perpetrator, and leading back to Marie and her account of events which had been labelled as false.

The introduction is very brief, just over 370 words, and utilises an in medias res technique, which we also identified at the beginning of 'Snow Fall' (Branch, 2012). The lead phrase, 'No one came to court with her that day, except her public defender' (Miller and Armstrong, 2015), provides a starting point which puts the reader 'into the middle of the action' (O'Nolan, 1969: 126) in a visual environment dominated by elements as the title and the phrase 'An 18-year-old said she was attacked at knifepoint. Then she said she made it up. That's where our story begins' (Miller and Armstrong, 2015).

At this point, the reader knows that the person at the centre of the story is an 18-year-old female and that she first reported a rape that she then retracted. The narration begins with the protagonist alone in court, while in the following lines, the introduction provides additional information to the reader: the story is set in 2008, the victim's middle name is Marie, and she was charged with falsely reporting a rape and sentenced to pay a 500-dollar fine and undergo mental health counselling. The narration abruptly halts as the introduction ends and the first chapter begins.

The first chapter which follows the introduction is set in Golden, Colorado, in 2011. As in Chapter 3 while analysing 'Snow Fall' the 'beginning *in medias res*' is followed by a halt in the narration, and a 'return to an earlier period of time' (Genette, 1980: 30). A new character, detective Stacy Galbraith, is introduced. While presenting a different crime scene, the story continues without any further mention of Marie or any elements of the previous narrative line set in Lynnwood, Washington in 2008. The first chapter mixes direct quotes from interviews with statistics, 'Rapes by strangers were uncommon – about the 13 per cent of cases' (Miller and Armstrong, 2015) and, as the chapter draws to a conclusion, provides a significant hint on what 'An Unbelievable Story of Rape' is centred on:

> In that way, rape cases were unlike most other crimes. The credibility of the victim was often on trial as much as the guilt of the accused. And on the long, fraught trail between crime and conviction, the first triers of fact were the cops. An investigating officer had to figure out if the victim was telling the truth. (2015)

In the second chapter, the narration moves back to Lynnwood, Washington and to Marie's case. Any further mention of the introduction is absent, as the writer focuses on Marie's biography, using a repetitive phrase structure to enhance his narration.

> She does not know if she attended kindergarten.
> She remembers being hungry and eating dog food.
> She reports entering foster care at age 6 or 7. […]
> She met her biological father only once.
> She reports not knowing much about her biological mother, who
>   she said would often leave her in the care of boyfriends.
> She was sexually and physically abused.
>   (Miller and Armstrong, 2015)

The writer mixes quotes from a report on Marie with direct quotes from the victim, in a constant process of construction of Marie's character and its evolution through time, right to the moment she has become a young adult and is living on her own. Again, the narration stops as the chapter ends.

The third chapter is once again set in Colorado in 2011, establishing a rhythm to the whole structure that shall be maintained until the end of the long-form journalism story. The reader can now establish with certainty that there are two different storylines, one centred on Marie in 2008 and the second on a rape investigation set in Colorado in 2011. The story's structure hints that the different storylines might intersect at some point, yet it is still unclear what might be the unifying factor between the two narratives. At the end of the third chapter, the writer makes a reference to the fact that the Colorado investigation has to do with a single, unifying subject, the perpetrator: 'If you drew a map, it was almost like the rapist was circling the compass points of Denver's suburbs' (Miller and Armstrong, 2015).

Chapter 4 returns to focus on Marie, further reinforcing the story's alternating structure. The narration is now focusing on the aftermath of the violence – which is not part of the narration – and the conduct of law enforcement officials, describing in detail procedures and investigation activities. Moreover, a special focus is placed on two of Marie's foster parents, which describe their doubts regarding the victim's account. As in the first chapter, statistical data is used. In this chapter, in proximity to the accounts of Marie's foster parents provides a sort of implicit counter-balance, as 'most recent research suggests that false reporting is relatively rare. FBI figures show that police annually declare around 5 per cent of rape cases unfounded, or baseless' (Miller and Armstrong, 2015).

The fifth chapter describes in detail the search for the suspect in the Colorado rape cases. Again, the chapter ends on the verge of a significant event, a technique that has been utilised before, for example, in the introduction. The narrative crescendo of this storyline is progressing, as the investigators are closing in on the suspect, yet the alternating storylines provide the writer with a tool to generate suspense in the reader.

While the fifth chapter finished with the account of the investigators' activity closing in on the suspect, the sixth chapter begins with a harrowing account of all the mistakes made in investigating Marie's case. Scenes from the victim's interrogation are narrated through indirect quotes of law enforcement officials, alternated with direct quotes from Marie. This alternation is allowed by the use of two different sources of information, as which are the detectives' notes and Marie's first-person account. The chapter, one of the longest in the whole long-form story, goes on to describe how Marie was charged with false reporting, the pressure she was subjected to by law enforcement officials, who did not believe she was raped. Finally, the different storylines begin to converge, as the chapter concludes with an account of a rape similar to the one experienced by Marie.

Chapter seven begins where chapter five ended: the suspect in the Colorado investigation is taken into custody as this storyline appears to come to a conclusion. However, the end of the chapter reveals to the reader how the two different storylines of the long-form story, which have been narrated in parallel, might intersect. Without describing all the elements, a first direct reference to Marie is made in this storyline, 'It was a picture of the woman's learner's permit, placed on her chest. It had her name. And it had her address. Lynnwood, Washington' (Miller and Armstrong, 2015). Hence, the reader is made indirectly aware that Marie's account was true, and she was not believed by the police.

The final chapter begins, once again, in medias res. The reference to Marie made in the previous chapter is absent from the narration of this chapter. This mechanism serves a purpose which is to keep the reader attentive through a story which is now about 10,000 words long, thus progressing towards the end, as the whole story is 12,000 words. The reader, taken back and forth between the two different storylines, sees them converge in this chapter, with a detailed description of what happened to Marie. The chapter ends with a small audio player, and the choice of a different medium helps the reader to identify this as a vital piece of information. In fact, it is the victim's voice, recalling the events. The sound clip is an unedited and harrowing, first-person account:

> I got off the phone and went to sleep. And then opened my eyes and there was someone in my house. It was very, very scary. He had a knife in his hands and was wearing a mask and told me to turn around in the bed and face the pillow. And he blindfolded me and gagged me and tied my hands behind my back so that I couldn't do

anything. And he basically raped me and took pictures of (both) my parts. I didn't say a word to him. I just prayed in my head that I would live. (Miller and Armstrong, 2015)

The two different storylines definitively join in the epilogue as the man is sentenced to prison. Moreover, the ending is dedicated to the description of all the flaws in Marie's case, how she was coerced into retracting her statements and victimised twice. The story concludes with an account of what happened to all the individuals involved, from law enforcement officials to the victim, Marie. The finale is a direct quote from her, describing how she reported the rape 'so nobody else would get hurt. They'd be out there searching for this person who had done this to me' (Miller and Armstrong, 2015).

'An Unbelievable Story of Rape', while built mainly around a text-based narration, was capable of captivating the readers for a significant amount of time (as data provided by *ProPublica* in Table 4.1 shows), both utilising classic narrative techniques such as in medias res beginnings, alternating storylines and combining them in a discreet yet powerful evocative multimedia environment, built around illustrations, where photographic material is mainly used not for aesthetic reasons, rather as a manner to provide context.

The use of a different medium only at the end of the story automatically helps readers in identifying it as a fundamental part of the narration. As we have seen, this long-form journalism story, while profoundly different from 'Snow Fall', which made a much more extensive use of multimedia elements, was equally capable of creating a captivating environment with extensive use of tools which, while not native of the digital landscape, can still be applied with successful results.

'An Unbelievable Story of Rape', since its publication as a long-form journalism story at the end of 2015, has evolved first into a podcast of *This American Life* series, co-written with the original authors (This American Life, 2016). After this experience, Miller and Armstrong developed the story into a book, entitled 'A False Report: A True Story of Rape in America' (Miller and Armstrong, 2018), which was subsequently republished as 'Unbelievable' (Miller and Armstrong, 2019). While the relationship between book publishing and long-form journalism has been a constant feature, the renewed interest regarding 'An Unbelievable Story of Rape' was also motivated by another factor. In June 2018, the web-streaming service Netflix announced that a series was being developed from 'An Unbelievable Story of Rape'. The eight-part series, entitled 'Unbelievable' debuted on 13 September 2019. Earlier the same year, Netflix started publicly disclosing viewership figures, something that it had not done earlier. A month after 'Unbelievable' was released, *The New York Times* published a story with figures provided by Netflix showing that in just over a month, 'Unbelievable' had become the eight most-viewed series of the period between October 2018 and September 2019, with thirty-two million views (Koblin, 2019). Netflix, Koblin explains, 'the counts a view as a streaming of 70 per cent of one episode within four weeks of the day it appeared on the service' (Koblin, 2019). Data from Google (Google, 2020) demonstrates that in the week of Netflix's release of 'Unbelievable', searches for 'An Unbelievable Story of Rape' recorded their historical maximum, albeit in a proportion which was fifty times smaller than the searches for the newly released series.

The creation of a series from a long-form journalism article such as 'An Unbelievable Story of Rape' and its success, resonates in the data underlined in an article published on *The Wall Street Journal* in February 2020 (Trachtenberg, 2020). According to the author, 'Collectively, streaming platforms are expected to spend $30 billion annually on content in the U.S. alone by 2024, according to GroupM's Brian Wieser – an explosion of new offerings that will keep fuelling demand for original content' (Trachtenberg, 2020). Moreover, the article underlines how a number of news media groups, including the Condé Nast group (which includes *Vanity Fair, WIRED, GQ, Vogue* and *The New Yorker*), The New York Times Company, Vox media Inc. and others are all either partnering with streaming services or aiming to create studios to produce their content.

Thus we can assume that 'An Unbelievable Story of Rape's' adaptation by Netflix and its success, paired with the rising role of streaming platforms in the demand of original content deriving from long-form journalism stories, could become pivotal in the re-imagination and re-use of this type of news media production.

Both long-form journalism stories which we analysed were written using features such as in medias res leads, to attract readers from the start and allow them to grow interested in these two different long-form journalism stories. As we have seen in Chapter 2, long-form journalism in the digital landscape shares a number of features with 'New Journalism' as defined by (Murphy, 1974). Murphy identified three main features of 'New Journalism', such as 'dramatic literary techniques; intensive reporting; and reporting of generally acknowledged subjectivity' (Murphy, 1974: 16). More specifically, according to (Berning, 2011), 'the features of the Internet allow for new forms of multiperspectival narration' (Berning, 2011: 4), which we have encountered in our two case studies in Chapter 3 and in this chapter. Moreover, we have identified two of the three identifying features of 'New Journalism', such as 'dramatic literary techniques; intensive reporting' (Murphy, 1974: 16) combined with a 'multiperspectival narration' (Berning, 2011: 4) as defining element of both 'Snow Fall' by *the New York Times* and 'An Unbelievable Story of Rape' by *ProPublica* and *The Marshall Project*.

Thus, long-form journalism, as analysed in the two case studies, has demonstrated to be resulting from the application of techniques which while deriving from print-era journalism, have been adapted to the contemporary digital landscape. Moreover, the digital landscape has opened up new possibilities for such techniques to be implemented more effectively, enabling the use of different multimedia sources, including video and audio. While these techniques serve a specific purpose within each long-form journalism story, they are also implemented in order to captivate reader 'cybertime' (Berardi, 2012). The value of reader 'cybertime' derives directly from one of the defining features of the digital landscape, as it is 'the fight for attention which dominates its everyday culture' (Franck, 1998: 3). Moreover, Franck underlines that the struggle for attention traces back to a specific conception of media which is based on their capacity of attracting 'the attention of the general public' (Franck, 2019: 36). For media organisations, attention is not an end in itself, but it is rather 'is what the advertising industry is desperately seeking' (Franck, 2019: 36).

Thus, we can conclude that through the analysis of our case studies we were able to identify and assess factors that are, on the one hand, strictly connected to the contemporary nature of these long-form journalism stories and, on the other hand, derive from a specific need for news media outlets to captivate readers within the contemporary digital landscape.

PART III

Archives in the Digital Landscape

CHAPTER 5

Archives, the Long-Term Memories of the Digital Landscape

Archives in the Digital Landscape: Memory and Use

Time in the Digital Landscape: Continuous Present and 'Feed Fruition'

In the previous three chapters, we focused on providing insights into long-form journalism, through a broad outlook on the relationship between news production and the digital landscape and through two case studies: *The New York Times*' 'Snow Fall' in Chapter 3 and *ProPublica* and *The Marshall Project*'s 'An Unbelievable Story of Rape' in Chapter 4.

In this chapter, we shall connect our assessment of long-form journalism with the role of news outlet archives and their function within the digital landscape. While describing the digital landscape and its main actors in Chapter 1, we identified relevance over time and distribution practices as elements that highlighted a possible common ground between long-form journalism and news outlet archives. Assessing this evolution led to the analysis of shifting distribution practices and the role of the digital public sphere, which has seen the rise of ephemeral content production and consumption. Our approach highlighted a possible correlation between the nature of news media content and its life cycle within the digital landscape (See Chapter 2).

In this chapter, we shall explore the role of past news outlets' production within the digital landscape, focusing on archiving practices and archive access within the digital landscape. Our analysis aims to explore if long-form journalism and news outlet archives share common trajectories in fields such as life cycle and aggregation and curation practices. While we will focus on these possible common traits in the following chapters, in this chapter we shall investigate the role of news outlet archives in the digital landscape. At the end of Chapter 2, while we were outlining a possible intersection between the nature of long-form journalism and archives we referred to the notion of information as a 'flow resource' (Hess and Ostrom, 2003: 132). Hess and Ostrom (2003) confer value to information as long as it is capable of being transmitted between individuals. Hence, within our field of interest, distribution practices constitute one of the defining elements of information. As we have seen, content distribution in the contemporary digital landscape is largely dominated by actors such as platforms rather than news media outlets. Moreover, there is an ongoing shift towards content consumption that is not only mediated by platforms and aggregation services but takes place within their 'walled gardens' (Berners-Lee, 2010: 83) as we have seen in Chapter 2. These elements concur to define an environment where content consumption and production are undergoing extensive modifications.

Before analysing the role of news media outlet digital archives, it is vital to assess the notion of time within the digital landscape. Writer and critic Mark Fisher in his book, *Capitalist Realism*, describes the contemporary and its relationship with time, underlining how

> this is a culture that privileges only the present and the immediate – the extirpation of the long term extends backwards as well as forwards in time (for example, media stories monopolise attention for a week or so then are instantly forgotten); on the other hand, is a culture that is excessively nostalgic, given over to retrospection, incapable of generating any authentic novelty. (2009: 59)

Fisher describes contemporary culture as being directly influenced both in production and fruition by a specific conception of time, which he credits Fredric Jameson for, defined as 'continuous present' (Fisher, 2009: 58). Jameson, in his work *A Singular Modernity: Essay on the Ontology of the Present*, argues that an ontology of the present 'would not only wish to register the forces of past and future within that present; but would also be intent on diagnosing, as I am, the enfeeblement and virtual eclipse of those forces within our current present' (Jameson, 2002: 214). Within this conception of time, news media consumption – as described by Fisher – is an activity perfectly adherent to the contemporary. According to Fisher, the dissolution of long-term perspectives regards the future: 'forwards in time' (Fisher, 2009: 59). Hence, this notion of the future and its absence in the contemporary echoes the one elaborated by Franco 'Bifo' Berardi in his book *After the Future*. Berardi underlines:

> I will try to develop the idea that the future is over. It is not a new idea, as you know: born with punk, the 1970s and '80s witnessed the beginning of the slow cancellation of the future. […] when I say 'future' I am not referring to the direction of time. I am thinking, rather, of the psychological perception, which emerged in the cultural situation of progressive modernity, the cultural expectations that were fabricated during the long period of modern civilization, reaching a peak in the years after the Second World War. (2011: 18)

Thus, time conception in the contemporary digital landscape has altered both the perception of the future (Berardi, 2011) and the past (Jameson, 2002), modifying the present (Fisher, 2009). As we are attempting to define the nature and role of past news media production within the digital landscape, this is a particularly relevant point of view. Moreover, one of the underlining ideas behind the creation of the World Wide Web – a key part of the digital landscape – was to create 'a distributed information system' that would offer a possible solution to information loss (Berners-Lee, 1989). Hence, a system that had been envisioned as a means to assess the issues posed by information loss has become a central part of the contemporary digital landscape in a time frame dominated by the present, without past or future (Fisher, 2009). Within our analysis of the role of news outlet archives, this is highly significant as it implicitly describes past news media production and its archives as a factor with limited impact in the contemporary digital landscape.

Moreover, in opposition to a prominent role of past news media production as an accessible information resource, this 'continuous present' (Fisher, 2009: 58) seems to be defined by a practice that is typical of the contemporary digital landscape that can be defined as 'feed fruition'. We define 'Feed fruition' as

> a specific practice where individuals browse autonomously updated and personalised lists.

One of the first insights into 'feed fruition' was provided by Ruchi Sanghvi while introducing Facebook's News Feed as 'a personalised list of news stories throughout the day' (Sanghvi, 2006). While introducing this new element, Sanghvi underlined that 'these features are not only different from anything we've had on Facebook before, but they're quite unlike anything you can find on the web' (Sanghvi, 2006). After a decade, the News Feed's definition provided by Facebook has somewhat changed. Currently, it is defined as 'the constantly updating list of stories in the middle of your home page. News Feed includes status updates, photos, videos, links, app activity and likes from people, Pages and groups that you follow on Facebook' (Facebook, 2012).

This 'constantly updating list of stories' (Facebook, 2012) is a defining element not only of Facebook but other platforms and social networks in particular. In Chapter 1, we saw how, within these platforms, individuals (clustered in crowds) became 'produsers', which, according to Bruns, are 'users that are always already necessarily also producers of the shared knowledgebase' (Bruns, 2008: 2). Moreover, their 'permanent activity' (Fuchs, 2010: 192), organised around 'feed fruition', transforms individuals from an audience into a 'produsage/prosumer commodity. The category of the produsage/prosumer commodity does not signify a democratization of the media toward a participatory or democratic system, but the total commodification of human creativity' (Fuchs, 2010: 192). This production dynamic, well exploited by Facebook, has other effects. As Forestal (2020) underlines: 'By making it difficult for citizens to recognize their membership in any number of publics on the site, Facebook keeps its publics disorganized. Users cannot easily identify other users they share interests with and are therefore unable to communicate and act to manage those interests efficiently.'

Another social network that revolves around what we have defined as 'feed fruition' is Twitter. 'Twitter users follow others or are followed. […] A user can follow any other user, and the user being followed need not follow back. Being a follower on Twitter means that the user receives all the messages [called tweets] from those the user follows' (Kwak et al., 2010: 591). Hence, each Twitter user develops its feed from the users he or she follows, in an individual fashion. Twitter's website describes how 'following someone means you've chosen to subscribe to their Twitter updates' (Twitter, 2017). If you follow another user, 'every time they post a new message, it will appear on your Twitter Home timeline' (Twitter, 2017). Thus, by accessing a social network such as Twitter, organised around 'feed fruition', each user's home timeline automatically updates in real-time with messages, generating a succession of feeds which is the unique result of a user's choices as to which feeds he or she subscribes to, together with advertising featured in users' feeds, which is the most significant source of income for Twitter, constituting 86 per cent of overall revenues for the company according to the 2018 first quarter (Q1) shareholders letter. Hence, in the contemporary digital landscape, while 'feed fruition' is a tailor-made experience, it is also a non-replicable experience, as underlined by Bakshy, Messing and Adamic (2015) in their description of Facebook's News Feed:

> The media that individuals consume on Facebook depends not only on what their friends share, but also on how the News Feed ranking algorithm sorts these articles, and what individuals choose to read. The order in which users see stories in the News Feed depends on many factors, including how often the viewer visits Facebook, how much they interact with certain friends, and how often users have clicked on links to certain websites in News Feed in the past. (2015: 1130–1131)

The non-replicable and individual dimension of 'feed fruition' is an especially significant factor, as it well portrays the ad hoc nature of platform services, which require individuals to cluster in crowds in order to develop themselves. Each platform builds and feeds back to individual parts of the crowd, increasingly drawing from their data usage (Bakshy, Messing and Adamic, 2015). This interaction, which we have explored in Chapter 1, is one of the fundamental elements of the contemporary digital landscape. The tailor-made environments that individuals experience in platforms rely on user-generated data in order to be aggregated and exploited. This process is generally confined in the hands of platforms, as is it not shared with crowds. To assess the relevance of 'feed fruition' within the contemporary digital landscape, it is useful to analyse data on time spent by individuals in this type of environments. Moreover, it is especially relevant to focus on how individuals spend time on their mobile devices. According to the Global State of Mobile 2019 report

(Comscore, 2019), which provides data on usage from Canada, the US, Argentina, Brazil, Mexico, Italy, Spain, UK, India and Indonesia, online time is on the rise (almost by half in the US between June 2017 and June 2019). Mobile usage is dominant, as in none of the ten countries it represents less than three-quarters of the overall time spent online (Figure 5.1).

According to Comcast 'more than 80 per cent of mobile minutes in all markets reported are spent on apps' (Comscore, 2019), making platforms truly dominant if compared to mobile web browsing and overall. The percentage of users that uses mobile to access social media and instant messenger services has reached 88 per cent, with an eight per cent rise in two years, and 'mobile-first categories are becoming entrenched' (Comscore, 2019). Thus, applications that are based on 'feed fruition', such as social networks, comprise a significant portion of the time spent by individuals on their mobile devices. The notion of time as 'continuous present' (Fisher, 2009: 58) is reflected in the manner in which individuals,

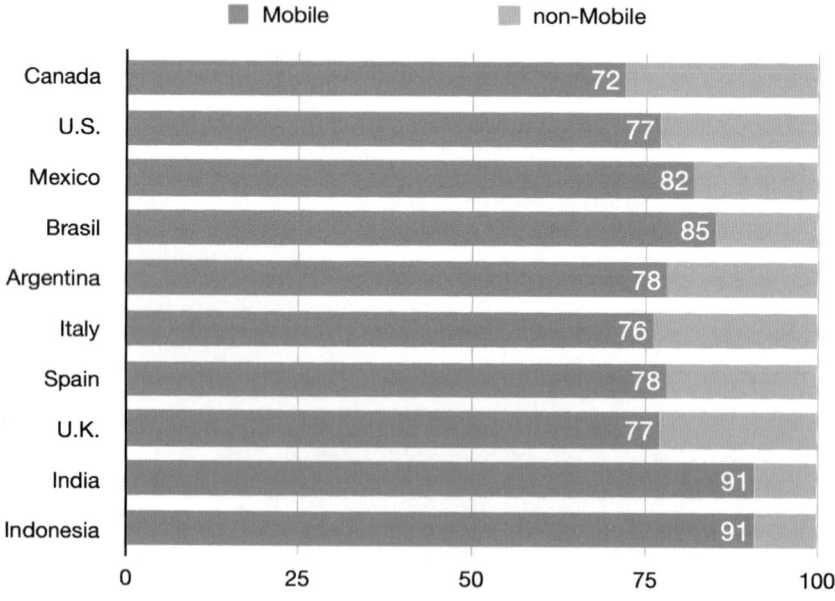

Figure 5.1 Percentage of online time between mobile and non-mobile
(Source: Comscore)

clustered in crowds, constantly access updating content feeds through their mobile devices. Moreover, the relationship between the continuous present and 'feed fruition' is strengthened by 'feed fruition's' role, which enhances crowds' tendency to cluster in environments such as platforms and specifically social networks.

In our analysis, after assessing the notion of time within the contemporary digital landscape, we shall now explore the relationship between time and digital archives, with a specific focus on news outlets digital archives. Having seen how time in the digital landscape is defined by feed fruition within a 'continuous present' (Fisher, 2009: 58), what is the role of archives? According to Adrian MacKenzie, 'we can point to two basic dynamics of virtualisation: real time processing and the archive drive. They stand as two cultural-technological poles or limits within which the virtual unfolds' (Mackenzie, 1997: 60). While 'real-time promises an experience of now' (Mackenzie, 1997: 60), the archive drive 'produces a locational "there" composed of text, images, indexes and records' (Mackenzie, 1997: 61). The relationship between these two poles produces what Mackenzie defines as 'the experience of the virtual' (Mackenzie, 1997: 62). In Chapter 1, we defined the contemporary digital landscape as

> sets of interaction ecosystems, which comprise three entities: individuals, crowds and platforms, which interact in an apparently frictionless manner. The digital landscape is defined by two main features, its nature as constant flux and a disruption enhancer.

Hence, we can assimilate 'the experience of the virtual' (Mackenzie, 1997: 62) to what individuals experience in the digital landscape, which can be considered a product of the constant dynamic between the 'real-time experience' (Mackenzie, 1997: 60) and 'the archive drive' (Mackenzie, 1997: 61).

Archives in the Digital Landscape

In the previous section, we explored the notion of feed fruition and 'continuous present' (Fisher, 2009: 58) as part of the 'real-time experience' (Mackenzie, 1997: 60) of the digital landscape. We shall now focus on the second pole described by Mackenzie, 'the archive drive' (Mackenzie, 1997: 60). According to Marlene Manoff 'most writers exploring the concept share a notion of an archive as a repository and collection of artifacts' (Manoff, 2004: 10). However, the author specifies that the term 'archive' can indicate a variety of entities.

> Frequently, the term archive refers to the contents of museums, libraries, and archives and thus the entire extant historical record. Some writers distinguish between archives as repositories of documents, manuscripts, and images; libraries as repositories of published books, journals, and other media; and museums as repositories of yet other kinds of cultural objects. Sometimes they do not. Writers focusing on the digital archive may use the term to refer to everything currently existing in digital format anywhere or they may use it to refer to some small subset of such material, typically a discrete collection of related electronic documents. Even librarians and archivists have become somewhat careless in their use of the term. (Manoff, 2004: 10)

In Manoff's analysis, the usage of the term 'archive' helps us to understand the numerous implications that the word has within the digital landscape. As we are trying to assess the possible relationship between the 'real-time experience' and the 'archive drive' (Mackenzie, 1997: 62), we shall focus on a specific aspect of the archive, the digital archive and more specifically on the news outlets digital archives. Hence, we can describe the digital archive within the digital landscape as 'everything currently existing in digital format anywhere' (Manoff, 2004: 10). While this is a very broad definition, it is a useful element in order to assess the changes that the digital landscape has undergone, transforming the open, distributed nature of the World Wide Web into its contemporary form. In Chapter 1, we have seen how the digital landscape has morphed from an open environment to a cluster of semi-closed platforms (Anderson and Wolff, 2010). Moreover, the World Wide Web has transformed into a platform for applications and content that interacts with a second force, crowds (Blanke, 2014). These changes within the nature of the World Wide Web can be framed within its nature as an archive and, according to French philosopher Jacques Derrida (1996), there is a direct relationship between who controls the archive and who holds political power. 'There is no political power without control of the archive, if not of memory. Effective democratisation can always be measured by this essential criterion: the participation in and access to the archive, its constitution, and its interpretation' (Derrida, 1996: 4).

Hence, if we conceive the World Wide Web as an archive, the issues of which entities constitute it, what is done with it and how participation develops, all directly influence its nature. As we have seen in Chapter 1, individuals, clustered in crowds, generate data which is increasingly harvested by platforms which are able to quantify and economically exploit it. If democratisation can be measured by 'the participation in and access to the archive, its constitution, and its interpretation' (Derrida, 1996: 4), we have to underline that the digital landscape, in its contemporary form, has reinforced the role of platforms at the expense of individuals.

However, archives are flourishing within the digital landscape. As underlined by Jussi Parikka in his Introduction to Wolfgang Ernst's *Media Archaeology,* 'suddenly archives are popping up everywhere. A lot of our software-based interaction online now has to do with archival metaphors' (Ernst, 2013: 1). Parikka defines individuals as 'miniarchivists ourselves in this information society, which could be more aptly called an information *management* society' (Ernst, 2013: 2). Moreover, he underlines

> we see the business of cloud storage, mobile storage, and such flourishing. We also see this in business models of social media: the so-called free platforms we are using to connect to friends and to share ideas, links, and preferences for films and music are all material for data mining, which is the new form of subsumption of our lives into capitalist production and accumulation of value. This algorithmic unconscious of social media cultures knows a lot about us and is often keen not only to keep but to sell those data to third parties. (Ernst, 2013: 2)

Thus, archiving in the digital landscape is an action performed by individuals, clustered in crowds, which takes place strictly in platforms which control the archive and its access, and thus power as underlined by Derrida (1996). While the contemporary has reached a stage in which each performs as archivist of his or her self, these actions are performed within the relationship between crowds and platforms. However, archiving is also mediated by machines and networks that within the contemporary digital landscape are becoming gradually more invisible, as we have seen in Chapter 1.

According to French philosopher Gilles Deleuze, 'types of machines are easily matched with each type of society – not that machines are determining, but because they express those social forms capable of generating them' (Deleuze, 1992: 6). Hence, Deleuze (1992) clarifies that computers constitute a type of machine that is the result of a mutation within capitalism. If the digital landscape's machines are reflective of the contemporary (Deleuze, 1992), they have likewise influenced not only how content is produced, but also how it is archived. Moreover, Ernst explores this relationship within different models of archives, underlining: 'Different media systems, from library catalogues to microfilming, have influenced the content as well as the understanding of the historical remains of the archive itself' (Ernst, 2013: 28).

In conclusion, the role of the archive in the digital landscape is defined by multiple factors. Individuals within this environment actively engage in archiving practices, which are influenced by the relationship between crowds and platforms. Moreover, these archiving practices are also conditioned by the means through which archiving is performed: machines and their nature are directly connected to what becomes part of the archive (Deleuze, 1992). Finally, the role of the archive itself influences what can be archived. Marlene Manoff sums up this relationship as expressed by Derrida in *Archive Fever*:

> One of Derrida's most valuable contributions is his elaboration of the notion that the structure of the archive determines what can be archived and that history and memory are shaped by the technical methods of what he calls 'archivization'. [...] The methods for transmitting information shape the nature of the knowledge that can be produced. (2004: 12)

Different News Outlet Archives in the Digital Landscape

Differences in News Outlet Archives in the Digital Archive

Our analysis to this point has been focused on time in the digital landscape, and we have explored the possible relationship between the notion of 'continuous present' (Fisher, 2009: 58) and feed fruition. Afterwards, we have assessed how the digital landscape has changed the notion of the archive. We shall now focus on digital media archives and their interaction with the digital landscape.

According to Manoff, one of the possible definitions of a digital archive is 'everything currently existing in digital format anywhere' (Manoff, 2004: 10). While this is a broad definition, we have also seen how archiving in the digital landscape is influenced by individual practices, devices and the archive itself. Within this framework, we shall now concentrate on a specific type of digital archives: news outlet digital archives.

Among news outlet archives in the digital landscape, there are different types of archives which originate from different practices and different eras of news media production. News outlets' digital archives based on textual sources are generally the product either of early print materials, which have been converted into a digital format, or the product of digital archives generated by articles originally published in a paper format which have also been published on the World Wide Web. Nicholson describes the shift introduced by the extensive digitisation process of hard-copy archives, underlining how 'the rapid digitisation of newspapers and periodicals has transformed even the recent past into a foreign country' (Nicholson, 2013: 59). Alongside this process, which has regarded these two types of archives which retain some relationship with their hard-copy version, there are digitally native news media outlets that publish exclusively on the World Wide Web. Hence, these outlets have created archives which entail a direct relationship only with the digital environment rather than a hard-copy source. As such, this process represents a departure both from hard-copy archives and their digitised versions. However, there is a further difference between hard-copy archives and their digitised versions as they are not the same:

> A hard copy of a newspaper is fundamentally different from a digitised version. At first glance, this difference seems obvious; one source is made from paper, the other exists as billions of 1s and 0s. However, the transformative effect of digitisation stretches beyond this material transition. Unlike microfilming, the creation of a digital newspaper does not simply produce what archivists term a 'surrogate', or stand-in, for the original. Instead, it creates something new; sources are 'remediated' and not just reproduced. (Nicholson, 2013: 64)

However, while there are numerous differences between different types of news outlet archives, there are also some unifying factors, common to all types of archives. Deacon identifies 'three perennial issues concerning the archiving of yesterday's news' (Deacon, 2007: 6). These three issues are storage, information retrieval and access and all have been greatly impacted by the digital landscape, as 'innovations in computer and information technology offer ways of alleviating the problems associated with storing, retrieving and accessing news material' (Deacon, 2007: 7).

Deacon identifies 'storage' as an issue that regards 'news material in its original format' (Deacon, 2007: 6), meaning news outlet production in paper or microfilm version. However, storage seems to be an issue in the digital landscape, as digital data is also prone to decay, as we had seen in Chapter 2, when we analysed the role of the digital public sphere and how it has adapted to the contemporary environment.

'Information retrieval' constitutes Deacon's second focus, meaning 'to what extent is it possible to locate specific pieces of information' (Deacon, 2007: 6). Again, this process has undergone a profound shift in the digital landscape, as the implementation of digital tools has revolutionised it. According to Nicholson, 'keyword search engines are widely recognised as a time-saving device […]. So far, in other words, the mainstream profession has treated digitalisation largely as a practical revolution – it has made research faster, easier, more convenient and more productive' (Nicholson, 2013: 61).

The final issue that Deacon identifies in news outlet archiving is 'access', connecting it to its physical dimension. Prior to the impact of the digital landscape, 'anyone wishing to consult conventional news archives had to be physically present to examine material, with all the attendant inconvenience this can cause' (Deacon, 2007: 6). Whereas the physical aspect is no longer present in the digital landscape, the issue of access has evolved in a different direction. As Mussell underlines, 'digital content enters an information economy that can only be monetised by the imposition of barriers to access' (Mussell, 2012: 65). Hence, within the digital landscape, there seems to have been a transition regarding access from a physical to an economic dimension.

All three issues – storage, information retrieval and access – regarding news outlet archives identified by Deacon (2007) have undergone significant transformations within the digital landscape. We shall now focus on different types of news outlet archives in the digital landscape, in order to assess the specific nature of each type of archive.

Early Media Production and Optical Character Recognition–Based Archives

Archives resulting from the digitisation of early newspaper production constitute a valuable starting point to trace the migration from a traditional, hard-copy archive to a digital archive. Thus, we shall begin by assessing this type of archive. Scholars, such as Bingham (2010) and Mussell (2012), have highlighted the differences between traditional archival search and the contemporary, digital archival search activity.

As noted by Mussell in this work, *The Nineteenth-Century Press in the Digital Age*, 'the digitization of our cultural heritage radically transforms our encounters with the past' (Mussell, 2012: 1). Mussell (2012) focuses on how digital tools applied to early news outlet production can provide new insight into nineteenth-century history. Before Mussell (2012), Bingham emphasised this radical alteration, underlining how 'it is clear even to the most casual observer of the historical profession that research practices are being gradually transformed by the digitisation of archives and primary sources' (Bingham, 2010: 225). Hence, according to Bingham (2010), digitisation has transformed the newspaper's role in a way which will increase its relevance. Digital archives of early newspapers can now be accessed more easily and searched using new digital tools that allow 'analysis to proceed in new ways. Digital searching enables newspaper content to be explored far more rigorously and sensitively' (Bingham, 2010: 228). Both authors underline how a physical entity, the newspaper, has been transformed in the digital landscape and how new results in research and writing are now possible thanks to the digitisation of hard-copy archives. However, Bingham also stresses that 'there is a danger in this process of forgetting that newspapers were material objects that were bought, read and passed around, and that the location and presentation of individual articles is of central importance in understanding how those articles were received by readers and how much significance was ascribed to them' (Bingham, 2010: 230). In Bingham's view, while the digitisation process of traditional hard-copy archives of early news outlets has opened new possibilities, it also requires researchers to focus on the broader and far from neutral issues that regard the digital dimension and its possibilities. In this regard, further insight is provided by Derrida (2005). The process that Bingham (2010) described regarding traditional news outlet archives in their new digital format is further assessed by Derrida his work *Paper Machine*, where it is defined as 'de-paperization' (Derrida, 2005):

> The 'de-paperization' of the supports if I can put it like that, is to begin with the economic rationality of a profit: a simplification and acceleration of all the procedures involved; a saving of time and space, and thus the facilitation of storage, archiving, communication, and debates beyond social and national frontiers; a hyperactive circulation of ideas, images, and voices; democratisation, homogenization, and universalization; immediate or transparent 'globalization' and so, it is thought, more sharing out of rights, signs, knowledge, and so on. But by the same token, just as many catastrophes: inflation and deregulation in the commerce of signs; invisible hegemonies and appropriations, whether of languages or places. (2005: 55–56)

For Derrida, the 'de-paperization of the supports' (Derrida, 2005: 55–56) or rather its transformation into new, digital forms, is a process implying multiple and ambiguous instances. Whereas it makes storage and archiving easier, it also makes this practice subject to economic dynamics – such as 'inflation and deregulation' (Derrida, 2005: 55–56) – highlighting the risk of 'invisible hegemonies and appropriations' (Derrida, 2005: 55–56). Moreover, in the same work, Derrida describes the digitisation process as 'always leading to new responsibilities, another critical culture of the archive – in short another "history"' (Derrida, 2005: 64). According to Derrida (2005), the digitisation process affects not only the archiving culture but, more broadly, the notion of history.

As we are focusing on the digitisation of hard-copy newspaper archives, it is important to underline that the technologies allowing the 'de-paperization' process (Derrida, 2005) have a direct influence both on the modus operandi of researchers and the results they are able to obtain from their activity. In particular, Optical Character Recognition (OCR) has proven widely popular in the digitisation of hard-copy sources. OCR involves a process that automatically recognises characters through an optical mechanism. Once sources are digitalised, they become storable, searchable and accessible as digitally native content. Regarding newspaper archives, 'it is far easier, for example to find out when a subject was first discussed in the press, or when a term was coined' (Bingham, 2010: 228). However, this technology does have limitations. More specifically Bingham (2010) underlines issues that arise especially in those newspapers which were composed with 'imperfect or irregular typefaces, and this can seriously limit the accuracy of keyword searches in pre-twentieth-century content' (Bingham, 2010: 228). Another critical aspect is highlighted by Deacon as the usage of OCR technology implies

> the loss of the visual dimension of news. This is a significant omission as the size and positioning of text and the use of photographs and illustrations are key mechanisms by which news-makers dramatize reports, assist reader' comprehension, corroborate the 'truth' of a reported event and, sometimes, qualify, or even subvert, the linguistic substance of a related news item. (2007: 10)

Hence, as we have seen, the digitisation process of hard-copy news outlet production opens a wide range of unforeseen possibilities, augmenting tools at disposal for the investigation of sources, and enabling new research paths to be followed. However, this process opens to all the possible critical aspects identified by Derrida (2005) in describing 'de-paperization', such as the effect of economic and power dynamics on archive digitisation. Moreover, while past news outlet production gains a digital dimension, it possibly loses other types of information that constituted its original version, such as the visual component, thus raising potential issues in its full assessment and comprehension.

Digitisation in Newsrooms and News Archives

Having begun our analysis of news media archives starting from early newspaper press converted in a digital format via Optical Character Recognition, we shall now focus on digital archives of news media that have been published both in a print and a digital version. The difference between these archives and archives that host early news media production converted in digital format is the technological process behind the archive's digitisation.

When computers became part of the toolset used daily by journalists, the term 'Computer-Assisted Reporting' started to be used. Significant signs of the beginning of this process can be dated between 1980 and 1985, as underlined by Scott R. Maier while describing computer usage in newsrooms. As Maier emphasises: 'In nearly every year since 1986, reporters have won Pulitzer Prizes for stories based on computer-assisted reporting. But only in recent years, as the new technology became easier and more versatile, have computers become a tool for everyday newsgathering' (2000: 96).

Moreover, there is a dual aspect of computer-assisted reporting application in newsrooms that has to be underlined, one regarding online-based newsgathering and the second database-oriented analysis (Garrison, 1997). The organising process of computer usage in newsrooms was transformative and resulted in the adoption of a new series of digital tools as described by Vigneaux, referring to 'newsroom computer systems' comprising 'data management software coupled with search-and-retrieval and word processing software. Newsroom computer systems make it possible to electronically store, catalogue, search for, and recall any of the textual information which they contained' (Vigneaux, 1996: 514).

Hence, since its early stages, the adoption of computers in newsrooms had multiple functions, which included implementation in archiving and search activities. Whereas 'a surrogate' (Nicholson, 2013: 64) is a digital archive that had a paper or microfilm origin, it seems to be clear that the introduction of computers had an impact on archiving practices within newsrooms. Archives started to be derived both from hard-copy digitisation and the progressive implementation of digital tools in day-to-day operations. However, as underlined for news outlet archives created with optical character recognition, archives of this type of news media production appear to suffer the same loss of the visual aspect.

In her article, *Archiving the Visual*, Nicole Maurantonio (2014) explores the absence of visual documentation within digital archives generated from news outlet archives in the era of Computer-Assisted Reporting. Her contribution is relevant as she uses a case-study: the 1985 bombing of the

MOVE house in Philadelphia, Pennsylvania, US Maurantonio underlines how 'digitized newspapers have altered the original text in crucial ways. Depending on the digital database, the changes to that newspaper text can vary widely' (Maurantonio, 2014: 89). Moreover, the author focuses on a further aspect, as 'the photograph's contingency, however, has made it a rather uneasy fit within digital archives in particular, given the latter's reliance upon linguistic schemas for organisation' (Maurantonio, 2014: 92) Browsing through the available digital archive repository, Newsbank, Maurantonio points out that visual elements are separated from the corresponding text and, in order to reconstruct the original composition, the only option is to work on hard-copy newspapers or their microfilm version. Maurantonio (2014) follows Olson, Finnegan and Hope in defining the visual dimension of news outlet production as not 'just images or visual media but the totality of practices, performances, and configurations of the visual' (Olson, Finnegan and Hope, 2008: xii). Hence, within archives produced when computers were implemented in newsrooms, there seems to be a loss not just of photographic material, but other visual aspects, such as the article's size, headline size and font type, position and space devoted to other elements in the page.

However, among this type of digital news media archives, *The New York Times* Archive has attempted to address the issue regarding the loss of the visual aspect of archived news. We have selected this particular outlet for this specific reason. *The New York Times* Archive also provides an example of how a news outlet can assess different challenges connected with the archival process and, more specifically, its digital possibilities and affordances. In its current form, the news media outlet archive hosts articles starting from 1851 and is divided into three different sections, each with its particularities regarding both access and material available. The main distinction within *The New York Times* Archive is the format in which articles are available: either in PDF (Portable Document Format) file format or online.

The articles available in PDF are divided into two different time periods. Articles published from 1851 to 1922 are available entirely for all visitors to *The New York Times* website without any monetary fee. Articles from 1922 to 1980 are fully available for those who visit *The New York Times* website and also have either a paid subscription or are willing to purchase single articles. Articles available online comprise those published from 1981 to date, accessible to all visitors to the website. However, visitors who are not paying subscribers can only access a set number of articles per month.

Articles available in *The New York Times* Archive that have been published from 1851 to 1980 do not include display or classified advertising. Moreover, photographs, graphs and other visual material might not be included in articles published after 1981. As *The New York Times* states on its website, some articles are available partially: 'Full archive articles include the full text of an article. Prior to 1981, most full articles are available only as PDF files. For these articles, the article page will display a partial article that includes only an excerpt or an abstract' (*The New York Times*, 2014b). It is evident that, even in a legacy news outlet such as *The New York Times*, the digital archive is the result of materials organised in multiple ways, which make content available to visitors in a variety of manners, with content either available entirely for free or rather available partially for paying subscribers.

However, *The New York Times* has developed an archiving tool aimed at retrieving and visualising articles in order to address the issue regarding the loss of the visual elements of its hard-copy paper production, as highlighted by Maurantonio (2014) and others. The tool, which is named 'TimesMachine', aims to provide 'over 150 years of *New York Times* journalism, as it originally appeared' (*The New York Times*, 2008). 'TimesMachine' debuted in 2008 after *The New York Times* decided to discontinue its first paywall, 'TimesSelect', which made articles by columnist and the newspaper archives available only for subscribers. Derek Gottfrid, *The New York Times* senior software architect and product technologist at the time described 'TimesMachine' as 'a series of large TIFF (Tagged Image File Format) images, associated metadata and article text capture from OCR. The metadata contains the location of each article within the TIFF images, which allows TimesMachine to know which article your mouse is hovering over' (Gottfrid, 2008). This description regards the first version of 'TimesMachine' which was operational from 2008 to 2013 when a new version was introduced. The new release of the 'TimesMachine' featured 'every article, every letter and every advertisement [is] included in a legible, linkable and shareable fashion' (Sandhaus, 2013). In a blog entry on *The New York Times* website, Sandhaus (2013) explained how this result was achieved. Since each edition of the newspaper is an image file of relevant size, the developers used a technique called 'tiling', commonly used in digital map development. According to Sandhaus

> with tiling, a large image is broken down into small tiles that are computed at several different zoom levels. When a user wishes to view the tiled image in a browser, only the tiles required to display the visible portion are downloaded. This approach dramatically reduces bandwidth requirements and has the further advantage of allowing users to zoom and drag the larger image. (2013)

Those editions of *The New York Times* that are available in the 'TimesMachine' provide readers with a fluid experience within their browsers, enabling them to experience every element on each page. Users can zoom on different areas of the page, click on articles and be presented with general information and the full text of the article. Hence, rather being a substitute of *The New York Times* digital archive, 'TimesMachine' provides full context, visual information and elements for each of the editions of the newspaper which are available on the service. Readers can experience, within a virtual frame, an archived version of the newspaper which is closer to a digital 'surrogate', which is how Nicholson (2013) defined the relationship between microfilm and its hard-copy source.

In 2016, *The New York Times* further expanded its 'TimesMachine'. Before this expansion, 'TimesMachine' featured every issue of the newspaper published between 1851 and 1980, comprising approximately 11 million articles in 2.5 million pages. After 2016, 'TimesMachine' also features all issues of *The New York Times* published between 1981 and 2002, and this expansion added 8,035 issues of the newspaper, 1.4 million articles in over 1.6 million pages. Hence, 'TimesMachine' then featured all content published on the newspaper editions of *The New York Times* published between 1851 and 2002, comprising around 12.4 million articles over 4.1 million pages. In the 2016 article that announced the expansion of 'TimesMachine', Jane Cotler and Evan Sandhaus explained in further detail how processing an edition of *The New York Times* into the 'TimesMachine' works. As we underlined before, developers used 'tiling' to provide readers with a fluid experience within the 'TimesMachine' which the authors describe as 'our virtual microfilm reader' (Cotler and Sandhaus, 2016). Cotler and Sandhaus (2016) describe the 'TimesMachine' process as the result of three different inputs: high-resolution scans of microfilm, XML (eXtensible Markup Language) metadata for each article and INI (initialization file format) files that provide the coordinates for the space that each article occupies in the page. As they write

> The pipeline first stitches the pages together into one large virtual image. The coordin-
> ates of every article on every page are then projected from Cartesian (x, y) coordinates
> into geographic (latitude and longitude) coordinates. These projected coordinates
> are combined with article metadata into a large JavaScript object describing the con-
> tents of a complete issue. The large virtual image is then cut up into thousands of
> 256×256 pixel tiles computed at several zoom levels. All of this data is uploaded to a
> content distribution network (CDN). (Cotler and Sandhaus, 2016)

Users who browse the 'TimesMachine' can access specific editions of the newspaper, as the software is designed to download the JSON object that contains the information on the specific edition of *The New York Times* and, instead of loading all the tiles that comprise each page of the newspaper, it limits itself to display what can be seen on the reader's screen (Cotler and Sandhaus, 2016). A JSON, or JavaScript Object Notation file, is a 'text based, language-independent data interchange format [...]. JSON defines a small set of structuring rules for the portable representation of struc-tured data' (ECMA, 2017). As the reader browses the webpage, moving across the page of the newspaper's edition, other data is loaded. Thus, *The New York Times* created a tool that can provide users with a browsing ex-perience into a 'digital surrogate' (Cotler and Sandhaus, 2016) of their paper edition which is both efficient and provides all the visual context for each edition which has been digitalised through this process.

The 2016 expansion of the 'TimesMachine' had to face an issue that we explored priory in this section: computer usage in newsrooms. As we under-lined before, from 1980 onwards, computer-assisted reporting started to gain momentum. Hence, articles started to be written, stored and archived in a digital format:

> Starting around 1981, *The Times* began keeping an archive of the complete digital
> text of every article published in print. In order to expand TimesMachine beyond

1980 and include links to the full text, we needed to know how our scanned print archive and our digital text archive aligned. (Cotler and Sandhaus, 2016)

The digitally developed computer archive and the digitised version of the archive originated from Optical Character Recognition had to be harmonised into a single archive, which was then processed to deliver each 'TimesMachine' edition of the newspaper. This process is significant as it demonstrates how the implementation of digital tools within newsrooms has raised issues in archiving practices. More specifically, the overlap between two digital versions of a single content – for example, an article – highlights very relevant harmonisation issues in news media outlets archives. With the rise in computer usage in newsrooms, archiving power became de-centralised and producing multiple versions of the same element – for example, an article – became a basic operation. However, the issue of harmonisation between different copies of the same source is extremely relevant as it is a process which has the task to generate a contribution to an institutional archive, as in the case of *The New York Times*, establishing which archived version is to become part of the archive itself.

Cotler and Sandhaus (2016) describe in detail how *The New York Times* addressed this issue to generate an archive which was established as a source for the 'TimesMachine'. The newspaper's team used an open-source optical character recognition engine named Tesseract, which 'was developed by HP between 1984 and 1994' and 'in late 2005, HP released Tesseract for open source […]. Now it is developed and maintained by Google' (Patel, Patel and Patel, 2012: 50). After performing this task with Tesseract, *The New York Times* team had two versions of each article: one version originated by the OCR scan and one from the digital text archive. The following step was to assess which articles matched between the two versions. In order to resolve this issue, a technique called 'shingling' was implemented by *The New York Times* team: 'We transformed the text of articles in both datasets into a list of tokens, and then turned the list of tokens into a list of n-token sequences called "shingles"' (Cotler and Sandhaus, 2016). The two authors underline that 'shingling' was chosen because articles that result from optical character recognition rarely provide an exact match, as we have seen in the previous section, and hence they could 'not align articles by simply testing for string equality. Instead, we used fuzzy string matching' (Cotler and Sandhaus, 2016).

The New York Times team then wanted to compare a list of articles that featured each shingle from the OCR scan produced version and the digitised version of the same article resulting from computer usage in its newsroom. Instead of applying this process to each article, work was performed on full issues of the newspaper from both the OCR scan produced version and the full-text version. Hence, the comparison was faster and more efficient. The difference between the two datasets was then expressed using a library – essentially, a tool – in the programming language Python. After processing the two versions with Python's difflib library, *The New York Times* team was able to match 80 per cent of the content from the OCR scan produced version and the full-text version (Cotler and Sandhaus, 2016). As to the remaining 20 per cent of the articles

> Some full text articles were represented as multiple regions in the scanned archive, and some single regions in the scanned archive corresponded to multiple items in the full text archive. We reconciled the disparity by splitting the data into paragraphs and carrying out a similar process to the one described above, on the paragraph level (Cotler and Sandhaus, 2016).

In conclusion, *The New York Times* produced a 'near-perfect, many-to-many matching of zones to the full text archive which is wonderfully searchable' (Cotler and Sandhaus, 2016). As we have seen, *The New York Times* had to undertake an extensive set of actions in order to provide users with a tool addressing many of the issues posed by digital archiving of traditional news outlet production. Moreover, as this digitisation process progressed to an era when computer-assisted reporting came into play, new issues arose. In order to produce a searchable, browser-friendly archive which provides all the visual context possible, *The New York Times* had to undergo an extensive process of comparison between two different versions, both developed within the digital landscape, one originating from OCR scans and the other from digital versions of articles published in the newspaper's editions. Thus, 'TimesMachine' is a result of this harmonisation process and describing how this process has evolved is relevant to assess the issues that arise from archiving news media production in the digital landscape.

The 'TimesMachine' is a tool that provides a new, digital version of archived content that was originally published on paper. However, *The New York Times* Archive also comprises content that has been published only on its website. Hence, it is relevant to analyse how the news media outlet has modified its digital publishing system to store digitally native content alongside content originating from hard-copy editions. In a blog entry published on *The New York Times* 'Open' blog, entitled 'The Future of the Past: Modernizing the New York Times Archive', Sofia Van Valkenburg and Evan Sandhaus describe how the news media outlet has harmonised all its content during its 2014 redesign and what this process has led the news media outlet to understand about its archive (Van Valkenburg and Sandhaus, 2016). The originating issue behind this process was converting articles published between 1851 and 2006 into a format that would work within the current CMS [Content Management System] in use at *The New York Times*, named 'Scoop'. The issue experienced by *The New York Times* is very relevant, as Content Management Systems (CMS) are at the heart of news outlet operations in the digital landscape. According to Deanne Barker, author of *Web Content Management: Systems, Features, and Best Practices*, a content management system can be defined as

> a software package that provides some level of automation for the tasks required to effectively manage content. A CMS is usually server-based, multiuser software that interacts with content stored in a repository. […] A CMS allows editors to create new content, edit existing content, perform editorial processes on content, and ultimately make that content available to other people to consume it. (2016: 9)

The importance of the process undertaken by *The New York Times* is clear as its goal was to harmonise content, created in different eras, within its current CMS. This process is moreover relevant as *The New York Times* has chosen, over the years, to develop a CMS capable of interfacing with all its production, whether originating from the archived content or produced for the hard-copy edition of the newspaper or produced for its website. However, the adoption of an internally developed CMS for all news outlet operations was complicated as, until 2006, *The New York Times* still used a CMS developed by a company named Fatwire, which was bought by Oracle in 2011.

In 2014, *The New York Times* provided an in-detail description of 'Scoop' on its own *Open* blog in a post by Luke Vnenchak (2014). The author underlined that the CMS system 'does not render our website or provide community tools to our readers. Rather, it is a system for managing content and publishing data so that other applications can render the content across our platforms' (Vnenchak, 2014). Vnenchak underlines how the news media outlet was planning to adopt 'Scoop' for both digital and print operations by 2015, as this CMS performed all operations required for working on content and its publishing process, alongside providing records of changes, suggesting tags and other material that might be connected to the article on which the writer or editor was working on (Vnenchak, 2014).

The importance of the transition undertaken by *The New York Times* is underlined by Giner (2014) as he describes the issues in adapting previously conceived content management systems to the digital landscape. According to Giner, it was much simpler for 'native multi-media CMS that were born digital […] to serve the print end of their system' (Giner, 2014). In 2017, *The New York Times* published a report focused on the future strategies of the news media outlet (*The New York Times*, 2017). However, it also provided insight into current operations, underlining that 'Scoop' is being continuously updated and is being adapted to the new requirements in digital publishing. As we have seen, a relevant feature of long-form journalism in the digital landscape is the presence of different content formats, such as visual content, audio, multimedia and datasets, into single suites. *The New York Times* report underlines that – as such – this issue has not been addressed within 'Scoop's' architecture, as 'our content management system, Scoop, makes the placement of visuals an afterthought. (The advent of Oak, our new story creation tool in Scoop, is encouraging because it is designed to address these problems)' (*The New York Times*, 2017).

We can see how the issues raised by news media archives in the digital landscape have impacted all the areas of the news production process. Moreover, even within content management systems that have been created in order to operate with different types of content, such as archived content, digitally native content and content for print versions within the same outlet, adapting to the digital landscape implies a continuous update of CMS systems in order to produce journalistic tools which are flexible, scalable and allow journalists to produce complex narrative forms such as contemporary long-form journalism.

The relevance of content management systems within news outlets in the digital landscape seems to be confirmed by the direction undertaken by *The Washington Post* after Amazon founder Jeff Bezos acquired it in 2013. Since 2013, *The Washington Post* has developed a new CMS and, alongside, a whole suite of tools named 'Arc'. Initially, 'Arc' was developed to overcome the usage of two different content management systems that were used simultaneously to publish content on two versions of the news outlet website, as 'each site happened to be called washingtonpost.com, and the exhausted designers and site engineers had to make sure readers couldn't see a difference' (Remington, 2016). In 1995, as Remington (2016) explains, the news media outlet launched its website and set up a separate CMS from the one used for the print version to operate in the digital landscape. After the print and digital newsrooms were merged in 2010, *The Washington Post* 'replaced its print and web CMS systems with a single solution that supported both print and digital publishing. But – as is so often the case – the all-in-one solution wasn't equally good at everything. It behaved like a legacy print CMS, where digital was an afterthought' (Remington, 2016). Hence, the choice was to implement tools from WordPress, an open-source platform, alongside the in-house CMS, creating de facto two different websites, which appeared identical. The first step to overcome this situation was to create a new tool named 'PageBuilder' (Kim, 2015). According to Timothy Kim, lead developer at *The Washington Post*, the new tool's objective was to separate the system dedicated to content creation from the one tasked with website publishing:

> By separating the rendering components from the rest of a unified CMS, it allows The Post to cleanly separate the concerns of presentation and content production / storage. This in turn, makes it significantly easier to create any arbitrary number of presentations for any set of content. (2015)

'PageBuilder' was one of the first steps that led to the creation of a completely new CMS within the news outlet. This new system has redesigned the whole architecture within *The Washington Post* and, as of 2017, has begun to be sold as 'SaaS' (Software as a Service), producing revenue for the company. 'SaaS' is defined as a practice that 'focuses on separating the *possession* and *ownership* of software from its *use*. Delivering software's functionality as a set of distributed services that can be configured and bound at delivery time' (Turner, Budgen and Brereton, 2003: 38). The new system developed by *The Washington Post* was licensed to competitors, such as the Tronc group, which owns major US newspapers such as *The Los Angeles Times*, *The Chicago Tribune*, *The Baltimore Sun* and *The Orlando Sentinel*, and other outlets including French newspaper *Le Parisien*, the *New Zealand Media and Entertainment* group and the Canadian *The Globe and Mail*. According to an article published on *Fortune* by Matthew Ingram, the goal within the development of the 'Arc' platform suite was to 'make it easier to produce various kinds of content both for the web and for mobile apps, and then to manage the editing and publishing of that content, as well as the monetisation of it through advertising and other methods' (Ingram, 2017).

It is relevant to underline that the whole operational dynamic within 'Arc' is directly inspired by Amazon, whose founder owns the news outlet. Shailesh Prakash, chief information officer at *The Washington Post*, clearly defined the relationship between Amazon and *The Washington Post* regarding 'Arc'. 'We have taken a page out of Amazon's playbook. It is completely hosted. We run it, we administer it and we get paid consistently every month. The great thing is if a site grows and gets more traffic, we get paid more' (Alpert, 2016). According to an article by Shan Wang published on *Nieman Lab*, as of February 2018, 'Arc' has dozens of customer, ranging from small news media outlets to larger ones, which constitute the core of 'Arc' clients and the future prospects involve providing 'a completely automated, self-service option' which is currently in the works, with 'parts of deployment [that] are starting to be automated, and certain developments, like a ticketing system for troubleshooting, set it on a path to scaling faster' (Wang, 2018). As described above by Alpert (2016), 'Arc' stems from Amazon's modus operandi, which is described by Blanke (2014): after deciding to 'offer its spare server capacities to others and develop a new business' (Blanke, 2014: 49). Amazon allowed other entities to 'transfer the responsibilities of running the systems to people specialised in this task and most often this will come at a lower cost than was originally anticipated'

(Blanke, 2014: 49). However, Blanke underlines that 'by handing over the responsibilities, one also gives away control' (Blanke, 2014: 49–50). Thus, while 'Arc's' operations are beneficial to *The Washington Post* as a revenue resource, they also raise issues regarding Amazon as, through 'Arc', it is operating both as a cloud computing service provider and a platform provider, while its founder is the owner of a major news media outlet such as *The Washington Post*.

As we have seen in the examples provided by *The New York Times* and *The Washington Post*, the importance of CMS within publishing in the digital landscape is an increasingly relevant factor as it determines both how content is published and how vital harmonising processes work. Yet, it is due to underline that, aside from *The New York Times* and *The Washington Post*, the majority of news outlets generally use Content Management Systems provided by a number of third-party companies, as shown by the results of a research published on the *Donald W. Reynolds Journalism Institute Missouri School of Journalism* website (Golding, 2015). The capacity to create in-house content management systems introduces a further differentiation among news media outlets in the digital landscape, as this type of activity is a resource and labour-intensive task, which not all news media outlets are able or willing to undertake, making third-party providers a very likely source of tools.

Having assessed the relevance of content management systems within the digital publishing process, the harmonisation issue experienced by *The New York Times* between its CMS and its digital archive appears increasingly relevant. Before focusing on the role of content management systems, we were describing how *The New York Times* team was faced with the task of 'converting the approximately fourteen million articles published between 1851–2006 into a format compatible with our current CMS and reader experiences was not so straightforward' (Van Valkenburg and Sandhaus, 2016). The process regarding archived content published between 1851 and 1980 (before the implementation of computer-assisted reporting) is described as simple (Van Valkenburg and Sandhaus, 2016). However, numerous issues arose for articles published between 1980 up to 2006, as *The New York Times* team discovered that 'there were possibly hundreds of thousands of online-only articles missing from the archive, which reflected only what appeared in the print edition' (Van Valkenburg and Sandhaus, 2016). In order to harmonise content within the CMS in use, the news outlet worked to produce a definitive list of all the content which was published online. The list's elaboration was not a straightforward process, rather a multi-sourced effort: 'To construct this list we consulted several additional data sources including analytics, sitemaps and our database of book, film and restaurant reviews' (Van Valkenburg and Sandhaus, 2016). The two authors describe the archive migration pipeline that they implemented in detail, explaining how each task was performed, from raw HTML and XML scraping to URL re-writing and duplicate content handling.

The whole digitisation process within newsrooms, as we have seen, presents complexities and issues. Moreover, it is directly influenced by a number of factors which have a profound impact on how content produced in the past is harmonised in the digital landscape. Hence, the development of hybrid archives that host content previously published in paper format and digitally native content raises a series of issues regarding the loss of information and harmonisation processes. As we have seen, there has been a significant effort by two legacy news outlets such as *The New York Times* and *The Washington Post* to enhance archive practices and to develop archive fruition tools. However, it appears relevant to continuously keep track of changes within news outlet archives as they merge with content distribution systems. Within this process, the adoption of content management systems separately tasked with print and online operations has led to increasing issues, which have not been resolved by the adoption of a single CMS for both operations, requiring further harmonisation processes, which have proven more complex as the harmonised content was produced within the computer-assisted reporting era.

Digitally Native Publishers and Archiving

The archive digitisation and harmonisation processes within newsrooms that operated prior and during the era of computer-assisted reporting has proven to be a complex process, raising further issues as the impact of the digital landscape becomes more relevant. However, we shall now focus on a different type of news media outlets and their archival practices, by concentrating on digital-only news media outlets, which are defined by their distribution practices, as 'they rely solely on new media to distribute content' (Adornato, 2017: 34). We shall investigate how they have faced the issue of content archiving and to which degree these news outlet archives are accessible.

To begin our analysis, we shall focus on a special issue devoted to this matter by *The Newspaper Research Journal*, entitled 'Capturing and Preserving the First Draft of History in the Digital Environment'. As underlined by the issue's editors, there are multiple archiving practices within different types of news media outlets in the digital landscape (Hansen and Paul, 2015). The first identifiable archiving practice regards digitally scanned of printed newspapers, as we have described before in this chapter. The second archiving practice regards 'print/online publications' as we have analysed in the previous section. The third archiving practice identified by Hansen and Paul regards what they define as ' "born digital" news' (Hansen and Paul, 2015: 290). Hansen and Paul underline that, while preservation has always challenged all stakeholders interested in archiving news content, these issues

> are even more pressing with the growth of 'born digital' publications or digital-only publications, 'big data' projects, interactive visualisations, social media content, user-generated content and comments and all the other formats and platforms on which news content is created and delivered. (2015: 290)

Hence, we must consider that digitally native publications face issues that – while being long present in archiving news content – appear to be stronger and more difficult to face, as sources and formats increase while newsrooms generally shrink in size. However, there is a more general issue, as underlined by McCain:

> Years, perhaps decades, of journalistic work they contain will be partially or entirely lost. It's not the fault of the software architects or hardware manufacturers; media executives tasked them with designing a system to speed up production and publication of news content, not to ensure its long-term survival. (2015: 338).

Hence, the influence of content management systems, on which we focused on in the previous section, is an issue that has needs to be taken into consideration together with a second, decisive factor regarding content produced solely in digital format. Moreover, McCain states that 'unlike content digitized from analogue media, born-digital often has no physical surrogate to serve as an effective fallback' (McCain, 2015: 338). Hence, once a loss of content takes place within the digital landscape, in the absence of a surrogate, there is effectively little that can be done to retrieve the original digitally native content. As we have seen in Chapter 2, the issue of information deterioration in the digital landscape regards all types of content and specifically news media outlet production. We must underline that the archiving responsibility for news media outlets clashes with their current status in the digital landscape, heavily influenced by increasing economic pressure, making this task especially complex. The issue of digitally born content frailty is likely influenced by the shift that has taken place regarding how news media outlets publish their content, as platforms have gained importance in this field, as we have seen in Chapter 2.

However, it is relevant to investigate how major news media outlets are archiving their content on the World Wide Web. In order to do so, we shall focus on a specific form of archiving practice within news media outlets in the digital landscape. We shall concentrate on Web archives created and maintained by digital-only news media outlets, as they appear to be the ones more directly influenced by the issues raised by McCain (2015). Moreover, we have chosen to focus on digital-only news media outlets on the World Wide Web, which have never operated using in other distribution formats.

We have chosen two case-studies, *The Huffington Post* and *BuzzFeed*. *The Huffington Post* is commonly described as a 'news aggregator'. A news aggregator is defined by Isbell as 'a website that takes information from multiple sources and displays it in a single place' (Isbell, 2010: 2). However, among news aggregators, Isbell identifies different typologies: *The Huffington Post* is described as a 'blog aggregator [...] a website that uses third-party content to create a blog about a given topic' (Isbell, 2010: 5). *The Huffington Post*, which has been online since 2005 and was acquired by AOL in 2011, as of May 2017 had seventeen different international versions. Its archive for the United States version is currently online, and a link can be found on its homepage. Entries are divided per year, month and day. The website does have a custom search engine for readers to search among the news media outlets' content, yet the search bar is absent from the homepage and cannot be accessed from the foldout menu. However, the archive itself does not feature any type of publicly accessible tool to explore its content, which is only available through a series of links divided in chronological order.

BuzzFeed (which was founded in 2006 by one of *The Huffington Post* co-founders, Jonah Peretti) is described by Lucy Küng as a 'viral content company that has only moved seriously into news provision in recent years' (Küng, 2015: 2), as *BuzzFeed*'s initial focused 'on investigating and creating viral content left it perfectly positioned to exploit the growth of social and mobile media' (Küng, 2015: ix). Whereas a lot of the content produced by *BuzzFeed* might appear as ephemeral, Küng underlines that the news media outlet 'is about data science, about analyzing user data to decode how and why content is shared and distributed' (Küng, 2015: 58). However, it is also important to emphasise how, in recent years, *BuzzFeed* has invested in dedicating part of its newsroom to investigative and long-form journalism. Alongside the news media outlet's website, its content is widely distributed among platforms, such as Facebook Instant Articles, which we have described while examining platform influence in news publishing methods in Chapter 2. According to an article published on *Fast Company* by Noah Robischon 'across all the platforms where it now publishes content, the company generates 5 billion monthly views [...] Traffic to the website has remained steady [...] even though as much as 75 per cent of BuzzFeed's content is now published somewhere else' (Robischon, 2016). A pivotal element for *BuzzFeed*'s success is its custom-made CMS, which has been described by Peretti as part of a broader strategy. According to Peretti, one of the main advantages of *BuzzFeed* is its internal technological development, as

> we manage our own servers, we built our CMS from scratch, we created our own real-time stats system, we have our own data science team, we invented own ad products and our own post formats, and all these products are brought to life by our own editorial team and our own creative services team. (Apfelbaum and Cezzar, 2014: 64)

Hence the CMS is integral to how the whole of *BuzzFeed* is produced, distributed and archived. As we have seen in the previous section, while analysing CMS development within both *The New York Times* and *The Washington Post*, content management systems appear to be not only at the core of digital operations for news media outlets but are also capable of directly influencing how content is created and subsequently made available to readers.

BuzzFeed's archive page is available on the World Wide Web but not directly reachable from the news media outlet's homepage. Its layout is similar to the one currently found in *The Huffington Post*, of which Peretti co-founded. However, *BuzzFeed* does feature a search bar on its archive page, which is a feature currently absent from *The Huffington Post*'s archive page. Content is organised in months and years, dating back to November 2006 when the news media outlet first started operations on the World Wide Web. *BuzzFeed*'s model is strongly rooted in distributing content over platforms, though the development of in-house tools which are designed to enhance reader interaction and diffusion over social networks through their proprietary real-time statistical system, the approach to its public archive page is mainly to have a repository function.

As we have seen, the two digital-only news outlets we chose as case studies do not host an archive that provides any kind of curation. However, the news media outlets which we have examined, while currently attracting a vast number of visitors, do not seem to devote resources destined to provide archive curation to readers. While this analysis focused only on the public, online archives of these two news media outlets, it does indicate a relevant trend. As we have seen in the previous section, news media outlets that have started their activity in paper format and subsequently have developed a presence within the contemporary digital landscape appear to have established their archives starting from the digitisation of their paper editions and harmonising their content created over different platforms as computer-assisted reporting became a modus operandi within newsrooms.

On the other hand, digitally native outlets appear to be less concerned with providing a curated version of their digital archive for readers to navigate. It seems to be evident that digitally native content is frail by nature (McCain, 2015) and even if stakeholders identify news organisations as the entity that should be engaged in its archiving (Moore and Bonnet, 2015), among online archives of digitally native news media outlets that we have analysed, public archiving practices seem to be separated from curation practices. However, while we were analysing *ProPublica*'s and *The Marshall Project*'s 'An Unbelievable Story of Rape' in Chapter 4, we underlined how *ProPublica* had built its production around 'Series', which is also reflected in its website's architecture. 'Series' allow the news media outlet to provide readers with suites dedicated to single stories, which are constantly updated with entries of different nature and produced in different timeframes. A *ProPublica*'s 'Series' page hosts a curated version of their archives, as the suites are grouped into different page elements, which are arranged on the page either by editorial decision – in 'Featured' section – or in chronological order – in the 'Recently Updated' section. Hence, in a news media outlet which roots its production in long-form journalism, there has been a strong effort to organise its archive in a curated form that represents a convergence model between long-form journalism and archives in the digital landscape.

Regarding the digital-only news media outlets we have examined, we can conclude that their nature seems to have a strong influence on their archival and curation practices. Among the different types of news media outlets which operate only in the digital production of content, such as news or blog aggregators or outlets focused on long-form journalism, their aim and scope appear to be a decisive factor in how their public archives are formed and made available to the public.

In this chapter, we have explored the specificity of time as a factor within the digital landscape, connecting it to the notion of what we have defined as 'feed fruition'. Subsequently, we have analysed the possible role of news media outlets archive and its different typologies among the digital landscape. The first type of news media outlet archive we have focused on is based on early media production and Optical Character Recognition technology. We then analysed digital archives which are the product of news media outlets which have been engaged in paper and digital operations and have subsequently devoted resources into the digitisation and harmonisation process in order to create fully functioning and comprehensive archives as in the case of *The New York Times*. Finally, we focused on available online archives of digitally native publications and their archival practices.

PART IV

Present and Future of Long-Form Journalism and Archives

CHAPTER 6

The Shared Trajectory of Long-Form Journalism and Archives

Common Traits between Long-Form Journalism and Archives

Long-Form Journalism and Archives: Relevance Over Time and Accessibility

After focusing on news outlet archives in its current forms in the previous chapter, we shall now investigate if the two entities at the centre of our research, long-form journalism and archives, share common traits within the digital landscape. Moreover, we shall focus on long-form journalism and archive aggregation and curation processes through a case-study. Our analysis will identify a series of tools which have been developed by researchers, news media outlets and third-party companies. We are focusing on these tools as elements of a possible fruition template centred on news outlet archive curation in the digital landscape.

We shall begin our analysis of the possible common traits between long-form journalism and archives in the digital landscape by referring to the long-form journalism definition we provided in Chapter 2. We defined long-form journalism in the digital landscape as

> built with the participation of many different professionals aside from the sole journalist, uniting text, audio and visual content together with data visualisation tools and specifically built datasets. However, these elements can be combined differently, without any being compulsory. Long-form journalism is likewise defined by its capacity to attract reader time rather than the number of words.

In our definition, we underlined that – due to the nature of the digital landscape – these different elements could be combined in different manners, without any being compulsory. Our definition's focus was placed on the function of long-form journalism in the digital landscape, which is tasked with providing in-depth narratives, rather than by the element it comprises. Moreover, as we have seen in Chapters 3 and 4, while we analysed two different long-form journalism examples, long-form journalism is typically a labour-intensive task, usually performed by a number of different professionals, such as journalists, editors, programmers, multimedia editors and content management specialists.

However, we can add a further feature to long-form journalism in the digital landscape, as it is a form of journalistic production that maintains its relevance over time. Smith, Connor and Stanton (2015), through the elaboration of a corpus of 5.2 million long-form journalism stories, were able to establish some defining aspects of long-form journalism in the digital landscape, one being its relevance over time. The three authors described it as a distinctive quality of long-form journalism as they quantified the number of new references to a long-form journalism story after its publication date on the World Wide Web. Smith, Connor and Stanton underline

> longform articles tend to maintain external links, a proxy for interest, longer than typical news articles. Some of the larger longform outliers retain anchors for nearly three months, which is significant given that most articles fall out of popular interest within a single day of being published. (2015: 2117)

Moreover, while producing the overall observations on their long-form journalism corpus, Smith, Connor and Stanton add that 'readers interact with the content for longer, and publishers are more likely to bring older longform content online' (Smith, Connor and Stanton, 2015: 2117). Thus, we can identify relevance over time as a defining quality of long-form journalism in the digital landscape. Moreover, being a form of journalistic production which is capable of retaining readers' interest for longer periods of time if compared to ephemeral news content, it is more likely that news media outlets will potentially engage in curation activities, sourcing long-form journalism from their archives. This constitutes a first, possible connection between long-form journalism and archives in the digital landscape, as it indicates that archive curation and distribution practices performed by news media outlets can enhance interest in long-form journalism production.

It is useful to focus on data provided by the former *The Guardian* readers' editor, Chris Elliott, to assess if news outlet archives are capable of attracting relevant interest if compared to long-form journalism stories. In an article published on *The Guardian*'s website, he underlined how

> *The Guardian*'s digital archive holds more than 1m articles. It's a rich resource of more than a decade's worth of print, podcasts and video material. And it is very popular. Nearly 40 per cent of content viewed on the website is more than 48 hours old. (Elliott, 2012)

Elliott's data is valuable as it provides insight into a major publication's digital archive capacity to attract readers within the digital landscape. A month after Elliott's article, *The Guardian* reported record traffic on its website, with over 71 million unique browser views per month and an average of 3.9 million daily unique browser views. Moreover, in the following years, traffic directed to *The Guardian*'s website has kept growing. The following figure is an elaboration on data extracted from the Digital Market Overview produced by UKOM, the *UK Online Measurement* (2020) – which owned in equal parts by the Association of Online Publishers (AOP), the Internet Advertising Bureau (IAB) and the Incorporated Society of British Advertisers (ISBA) – and shows *The Guardian*'s performance in the years between 2016 and 2019. Data is provided on a quarterly basis and shows how *The Guardian* has always been among the top twenty most visited websites and platforms in the United Kingdom per monthly unique visitors.

As we can see in Figure 6.1, *The Guardian* has consistently had more than twenty million monthly unique visitors from 2016 to 2019 in the United Kingdom. While Elliott's data dated back to 2012 and did not differentiate what type of content was accessed, it did underline a strong interest in the archived content. The data provided by Elliott (2012) seems to support the hypothesis that news media outlet archives attract a significant amount of interest in the digital landscape. Moreover, in order to evaluate this figure, a relevant factor is the absence of paywalls to access *The Guardian*'s website, a characteristic which has been maintained since its inception.

As we are attempting to establish if long-form journalism and archives withhold the same relevance over time in the digital landscape, it is useful to underline a further aspect. As digital news archives are primarily

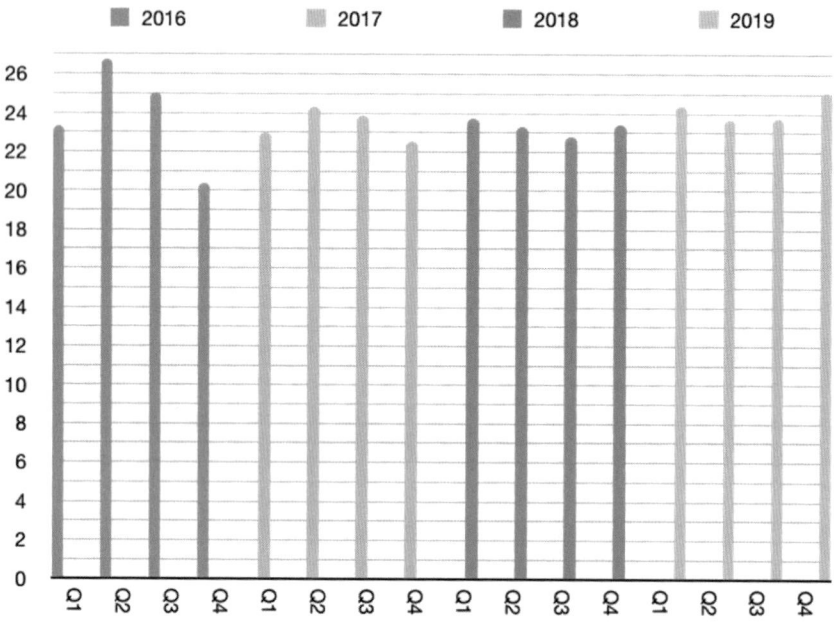

Figure 6.1 *The Guardian* unique visitors (numbers in millions)
from 2016 to 2019 (Source: UKOM)

created, organised and operated by news media outlets, it is important
to assess what type of content they choose to provide to readers and in
which form. As we have seen in Chapter 5 while we were analysing the
digitisation of *The New York Times*' archive, the harmonisation process
within news media outlets that operate both in print and digital format
is complex and technically challenging. Hence, while not all news media
outlets might be able to engage in a full digitisation process such as the one
undertaken by *The New York Times*, it is relevant to establish if they focus
on long-form journalism in their digitisation processes. Smith, Stanton
and Connor underline that, in the analysis of their 5.2 million corpora
of long-form stories, 'older longform articles at all ages are nearly twice
as likely to be put online than news, including quite old articles, such as
those published 15 years prior to coming online. This indicates that there
may be more interest in these archived articles, either from the readers or

publishers themselves' (Smith, Connor and Stanton, 2015: 2117). Hence, this might indicate that news media outlet themselves perceive long-form journalism content as more valuable and are more drawn to its digitisation, regardless of its first publication date.

However, for news media outlets finding and curating archived long-form content can be a complex process. In Chapter 5, we described how content management systems are the core element of news media outlet digital operations and often require custom-built tools in order to be fully accessible. As we have seen in this chapter, news media outlets perceive long-form journalism as a valuable asset and are more inclined to make it available to readers, as it is capable of generating interest for a longer period of time. However, this retrieval process poses distinct challenges to content management systems which within newsrooms are used for a number of activities ranging from content creation to editing, publishing and distri-bution (Barker, 2016). Thus, content retrieval in general, and long-form journalism retrieval from news outlet archives more specifically, poses a difficult challenge within the usage of content management systems.

A specific example of how these challenges have been addressed within a news media outlet is detailed by Bøerge Svingen, director of engineering at *The New York Times*, as he describes the challenges of making the news outlet published material available across all the different platforms *The New York Times* uses, which range from its website to mobile applications, personalised feeds and newsletters (Svingen, 2017). Svingen underlines that 'whenever an asset is published, it should be made available to all these systems with very low latency – this is news, after all – and without data loss', and describes the system the news media outlet has put in place, based 'on a log-based architecture powered by Apache Kafka' (Svingen, 2017). Apache Kafka is defined on its website as 'a streaming platform that has three capabilities: Publish and subscribe to streams of records, similar to a message queue or enterprise messaging system; Store streams of records in a fault-tolerant durable way; Process streams of records as they occur' (Apache Kafka, 2016).

Essentially, by transitioning from an API [Application Programming Interface] based system to a log-based system, *The New York Times* has achieved an overhaul of its content organisation, based on a different philosophy. 'Whereas a database typically stores the result of some event, the log stores the event itself – the log therefore becomes an ordered representation of all events that happened in the system. Using this log, you can then create any number of custom data stores' (Svingen, 2017).

By implementing a log-based architecture, *The New York Times* has been able to develop 'Monolog', which is the new 'source of truth for published content' (Svingen, 2017) and contains 'every asset published since 1851. They are totally ordered according to publication time. This means that a consumer can pick the point in time when it wants to start consuming' (Svingen, 2017). *The New York Times* director of engineering underlines the main differences between the two systems, one based on databases and the second on logs. According to Svingen, the two systems differ not only in maintenance but also in flexibility and end usage: 'All content is coming through the same pipeline is simplifying our software development processes, both for front-end applications and back-end systems' (Svingen, 2017).

Thus, by revolutionising its internal content organisation, *The New York Times* has been able to develop more flexible tools which provide more accurate answers if compared to the traditional organisation of content within a news media outlet. Whereas this is especially relevant for a legacy publication such as *The New York Times* which, as we have seen in Chapter 5, houses content from different eras and produced in by different techniques, this process indicates that the development of systems capable of extracting content as efficiently as possible from news outlet archives is a central feature of content management in the digital landscape.

Digital News Outlet Archives as Distribution Sources in the Digital Landscape

Having explored relevance over time as a common trait between long-form journalism and news media outlet archives in the digital landscape, we shall continue to examine possible connections between the two entities at the centre of this work. As we have seen, long-form journalism is a type of content that maintains its capacity to attract readers over time and, as such, is more likely to be made available by news outlets. Hence, we can define long-form journalism as one of the factors promoting interest towards new media outlets' archives. More broadly, within the digital landscape, single news stories are organised in digital news archives that operate as distribution tools. Hence, we shall investigate how news outlet archives produce and distribute content within the contemporary digital landscape.

In Chapter 2, we have seen how Anderson describes the long-tail as a model based on 'infinite choice' (Anderson, 2009: 180). The long-tail has established itself as one of the leading production and distribution models within the contemporary digital landscape. According to this model, distribution has become cheaper, and variety has been amplified, with audiences tending 'to distribute as widely as the choice' (Anderson, 2009b, 180). According to Anderson, this new model has been embraced more efficiently by intermediaries rather than traditional producers. Anderson (2009b) mentions the media industry as one of the main examples of this dynamic: aggregators are performing more efficiently in distributing content if compared to traditional news media outlets. However, there are other relevant factors in the long tail, such as the democratisation of production and distribution tools and the connection through filtering between supply and demand (Huang and Wang, 2014). These authors also emphasise that the physical constraints that traditionally limit shelf space do not apply to digital firms as they are able to limit production, distribution and search costs (Huang and Wang, 2014).

It is relevant to assess how the long-tail model has impacted news media within the digital landscape, especially among news media outlets. For Anderson (2009b), a business model that is capable of expanding its offer in the highest number of niches is positively adapting itself to the long-tail model. News media outlets in the digital landscape are 'in a sense a legitimate example of bundling hits and niches by offering content that ranges from homepage news about local, national, and international affairs to pages like obituaries, crosswords and horoscopes' (Huang and Wang, 2014: 161). According to these authors, digitisation allows news media outlets to reach readers who seek different news items, ranging from the most popular to the niche ones: 'When news media go online, new efficiencies are created in manufacturing, distribution, and marketing. The unique capabilities of the Internet may influence the economic efficiency of online news and provide the foundation for a long tail economy' (Huang and Wang, 2014: 161).

In their research results, Huang and Wang (2014) identify content variety as the main driving force for website traffic, while other long-tail model factors, such as the democratisation of production and distribution tools seem to have a smaller impact on a news media outlet production. Thus, according to these authors, digital news media outlets have adopted a long-tail model in a range of different aspects, such as content and service variety (Huang and Wang, 2014). However, a quantitative study of French-language news media outlet production, performed in 2010 by Smyrnaios, Marty and Rebillard, underlines issues with the application of the long-tail model to news media outlets production, as

> our findings do not totally confirm this hypothesis. Our quantitative study of French-speaking news websites shows that their production has quite similar characteristics to those of traditional media. News appears to be both varied and very unevenly distributed. Indeed, our study illustrates a classic power law distribution, as old as those of Pareto, Zipf or Bradford: 20 percent of the most important topics of the news agenda generate 80 percent of the distributed articles. (2010: 1257)

Even considering these findings, it is possible to assume that the digital landscape and long-tail model have conditioned news media outlets production. Moreover, a study by Cook and Sirkkunen (2013) focusing on sixty-nine online-only news outlet start-ups in the 2011–2012 period has identified other impact factors of the long-tail model on digital news production. In their study, Cook and Sirkkunen (2013) divided their pool of online-only start-ups into two different groups, one for news outlets oriented towards storytelling and the second for service-oriented news outlets. According to the authors, 'correlating the storytelling sites to the long tail we found the major forces to hold true however as an oversimplification of the niche marketplace' (Cook and Sirkkunen, 2013: 76). However, journalism focusing on what the long-tail defines as niches 'could also be defined by customised content and service propositions that move beyond a maximization of audience share from mainstream news offerings' (Cook and Sirkkunen, 2013: 78). This finding adds a further element to other works cited above, (Huang and Wang, 2014) (Smyrnaios, Marty and Rebillard, 2010), and highlights a fragmentation of the digital news market as new digital-only news media outlets have been dedicated to specific niches. Hence, we can assume that the long-tail model has impacted digital news media outlets on two different levels: one regarding the production of single outlets, fostering variety in content production and the other encouraging the birth of specific, digital-only news media outlets with a focus on different niches.

The possible correlation between digital news outlets and the long-tail model is relevant in our overall analysis of common traits between long-form journalism and archives in the digital landscape. As we have seen, studies focusing on digital news production have underlined the function of content variety in news media outlets' adaptation to the long-tail model. However, these studies tend to focus on contemporary news media outlets production. As digital archives comprise a relevant portion of total visits to news media outlets' websites (Elliott, 2012), it is possible to explore their role within the long-tail model. In Anderson (2009b), the long-tail model is based on providing a choice that is capable of covering as many niches as possible, and distributors and aggregators are more efficient than traditional news media outlets in distributing digital news content. Moreover, there are examples of how a more efficient distribution, inspired by the long-tail model, can be performed on archived content within the contemporary digital landscape.

In March 2014, the film *12 Years a Slave* won three Academy Awards for Best Picture, Best Actress in a Supporting Role and Best Writing (Adapted Screenplay). *The New York Times* posted an update on its Twitter account, linking a story the news media outlet published in 1853 which narrates the events on which the film is based. However, the article did not draw considerable amounts of traffic, despite being a timely and relevant reference to the news media outlet's digital archive. In its 'Innovation Report' *The New York Times* provided insight into what happened:

> On Oscar night, *The Times* tweeted a 161-year-old story about Solomon Northup, whose memoir was the basis for *12 Years a Slave*. After it started going viral on social media, *Gawker* pounced, and quickly fashioned a story based on excerpts from our piece. It ended up being one of their best-read items of the year. But little of that traffic came to us. (2014: 28)

The story that the report is referring to was published on *Gawker* (Hedgecock, 2014), an outlet founded in 2003 with a focus on the media industry in New York, which later evolved into a publication with a national focus (Gandert, 2011). The description of the story in *The New York Times* 'Innovation Report' (2014a) is correct. While adding very little original content to the story published in *The New York Times* in 1853, *Gawker* (Hedgecock, 2014) succeeded in harvesting its content in a different format, by adding a snapshot of the motion picture coupled with a new, ad hoc created title. The same article from *The New York Times* did not attract a vast number of readers, as the news media outlet presented it on Twitter in the original format, without any modification.

According to the long-tail model we discussed above, the aggregation and distribution of content performed by *Gawker* proved to be more effective than the original news media outlet's distribution practice. Moreover, it is significant to underline that *The New York Times* itself could have implemented the process behind the creation of *Gawker*'s news item. As underlined in its 'Innovation Report', an outlet such as *The New York Times*, which has a rich archive, has many opportunities to repackage 'content so that it's more useful, relevant and shareable for readers' (*The New York Times*, 2014: 33).

The second example of a more efficient distribution performed on digital news archives is also derived from *The New York Times* 'Innovation Report' (*The New York Times*, 2014a). The authors of the report underline how senior product manager at the news media outlet Andrew Phelps created a collection of the most important obituaries published by *The New York Times* in 2014 using Flipboard, a digital news aggregator and mobile application. According to Rockley, Cooper and Abel, the collection created by Phelps proved to be one of the most popular in Flipboard's history and drove readers from the mobile application to *The New York Times*' website (Rockley, Cooper and Abel, 2015). Moreover, these three authors emphasise that *The New York Times* 'Innovation Report' (*The New York Times*, 2014a) did underline the importance of reutilising already published content

> but noted that manual reuse was slow, cumbersome, error-prone, and not scalable. Because their content was not intelligent – it was unstructured and the tools they

used to produce content were designed around a print publishing paradigm – the paper was unable to create collections as fast as their more nimble digital publishing competitors. (Rockley, Cooper and Abel, 2015: 34)

As we have seen in the previous section, retrieval and re-usage of already published material is an issue that has since driven *The New York Times* to implement a log-based architecture, in order to respond more swiftly to these issues (Svingen, 2017). However, emerging third-party platforms that organise and curate content are a significant phenomenon in the contemporary digital landscape (Rockley, Cooper and Abel, 2015). In the frame of the long-tail model provided by Anderson (2009b). Aggregation and curation services appear to adapt better to the contemporary digital landscape if compared to traditional news media outlets. Moreover, there are two further elements underlined by Rockley, Cooper and Abel while describing *The New York Times* Archives: the first is that the archives were constituted by unstructured content and the second was the lack of effective tools to create collections (Rockley, Cooper and Abel, 2015).

While exploring possible connections between long-form journalism and archives, we used the long-tail model in order to comprehend better how content organisation and distribution are relevant factors in the contemporary digital landscape. Moreover, we have seen how long-form journalism and archives are both entities which have a longer shelf life if compared to day-to-day ephemeral news production. However, Rockley, Cooper and Abel (2015) highlight a different common trait between long-form journalism and archives: both entities are – in their primary stage – unstructured content. Hence, this content, being unstructured, is often under-used by news media outlets as they need to develop tools to organise and curate it. Thus, it is relevant to focus on the unstructured nature of the entities at the centre of our research.

Within the contemporary digital landscape, long-form journalism and digital news media outlet archives yet to be fully datafied (Mayer-Schönberger and Cukier, 2013). Mayer-Schönberger and Cukier define 'datafication' as the process of organising a phenomenon 'in a quantified format so it can be tabulated and analysed' (Mayer-Schönberger and Cukier, 2013: 78). In Chapter 1, we introduced this concept in order to underline how data quantification and exploitation are two features of the contemporary digital landscape. However, while news media outlet archives in the digital landscape have a growing digital presence, stemming from the digitisation of physical archives, harmonisation of digital archives and digitally native archiving practices (as we have seen in Chapter 5), its content is yet to be datafied. As Blanke and Prescott underline 'there is a difference between a book which has been scanned to produce a digital image which has been made available as unstructured data, and a text which has been keyboarded and marked up for automated processing so that it is structured data' (Blanke and Prescott, 2016: 192). Moreover, the authors define the datafication process as 'different from the process of producing digital surrogate based on digitising originally analogue content by (for example) transferring a microfilm of a book to digital form or making an MP3 version of a taped interview' (Blanke and Prescott, 2016: 192). Hence, datafication is based on the principle that the process outcome can be transformed in a quantifiable format for it to be exploited in different manners.

However, it is important to underline how datafication is not a neutral process, as some aspects recall the issues raised by the 'de-paperization' process (Derrida, 2005), which we described in Chapter 5. While Derrida (2005) identified the potential benefits of the 'de-paperization' process, he also underlined the issues it raises, such as 'invisible hegemonies and appropriations' (Derrida, 2005: 55–56). In this regard, an example of the non-neutrality of the datafication process is provided by Mayer-Schönberger and Cukier's praise of the Google Books project as an example of successful datafication (Mayer-Schönberger and Cukier, 2013). In 2004, Google began scanning books, gradually building a digital library and, by 2015, the Google Books project had scanned 'more than 25 million volumes [...], including texts in 400 languages from more than 100 countries' (Heyman, 2015). This process, aside from creating an immense digital library, created economic value for Google. As Pybus, Coté and Blanke remark in their article *Hacking the social life of big data*

> scanning millions of books, hence datafying hundreds of millions of data points on every page that entered their vast digital archive, ultimately led to the creation of a new asset – Google Translate. Value for Google was not a simple effect of the data they extracted from all of the books they scanned; instead, it came through realising the relational potential within those datasets to create what is now the most used translation platform in the world. (2015: 3)

Hence, while this datafication process can be defined successful for Google, leading to the creation of an asset with sizable economic value and multiple future applications, it has likewise produced an 'invisible hegemony and appropriation', as Derrida warned while describing the potential issues with the 'de-paperization' process (Derrida, 2005). To further clarify the datafication process, it is also useful to recall the definition of 'big data' provided by Mayer-Schönberger and Cukier (2013). According to the authors, big data

> refers to things one can do at a large scale that cannot be done at a smaller one, to extract new insight or create new forms of value, in ways that change markets, organisations, the relationship between citizens and governments, and more. (Mayer-Schönberger and Cukier, 2013: 6)

Hence, for the authors, value extraction appears to be at the centre of big data and the datafication process. However, value extraction within the digital landscape is usually performed by platforms such as Google, which is coherent with the theorisation of aggregators performing on the long-tail more efficiently if compared to traditional entities such as news outlets (Anderson, 2009b). Mayer-Schönberger and Cukier describe in a similar manner book publishers, 'which saw the value of books as content, not as data [...] they never saw the need, or appreciated the potential' (Mayer-Schönberger and Cukier, 2013: 85). Hence, a new, incumbent and more efficient aggregating entity in the digital landscape, such as Google, was needed to envision book content as data, from which to harvest profit in the shape of services (Pybus, Coté and Blanke, 2015). While digital news archives have been digitised but not yet datafied, the development of a number of tools and services demonstrates they might be subject to a future datafication process.

One of the possible examples of digital news archives datafication is person-centric mining. Coll Ardanuy et al. (2016) present a software infrastructure, named 'ASINO', which has been developed to provide support for person-centric text mining, mainly in historical research. The authors describe how 'person-centric mining can be integrated in a general purpose text-mining environment' (Coll Ardanuy et al., 2016: 320) and underline how 'in a Humanities context – newspaper archives constitute "big data"' (Coll Ardanuy et al., 2016: 321). The authors clarify that this process is based on 'named entity disambiguation (distinguishing between different referents referred to by the same named entity expression) in addition to named entity recognition and tagging' (Coll Ardanuy et al., 2016: 322). Thus, 'ASINO' constitutes an example of a possible datafication tool of news media outlet archives, that can be used not just for person-centric mining, but also location and other types of search activities. Another possible example of datafication regarding news outlet digital archives focuses on geospatial information. A study by Yzaguirre, Smit and Warren (2016) describe the creation of a database regarding flood events using a newspaper archive. Their starting point was an unstructured corpus of two million articles published in *The Chronicle Herald*, a Canadian newspaper. The authors implemented 'a manual data cleaning/filtering step to remove non-news articles' resulting in '1.210,476 digital articles in XML format (6,54 GB) dating from January 1992 to February 2015' (Yzaguirre, Smit and Warren, 2016: 3). Their goal was to create 'a structured corpus that includes a date for the event, a geo-tagged location, a snippet from the full story text, a list of other places mentioned in the article, and a full citation of the article (author, headline, publication date)' (Yzaguirre, Smit and Warren, 2016: 3). The outcome of their work is a geospatial distribution display of their corpus in an environment built using Google Maps as a visualisation tool.

Yzaguirre, Smit and Warren (2016) describe how this study has led them to define a set of objectives in connecting users with archives following a datafication process such as the one they performed on their article corpus. These objectives include relevance, summarisation, geospatial significance, interactivity and visualisation and are described in Table 6.1. This user-centric approach is particularly relevant, as it explores datafication possibilities not limiting them to the entities involved in the process itself, but likewise considers the end-users as an influencing factor in how results are presented and, ultimately, used.

Yzaguirre, Smit and Warren (2016) succeeded in creating a user-centric interactive environment which is an example of datafication within news outlet digital archives. As we can see from Table 6.1, curation is a fundamental element in this approach, which is also heavily influenced by common practices within the digital landscape. In the 'Relevance' field, the authors make a direct reference to Google Search, which is one of the most

Table 6.1 The five objectives in connecting users to archives
after a datafication process

Relevance	Identifying only the data sought is important when expectations are set by Google's web search example.
Summarisation	Crafting a summary that reflects the story's value.
Geospatial Significance	Presenting accurately data tied to place, including the density of data.
Interactivity	Providing navigation tools that allow users to navigate through the data collection in an intuitive way that can be turned to their own interest.
Visualisation	Presenting data in an intuitive and accessible format that exploits temporal and spatial features.

common platform services, which is used as a benchmark for user attention to search results. Moreover, both 'Interactivity' and 'Visualisation' fields definitions reflect the need for tools to be developed from a user-centric perspective. Both objectives need to be developed in two directions, flexibility and accessibility. These qualities are typical of environments in the digital landscape, as we have seen in Chapter 1, while we described the apparent absence of friction as one of the unifying factors between platforms and crowds. In the first chapter, we underlined how platform services are being developed in the digital landscape to enhance participation by crowds. In the digital landscape, platforms need to promote a certain degree of simplification, flexibility and ease of use, in order to be relevant and attract crowd participation. However, the qualities described by Yzaguirre, Smit and Warren (2016) are generally relevant to enhance end-user familiarity and usage of tools resulting from datafication processes.

As we are examining long-form journalism and archives as potential datafication sources, it is relevant to underline that this process has been mainly undertaken by third parties rather than by news media outlets themselves. We have seen how both long-form journalism and archives could be a viable field for a future datafication process. Within this process, aggregation and curation appear to be a fundamental element of its potential success within the crowd-platform dynamic. In Chapter 5, while examining the different types of news media outlet digital archives, we have seen how archives are organised in a manner that seems to be influenced more by the origin of the archived content rather than by a user-based perspective. Thus, we shall now focus on a user-centric example of aggregation and curation that focuses specifically on long-form journalism and archives, a website and mobile application named Longform.org.

Long-Form Journalism and Aggregators: Longform.org

Longform.org as an Example of Long-Form Journalism Curation

In the previous section, we have assessed common traits shared between long-form journalism and news outlet digital archives in the digital land-scape. We underlined how relevance over time is a common feature between the two entities at the centre of this work. Moreover, we described the impact of the long-tail model on the news industry and how it has affected news production and distribution, with a specific focus on long-form journalism and news outlet digital archives. Finally, we identified long-form journalism and archives as possible sources of datafication (Mayer-Schönberger and Cukier, 2013), providing examples such as person-centric mining (Coll Ardanuy et al., 2016), and geospatial information, while underlining the role of user-centric tool development (Yzaguirre, Smit and Warren, 2016).

We shall now focus on distribution practices of news outlet digital archive content in the digital landscape. As we have seen, in the long-tail model, third-party content aggregators generally perform more efficiently distribution tasks, if compared to traditional entities and the news industry is an example of this phenomenon (Anderson, 2009b). Hence, we shall focus on content aggregators which revolve around the aggregation, curation and distribution of long-form journalism and archives.

Before providing an in-depth analysis of a single aggregator and distribution service, namely Longform.org, it is relevant to underline a series of findings by Smith, Connor and Stanton (2015) which we focused on in previously in this chapter. These authors underline how overall long-form journalism production in the digital landscape is increasing, yet it is doing so following a specific trajectory. As the study's authors emphasise, there is an increasing number of news media outlets producing long-form journalism and, among these, there is an increasingly strong presence of digitally native news media outlets (Smith, Connor and Stanton, 2015). Moreover, while the total quantity of long-form journalism produced in the digital landscape is increasing, it is doing so at a slower pace if compared to the overall growth in news production (Smith, Connor and Stanton, 2015). Finally, while there is an increasing number of news media outlets producing long-form journalism, only a small number of these news media outlets produce relevant volumes of long-form journalism stories (Smith, Connor and Stanton, 2015).

These findings describe the digital landscape as an environment where long-form journalism can be found in numerous news media outlets, but only a relatively small number of those have the economic and organisational strength to produce long-form journalism on a continuous basis, as also underlined by Bruns: 'Few journalistic organizations can afford to engage in much long-form, resource-intensive, investigative journalism' (Bruns and Highfield, 2012: 2). The increase in long-form journalism production in the digital landscape is the result of a large number of news media outlets producing small quantities of long-form journalism stories while increasing at a slower pace if compared to standard news production, this specific type of journalistic production is capable of remaining relevant for more extended periods of time (Smith, Connor and Stanton, 2015). Within this frame, it is moreover relevant to analyse long-form journalism aggregation and curation services which focus on news outlet digital archives. Among the various services currently active in the digital landscape, we have chosen to focus on a single aggregator to examine in-depth its activity.

Longform.org (Longform.org, 2010a) was founded in 2010 and begun by recommending recently published and digitally archived news items which were over 2,000 words long and already available on the World Wide Web. The difference between Longform.org and similar aggregators is the objective of its activity, as underlined in *Tales from the*

Great Disruption – Insights and Lessons from Journalism's Technological Transformation (Shapiro, Hiatt and Hoyt, 2015). Longform.org

> was to be an archive of great longform stories, both new and old, categorized by topic, like sex, war, crime, media, and politics, among others. […] Longform.org seems to be an anthology you can dip in or out of. But Longform doesn't hog the traffic; it simply pushes readers on over to the host site. (Shapiro, Hiatt and Hoyt, 2015: 175)

Longform.org's first online version dates back to 2010. It was released in parallel with the launch of Apple's iPad, by two individuals, Max Linsky and Aaron Lammer. One of the founders, Lammer, describes in an interview published by *The Timbre* the first steps of the website:

> We started Longform for fun. Two people doing it for fun. We did not think it would be – I don't even think we thought it through, actually. I was going to say that we didn't think it would be as successful as it was, but that's not really true. We didn't really think about it all. I would not have bet on it lasting more than a year. At first, we were just kind of juiced that people were into it at all. The audience that came just kept getting bigger and bigger without us doing much. (McQuade, 2015)

Since 2010, the aggregator has broadened its offer. In 2012, it added a fiction section, begun an intense podcast production and developed its first iPad application, which was priced at 5\$ (US dollars) and, as 2014, sold circa 60,000 copies (Bercovici, 2014). Moreover, according to an article published in *New York* magazine in 2014, the podcast service had reached 50,000 listeners (Kachka, 2014). In September of the same year, Longform.org released its first iPhone application, introducing the possibility for readers to build lists of specific writers to follow across different news media outlets and developed an algorithm regulating which articles were to be featured within the application (Mullin, 2014). However, as of April 2017, Longform.org's application is not available any more on both iOS or Android platforms (Longform.org, 2017). Founders Max Linsky and Aaron Lammer explained that this is due to the rejection by Apple of their newly developed version of the application:

> The app reviewer spelled out three changes we could make to be approved. We were torn. Two of the changes were flat-out impossible, and the third would require huge

amounts of ongoing developer labour while providing a worse experience for users. After some bummed conversations, we concluded that we simply don't have the time, money, or personal hubris to continue supporting the Longform app. (Longform.org, 2017)

While Linsky and Lammer underline how the tools that allow readers to access long-form content have significantly developed over the years, they also stress that – through Longform – they 'have sent over 100 million outbound links to publishers since 2012' (Longform.org, 2017). They also remark how Longform.org was not a competitor neither for Facebook or Apple News service. An assessment of Longform.org's team can be found in 'Slow journalism for a new digital audience. The case of Longform.org [2010–2015]' (Albalad Aiguabella, 2015):

> Longform.org's work team consists of two founders, Aaron Lammer and Max Linsky, along with six editors, one person dedicated to management-administration tasks, two professionals in the fiction area, two in the podcast production area a developer dedicated to the Web and one dedicated to mobile applications.[2] (2015: 16)

In the same article, the founders clarify that they perceive Longform.org as 'closer to a technology company than a communications medium'[3] (Albalad Aiguabella, 2015: 18). In the same article, the two founders provide a series of meaningful data regarding Longform.org. In 2015, 40 per cent of the traffic originated from mobile devices, whereas it was only 2 per cent of the whole traffic in 2010. Longform has relevant data on its readership which is described as mainly a 25–45-year-old American, highly educated, typically residing in the East or West Coast of the US, while other countries that draw a sizable number of visitors are, in order, the United Kingdom, Australia and India. Longform.org's website reaches half a million visitors per month. If access numbers from the application and newsletter were included, it would reach a million users per month.

2   Original quotation (my translation): 'El equipo de trabajo de *Longform.org* lo conforman los dos fundadores, Aaron Lammer y Max Linsky, junto con seis editores, una persona para tareas de gestión-administración, dos profesionales en el área de ficción, dos en la de podcast, un desarrollador web y otro de aplicaciones móviles.'
3   Original quotation (my translation): '*Longform.org* – apunta su propietario – se aproxima más a una empresa de tecnología que a un medio de comunicación.'

Further insight on Longform.org's readership was provided in 'Notes toward a Supreme Nonfiction: Teaching Literary Reportage in the Twenty-first Century', a keynote address by Robert S. Boynton at the International Association for Literary Journalism Studies (2013):

> Longform's demographic is the envy of any advertiser: young (50 percent of the readers are under 34), mobile (30 percent read primarily on phones or tablets), and well educated (42 percent have attended graduate school). Virtually every story posted receives at least a thousand reads, with the average being four thousand. […]. Usage is heaviest between seven p.m. and two a.m., peaking at nine p.m. The number of visitors to Longform doubles during weekends. A full sixty-five percent of visitors complete every story they read. (2013: 130)

Boynton underlines this last factor as very significant of the relevance over time of long-form journalism:

> The best narrative non-fiction – unlike basically every other content type on the web – doesn't lose appeal as it ages. A 1993 murder story from *Texas Monthly* was number nine on the 2012 list. George Orwell's "Why I Write" (1946) was number twenty. A total of three dozen older stories made it into 2012's top fifty list. In fact, Longform's readers are ten percent more likely to read an older story than a new one. The publication date carries almost no weight. Readers care more about an article's subject than whether it is new. (2013: 138)

According to Boynton's data, the aggregation and curation practices that Longform.org is centred on, demonstrate long-form journalism's relevance over time and the endurance of this type of content, as the first publication date does not influence readers' choices (Boynton, 2013). Longform.org shows how news outlet digital archives can be mined, highlighting a further connection between long-form journalism and archives in the digital landscape. While the content itself might be published even years before it is featured in aggregation and curation services, readers are drawn by the aggregator's activity (Boynton, 2013). Long-form journalism and archives in the contemporary digital landscape share not only relevance over time but also possible aggregation and curation practices which, if performed with a user-centric approach such as the one implemented by Longform.org, can provide a steady flow of readers to content which news media outlets host on their archives but which is substantially inactive as we have seen in the previous section, while we were analysing a datafication process aimed at retrieving geospatial information within a newspaper archive (Yzaguirre, Smit and Warren, 2016). A user-centric approach is fundamental in the development of tools and services in the digital landscape. Thus, it is viable to say that if the long-form content is presented through user-centric aggregation and curation services that focus on news outlet digital archives, this greatly enhances its possibility to attract readers. Moreover, it demonstrates how the function they perform is substantially different from the one performed by news outlet digital archives.

For news media outlets, the activity performed by aggregators such as Longform.org demonstrates that, within their digital archives, there are pools of resources, specifically long-form journalism stories, which are under-used as they are not aggregated and curated in order to enhance readership. While this aspect is moreover relevant for legacy publications, which own a great deal of archived content, it is also significantly relevant for news media outlets which have a shorter lifespan, as confirmed by readership data originated by Longform.org, as described by Boynton:

> the top twenty publishers on Longform – magazines like the *New Yorker, The New York Times Magazine, Vanity Fair, GQ* and *Esquire* – account for 52 percent of its total archive. Yet those same twenty publishers are responsible for only fifty-five percent of the most-read stories, which is a negligible increase. A well-known publication name doesn't move the needle much at all. That is, a *New Yorker* story is no more likely to get clicked than a piece from someone's personal blog. In fact, unknown publications often do better than brand names because readers are intrigued to see something new. (2013: 131)

These findings are consistent with those we presented in the previous section while investigating the possible common traits between long-form journalism and archives in the digital landscape. Having gathered insight on Longform.org's creation and the data resulting from its activity, we shall now confront them with a specific dataset we have extracted from Longform.org's activity in 2016. Thus, we shall assess if the critical factors identified in this section, such as the relevance over time of long-form journalism and the role of archives as resource pools, are coherent with the data analysis in the following section.

Longform.org's Activity in 2016, a Case-Study

We shall now analyse Longform.org's activity over the last year in which the application was still available on iOS or Android platforms, which is 2016. The generation of our dataset began by collecting all Longform.org entries from 1 January 2016 to 31 December 2016 – the dataset is publicly available online on the Open Science Framework (Braghieri, 2019).

Longform.org's website provides a page by page navigation that goes back to 1 April 2010 and, while the website's design has changed since it has maintained its organisation around a central column which features a feed of articles. The website's organisation appears to be in line our definition of 'feed fruition' in Chapter 5, which we described as a specific fruition practice where an individual browses an autonomously updated list. We obtained the necessary data for all Longform.org's 2016 via the World Wide Web, through a process named 'web scraping'. Web scraping can be defined as

> the practice of gathering data through any mean other than a program interacting with an API [or, obviously through a human using a web browser. This is most commonly accomplished by writing an automated program that queries a web server, requests data [usually in the form of the HTML and other files that comprise the web pages], and then parses that data to extract needed information (Mitchell, 2015: viii)

As such, web scraping is being used within the framework of digital methods (Rogers, 2013), intended as 'techniques for the ongoing research on the affordances of online media' (Venturini et al., 2018: 4), deployed to harvest 'information made available by Internet platforms' (Venturini et al., 2018: 2). In order to perform our web scraping operation, we used a browser extension for Google Chrome, named Data Miner, 'that assists you in extracting data that you see in your browser and save into an Excel spreadsheet file' (Data Miner, 2016).

To obtain the information we needed from Longform.org, we had to develop a series of 'extraction instructions that Data Miner uses to extract data from websites' (Data Miner, 2016), which are named 'recipes'. An ad hoc 'recipe' was created to obtain the largest possible amount of information from the scraping process. Once we provided the web scraping extension with our 'recipe', we were able to scrape fifty pages out of Longform.

org's website. The data was provided in a CSV (comma-separated values) file, which we then fed to OpenRefine, an interactive data transformation tool which we used to perform a data profiling and data cleaning processes. Data profiling was implemented to 'discover the true structure, content and quality' (Olson, 2003: 119). The data cleaning process was implemented in order to correct possible errors in our data 'in a semi-automated way' (Verborgh and De Wilde, 2013: 6). Hence, we shall now analyse the resulting data set, which is the outcome of our web scraping, data profiling and data cleaning processes.

In total, we scraped 1225 posts from 1 January 2016 to 31 December 2016. Typically, Longform.org elaborates posts which comprise a link to a single long-form journalism story, a summary and information on the author, news media outlet and date in which the long-form story was first published. However, alongside this primary type of entry, Longform.org has developed, over the years, other types of entries. The first is the 'Longform Guide' type of entry, which typically groups together long-form journalism stories from different news media outlets which focus on the same subject.

As Longform.org is an aggregator of already published content, this allows the production of theme-based collections, which are typically sourced from different news media outlets digital archives, all openly available on the World Wide Web. Alongside this type of entries, Longform.org publishes entries dedicated to a single author, which has already been featured multiple times in the websites single-story entries. In 2016, Longform.org produced seven of these entries, revolving around both fiction and non-fiction writers, such as novelist Zadie Smith and writer and journalist William Langewiesche. Besides the 'Longform Guide' entries and the entries dedicated to single authors, there are weekly entries dedicated to fiction writing. These entries are named 'Fiction Pick of the Week' and are commonly sourced both from specialist outlets and news media outlets which publish this type of content. In 2016, Longform.org produced fifty-one of these entries.

Aside from its long-form aggregation and curation activity, Longform.org has developed a significant original multimedia production, through a podcasting series. In the *Encyclopaedia of Media and Communication*, a podcast is defined as 'audio file containing information and music, which is available for downloading through the internet on media players or devices' (Bockarova, 2013: 520). In 2016, Longform.org produced fifty-five different podcast entries, the vast majority of which feature the participation of long-form journalism authors which analyse their work along with Longform.org's hosts.

Table 6.2 Longform.org's entries in 2016, divided by type

Single-story Entries	1074
Longform Guide Entries	30
Fiction 'Pick of the Week' Entries	51
Podcast Entries	55
Other types of Entries	15
Total Entries	1225

In Table 6.2, all entries scraped from Longform.org are divided by type. As we can see, the vast majority of entries regarded single-story entries, which are the ones we shall analyse in-depth. We will provide an assessment of the news media outlets selected by Longform.org to be featured in this type of entries, and we shall also focus on the publishing dates in which each long-form journalism story was first published. As we have seen in the previous section of this chapter, according to Boynton, for Longform.org's users 'the publication date carries almost no weight. Readers care more about an article's subject that whether it is new' (Boynton, 2013: 130–131).

As Longform.org is a curation service which acts as an aggregator in the long-tail model (Anderson, 2009b), it is especially relevant to examine its choices in detail, as its activity revolves specifically around long-form journalism and news media outlets digital archives in the digital landscape. Moreover, this activity is organised by Longform.org around what we have defined as 'feed fruition', which we described in Chapter 5. Hence, as we are investigating long-form journalism and archives, an in-depth analysis of an aggregator and curation service's activity can provide highly relevant insight regarding the correlation between these two entities.

We shall concentrate our analysis of the 1,074 single-story entries published by Longform.org in 2016. As the first publishing date for each long-form journalism story is provided within the entry, it is possible to establish how Longform.org has distributed its choice within news media outlets and different production eras. The 1,074 single-story entries on Longform.org in 2016 are drawn from an extensive time frame, as the oldest long-form journalism story that was featured in a single-story entry was first published in 1877. Year-wise, the most relevant group is the one which comprises stories published in 2016, the same year which we focused our analysis on, as single-story entries based on long-form journalism stories first published in 2016 were 77 per cent of the total.

As we can see in Figure 6.2, the time frame from which long-form journalism stories were chosen to be featured in single-story entries is very ample. However, approximately in the period ranging from 2009 onwards, choices tend to become more frequent. It is relevant to underline that Longform.org aggregates and curates solely content within news outlet websites or archives which do not implement a 'radical' paywall (Brock, 2013: 155), as we described in Chapter 2. This pre-condition does appear to affect the total pool of news media outlets this specific aggregator uses.

While the overall balance between first publishing dates among Longform.org single-story entries is clear, it is useful to further focus on those entries which have a first publishing date that precedes 2016. As we have seen in Figure 6.2 they comprise 23 per cent of the total single-story entries, but – in order to gain better insight on their distribution – we have divided all pre-2016 entries in decades, grouping together all entries referring to long-form journalism stories published before 1960.

Figure 6.3 shows how single-story entries which revolve around long-form journalism stories with a first publishing date that pre-dates 2016 increase gradually every decade. However, the increase in entries dated between 1990 and 1999 and the following decade is a record 171 per cent. As we have seen in Chapter 5, the newsroom digitisation process has had a significant impact on news media outlet digital archives, broadening their development and fruition, which seems to be confirmed by the number of stories sourced from the 2000–2009 decade. While digital news media outlet archives which originate from physical copies are labour-intensive

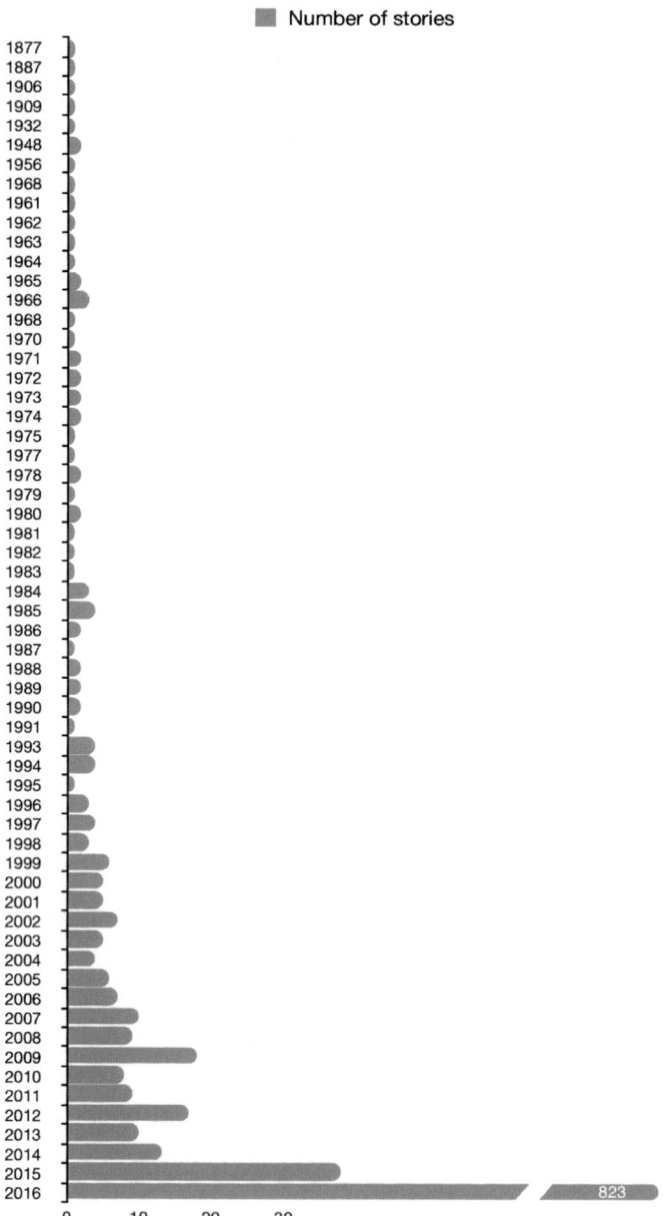

Figure 6.2 Single-story entries on Longform.org in 2016
divided per first publishing date

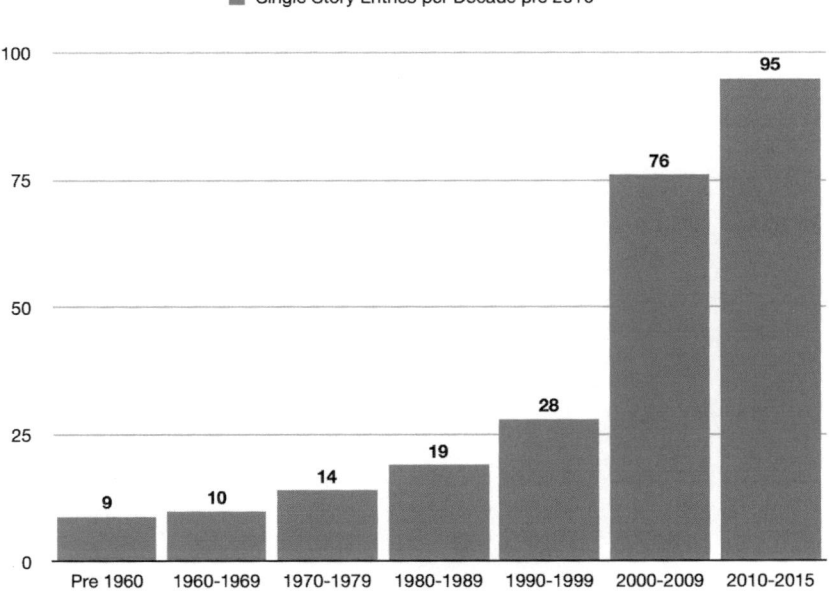

Figure 6.3　All Longform.org's 2016 single-story entries with first publication
date prior to 2016, divided per decade

to create, the newsroom digitisation process has brought broader access
to news archives. As we can see in Figure 6.4, news media outlets which
have significantly developed their digital news archives, tend to be more
represented.

　　Figure 6.4 shows slightly more than four out of ten long-form journalism stories selected to be featured in single-story entries by Longform.
org were published on outlets which are overall featured ten times or less
in the 1,074 entries. The total number of news media outlets featured in
single-story entries by Longform.org in 2016 is 221 and, out of these, only
25 news media outlets are featured ten or more times. Moreover, among the
196 news media outlets which have been chosen for ten or fewer entries,
the most relevant group comprises outlets selected once or twice. Out of
the 196 news outlets featured less than ten times, the most relevant group
are the news media outlets that have been chosen once, comprising 108
news media outlets.

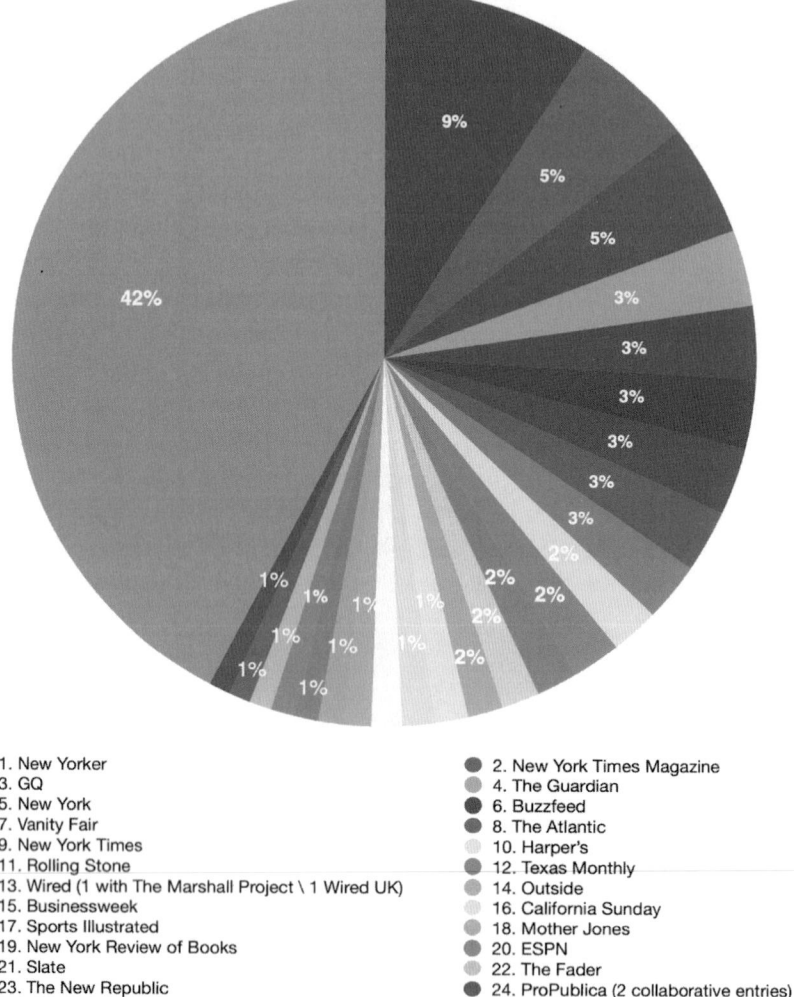

1. New Yorker
3. GQ
5. New York
7. Vanity Fair
9. New York Times
11. Rolling Stone
13. Wired (1 with The Marshall Project \ 1 Wired UK)
15. Businessweek
17. Sports Illustrated
19. New York Review of Books
21. Slate
23. The New Republic
25. Ten or less articles per outlet

2. New York Times Magazine
4. The Guardian
6. Buzzfeed
8. The Atlantic
10. Harper's
12. Texas Monthly
14. Outside
16. California Sunday
18. Mother Jones
20. ESPN
22. The Fader
24. ProPublica (2 collaborative entries)

Figure 6.4 News media outlets featured in Longform.org single-story entries in 2016, per number of entries

While the majority of Longform.org's selection revolves around a selected number of news media outlets, variety in news media outlet selection is a relevant factor among Longform.org's selection choices. This diversity is achieved not just by generally widening the number of news media outlets the aggregator sources its stories from, but by specifically choosing news media outlets which are featured fewer times. This selection activity seems to indicate that one of the major focuses in aggregator activity is variety in outlet selection. However, among news media outlets featured in single-story entries in 2016, there has been a particular focus on *The New Yorker*, featured in ninety-five entries.

In order to assess the consistency of the top news media outlets featured in single-story entries in 2016, it is possible to compare our dataset with the overall number of times a news media outlet has been featured on Longform.org. However, while this data is available directly on a specific page (Longform.org, 2010b) of Longform.org's website and is relative to 22 May 2017, the methodology with which Longform.org has elaborated its data is not specified.

Figure 6.5 essentially confirms the consistency between the data which we scraped from 2016 single-story entries and the overall data provided by Longform.org. While news media outlet selection seems consistent if compared across the two datasets, we can observe how there is a small number of outlets that have not been chosen as frequently in 2016, while being featured extensively in the past, such as *The New Republic, Slate, The New York Review of Books, WIRED* and *Rolling Stone*. However, it is possible to assume that the top twenty-five contributors in 2016 for single-story entries are representative of the overall news media outlet selection in Longform.org.

We can also see how, alongside outlet variety, the other factor at play in news media outlet selection operated by Longform.org is legacy. As outlet presence seems to be consistent in both datasets, the overall orientation in Longform.org's choices for its main contributors is decisively aimed at major news media outlets which have been active for an extended period of time, as among the top overall contributors we can find *New Yorker* magazine, *The New York Times Magazine, New York* magazine, *GQ* and *Vanity Fair* magazine.

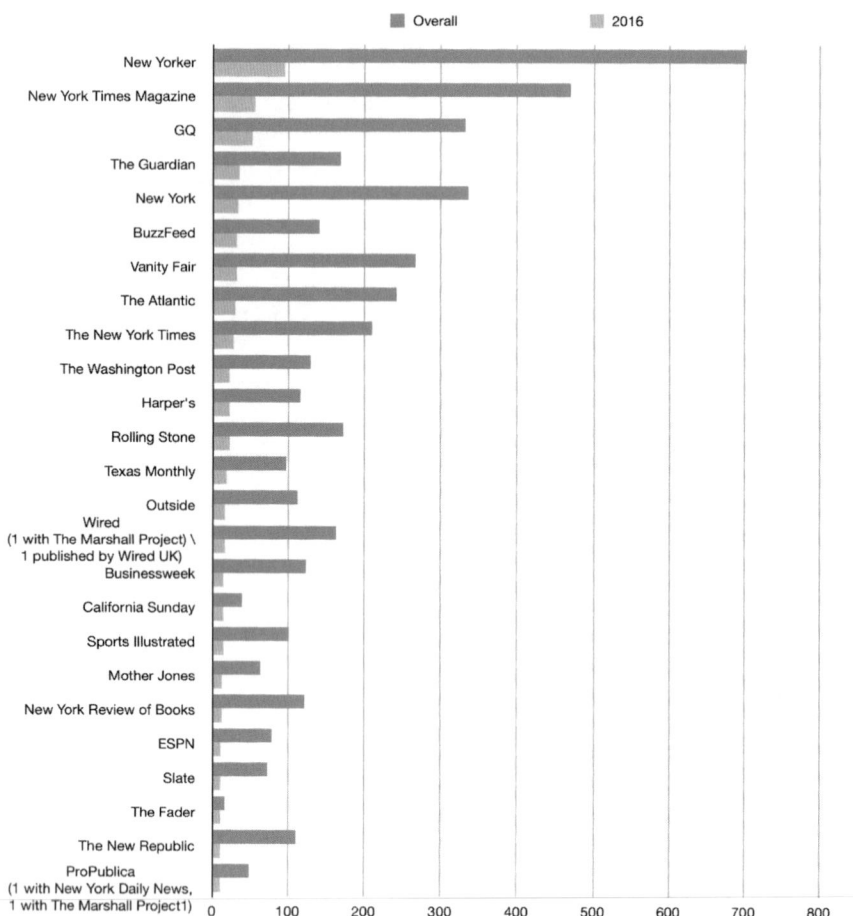

Figure 6.5 Top twenty-five news media outlets per single-story entries in 2016 and the respective data regarding overall production sourced from Longform.org's website

To further assess news media outlet relevance, we shall focus on news media outlets which have had at least two long-form journalism stories featured in Longform.org 2016 single-story entries. The number of news media outlets which have been featured at least twice in Longform.org 2016 single-story entries is 111, and they are responsible for 965 entries out of the total 1,074. As we have seen in Figure 6.5, news media outlets most frequently chosen in 2016 are consistent with the overall choices made by Longform.org since its inception in 2010. An analysis of the type of news media outlet responsible for these 965 entries could then provide more general insight on which type of news media outlets are more relevant among Longform.org's overall choices.

Out of the total 111 outlets which are featured at least twice in single-story entries in 2016, sixty-eight are magazines which retain a paper edition, thirty-two are digital-only news media outlets, eight are daily newspapers and three are websites developed by media companies which focus primarily on another type of medium, such as television or radio. The overall number of magazines which retain a paper edition is highly relevant, both if compared to other types of news media outlets featured in 2016 and to the top overall contributors to Longform.org. However, there is a significant number of digital-only publications (thirty-two in total) which are the second largest group among news media outlet types. The number of digital-only publications is moreover relevant as this group is four times larger than daily newspapers, which are only eight, namely *The Guardian, The New York Times, The Washington Post, The Boston Globe, The Los Angeles Times, The Tampa Bay Times* and *Dagbladet*, a newspaper published in Norway. Alongside magazines, digital-only publications and newspapers, there are three websites developed by media outlets which focus primarily on television or radio, which are *ESPN, MTV, NPR* and *Fusion*.

Figure 6.6 demonstrates the percentage of each news media outlet category among the overall single-story entries in 2016. Magazines are the most relevant type of news media outlets, accounting for 69 per cent of all single stories drawn from a pool of sixty-eight different outlets, which were 61 per cent of the total outlets. Digital-only news media outlets account for 18 per cent of all single stories featured but represented 29 per cent of the total news media outlets selected by Longform.org. Moreover, while daily newspapers account for 11 per cent of the single-story entries, they represent just 7 per cent of the overall news media outlets. A similar result can be found among other types of outlets which account for 4 per cent of the number of single-story entries but represented just 2 per cent of the overall news media outlets.

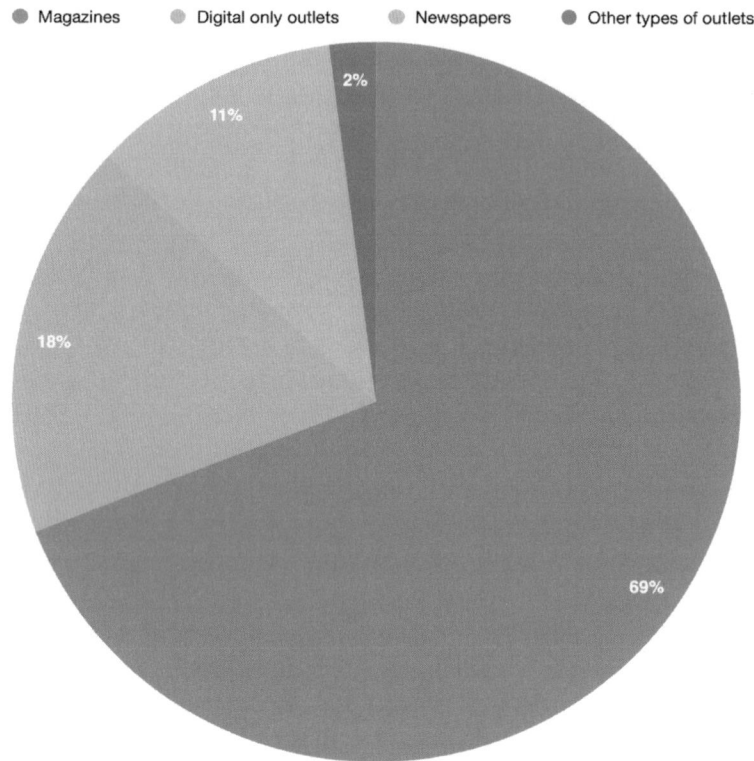

● Magazines   ● Digital only outlets   ● Newspapers   ● Other types of outlets

Figure 6.6 Number of entries per news media outlet type in 2016 on Longform.org

The percentage difference between news media outlet type and the number of articles selected from each group is significant as it shows that digital news media outlets are used as a source for a smaller number of articles. Thus, news media outlet variety is achieved by Longform.org mostly by choosing long-form journalism stories published by digital news media outlets. In comparison, magazine and daily newspaper production are both over-represented in relation to the total number of news media outlets in the two categories. Thus, Longform.org tends to privilege legacy news media outlets, as we saw in Figure 6.4. There is a further factor of influence in Longform.org's choices which can be clearly identified, as all but eleven outlets are based in the United States. These news media outlets are based in the United Kingdom, Germany, Norway, Canada and Australia and are *The Guardian, Der Spiegel, London Review of Books, Dagbladet, The Globe and Mail, Canadian Business,* the *BBC, The Economist, The Sidney Morning Herald, The Toronto Star* and *Toronto Life.* Among these news media outlets, *The Guardian* is the only one with a significant impact in terms of selection, as it was featured in thirty-five single-story entries in 2016. Overall, the number of single-story entries sourced from non-US based news media outlets is 56 out of 1074.

To further examine the selection process operated by Longform.org regarding specific news media outlets, we shall now focus on the first publication dates of long-form journalism stories sourced from the top ten contributors in 2016.

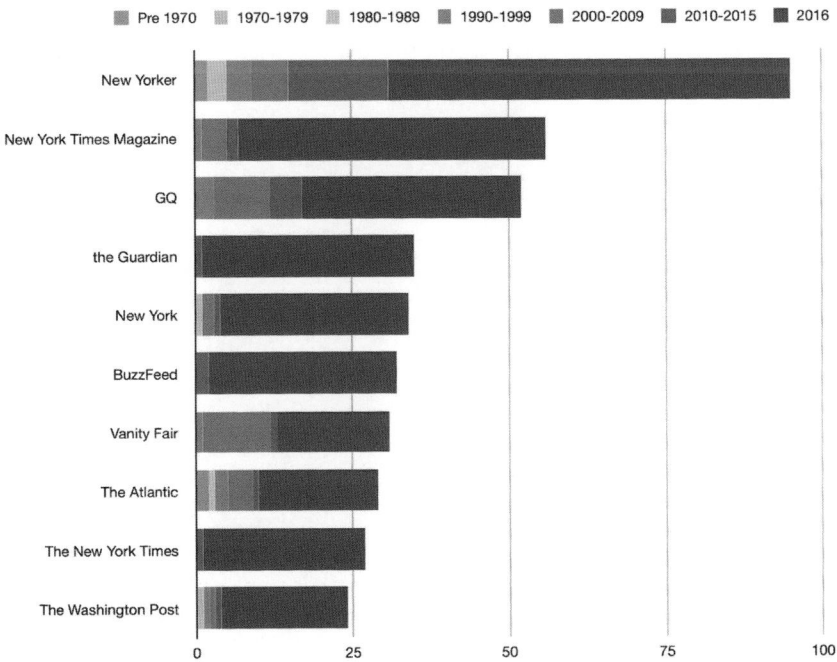

Figure 6.7 The top ten news media outlets in 2016 and the first publishing dates of their long-form stories divided per decade and in the year 2016

As we saw in Figure 6.4, single-story entries in 2016 were sourced from a wide variety of news media outlets, with 41 per cent of the total sourced from news media outlets which were featured once or twice in the whole year. Out of the top twenty-five news media outlets which were featured more than ten times in 2016, we shall focus on the top ten. In order to better understand how single-story entries from these news media outlets have been selected, we have tracked the publication date for each of the entries by *New Yorker, The New York Times Magazine, GQ, The Guardian, New York* magazine, *BuzzFeed, Vanity Fair, The Atlantic, The New York Times* and *The Washington Post.* We have divided first publication dates into seven different timeframes, one devoted to entries first published before 1970, followed by five decade-by-decade time frames, devoting the last time frame to entries first published in 2016. In Figure 6.7, the latter is by far the most represented category. However, only two news media outlets have entries which were first published in six different time frames, *New Yorker* and *The Atlantic.* Both are legacy news media outlets, as they were founded in 1925 and 1857 respectively. Moreover, we can see how *The New York Times Magazine, GQ* and *Vanity Fair* all have a similar pattern, with entries from the same four eras (1990–1999; 2000–2009; 2010–2015 and 2016). The only exclusively digital outlet featured among the top ten is *BuzzFeed,* yet its pattern is similar to the one developed by entries from *The Guardian* and *The New York Times,* which feature only single-story entries first published between the 2010–2015 period and in 2016. *The Washington Post* highlights a different pattern, with entries drawn from five different time frames. Hence, we can conclude that legacy magazines entries tend to be drawn from a more composite pool of publishing eras, with a more pronounced focus on entries which were first published before 2016.

After assessing the selection pattern among the ten most relevant news media outlets in 2016 per number of entries, we provide further insight on how a single outlet has been featured on Longform.org since its foundation, in April 2010. As we have seen in Figure 6.5, *The New Yorker* was the most relevant news media outlet per number of single-story entries in 2016 and overall, according to the data published on Longform.org's website. In order to establish in further detail how Longform.org has mined the *New Yorker'*s archive, we performed a scraping activity on all the entries which Longform.org has identified on its website with the tag 'New Yorker' or 'The New Yorker'. We chose the same Google Chrome extension (Data Miner, 2016) used to build our dataset. We then processed the data through Open Refine for data profiling (Olson, 2003) and data cleaning (Verborgh and De Wilde, 2013). We focused on all entries except those dated after 2016, in order to create a consistent dataset with the one we analysed previously. In total, Longform.org's website identified 650 entries by either 'New Yorker' or 'The New Yorker', with first publication dates ranging from 1933 to 2016, including both non-fiction and fiction long-form stories.

We grouped all entries in seven different time frames, ranging from 1933–1960 to 2010–2016. As we can see in Figure 6.8, while more recently dated long-form journalism stories are the vast majority of entries [67 per

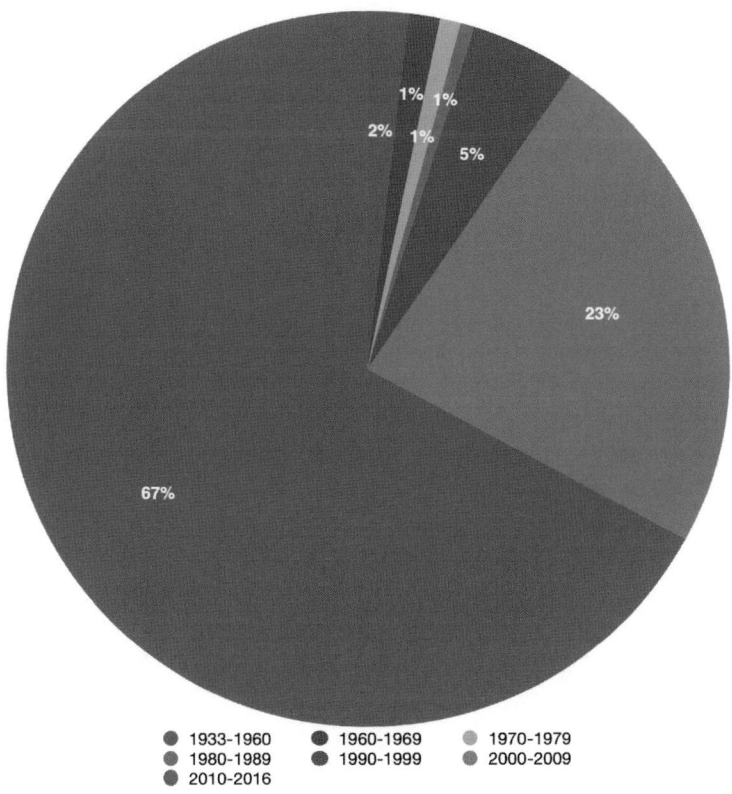

Figure 6.8 All *New Yorker* entries on Longform.org divided per publishing era

cent], there is a significant portion of entries [10 per cent] which are dated
before the year 2000. However, analysing the general trend, it is possible to
assume that a long-form journalism story's first publication date is a factor
in its possibility to be mined by Longform.org. Moreover, as Longform.org
started its operations in 2010, all entries prior to that date have been mined
from a period which pre-dates the aggregator's activity. In Figure 6.9, we
divided in the same seven time frames utilised in Figure 6.8, the *New Yorker's*
single-story entries which we scraped from Longform.org activity in 2016.
As we can see, if we compare the two figures, we can see how consistent
the 2016 dataset is if compared to the overall entries.

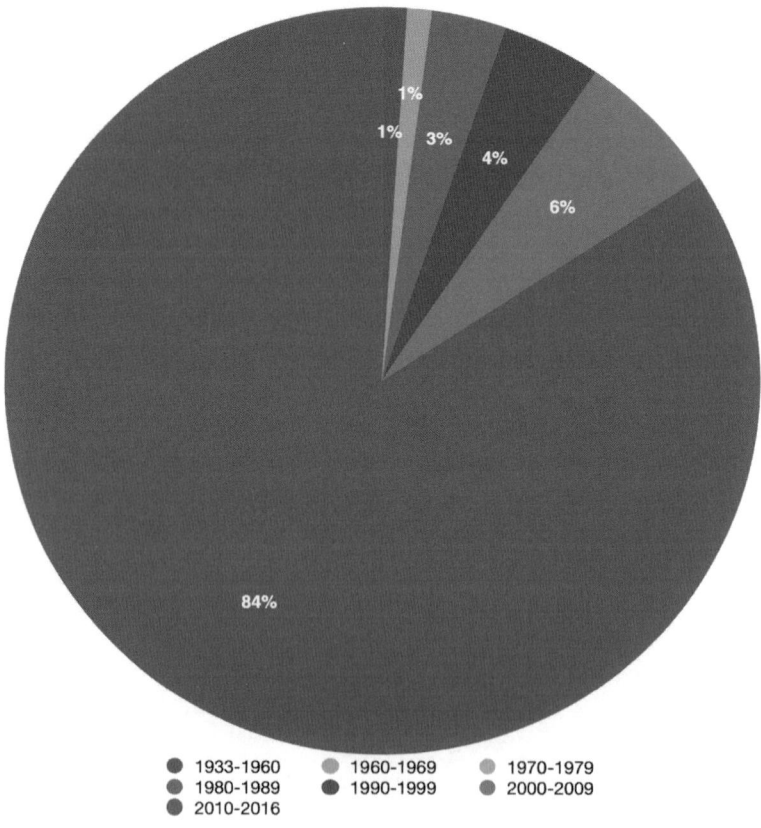

Figure 6.9 *New Yorker* single-story entries in 2016 per first publishing date

While single-story entries selected by Longform.org seem to be focusing more strongly in the period between 2010 and 2016, it is important to underline that all the other categories are present, except long-form journalism stories published between 1970 and 1979. Overall, among the wide mining of *New Yorker*'s archive operated by Longform.org since its birth, while the vast majority of choices focuses on the more recent content, there is a constant aggregation and curation activity that has regarded the older content published by *New Yorker*. The balance between recently published and older content appears to be a constant feature of Longform.org aggregation and curation activity. Thus, readers focus on the topic and appreciate the aggregation and curation activity itself, rather than focusing on the first publishing date in deciding to read or not a long-form journalism story (Boynton, 2013).

CHAPTER 7

The Future of Long-Form Journalism and Archives: Digitisation, Datafication and Curation

Long-Form Journalism Aggregation and Curation as a Template for News Archive Fruition

Curation by News Media Outlets and Aggregators

In the previous chapter, we focused on an aggregator such as Longform. org, providing data on its aggregation and curation choices. Assessing how these third parties perform their activity allowed us to identify a specific set of practices, such as news media outlet variety and a balance between more recent and older long-form journalism stories. We have seen how, in Longform.org's case, aggregator's selection is organised around the notion of 'feed fruition'. Among the news media outlets selected by a third-party aggregator such as Longform.org, we have found how legacy news media outlets tend to be featured more frequently as they provide an age-wise more diverse pool of long-form journalism stories to mine.

We shall now investigate how news media outlets engage in this type of aggregation and curation activity themselves. Aside from specific topics, this activity does not appear to be undertaken consistently by news media outlets. *The Guardian*, for example, curates a series named 'Burst your Bubble' (*The Guardian*, 2017) which is a weekly selection of articles published by conservative news outlets, which are summarised and linked on *The Guardian*, to provide a different point of view, mainly on political topics, to the news outlet readers. However, rather than being a self-standing curation and aggregation service, it appears as a complementary reading for *The Guardian*'s readers.

An aggregation and curation activity which is comparable to the one performed by Longform.org is performed by *The New York Times* Archive account on Twitter (*The New York Times*, 2014b). The account's description states 'Highlights from the 165-year-old archive of *The New York Times*. Links to the "TimesMachine" are publicly available for seven days after we tweet them' (*The New York Times*, 2014b). Hence, the account presents itself as a curation account for content in *The New York Times* Archive. This content is made available through the 'TimesMachine' which we described in-depth in Chapter 5.

The New York Times Archive account on Twitter has been active since April 2014, and in order to assess how *The New York Times* has used its Twitter Archive account as a curation platform, we have analysed all the tweets produced in 2016, applying digital methods (Rogers, 2013), data profiling (Olson, 2003) and data cleaning (Verborgh and De Wilde, 2013). Out of the approximately 1,030 tweets published in 2016, the overwhelming majority refer directly to an article in *The New York Times* Archive. Out of the total, we were able to identify 919 tweets with an explicit article reference. We must begin our analysis of this dataset by underlining that *The New York Times* is expanding its 'TimesMachine' service, which is currently hosting all the content published on the newspaper from 1851 to 2002, which comprise around 12.4 million articles and over 4.1 million pages (Cotler and Sandhaus, 2016). Hence, *The New York Times* Archive account on Twitter is acting as a content aggregator and curator, which has a very considerable yet not complete pool of articles to mine. It is relevant to underline that the choice of a Twitter account to perform this aggregation and curation activity is in line with the notion of 'feed fruition' which, as we have seen in previously in this chapter, was a distinctive feature of Longform.org's activity.

Articles featured in tweets by the *New York Times* Archive account in 2016 range from 1856 to 2012, and generally regard with more intensity the decades after 1960, with a special focus on the two decades between 1960 and 1980. As the Twitter account focuses mainly on material hosted on the 'TimesMachine' and being this service incomplete as it covers in full only the period between 1852 and 2002, we can see a steep decrease in references to articles published after the year 2000.

Tweets referencing to events occurred on the same day in which they were written appear to be a constant element of the vast majority, if not all, of the tweets that contain an article link. Moreover, article selection and curation are also organised around anniversaries or the first time *The New York Times* introduced a topic, as in the case of Labour Day: '*The Times* was highly sceptical of the first Labour Day in 1887. <http://nyti. ms/2b2ps7w>' (Twitter, 2016). However, thoroughly analysing the tweets from *The New York Times* Archive account, we were able to extract insights regarding the publishing dates of articles they featured. As said above, recent content is not featured as much as older content, being the account based on the 'TimesMachine' service, which does not comprise the whole of the newspaper's production, as *The New York Times* has not yet completed its archive conversion into the 'TimesMachine' (Cotler and Sandhaus, 2016).

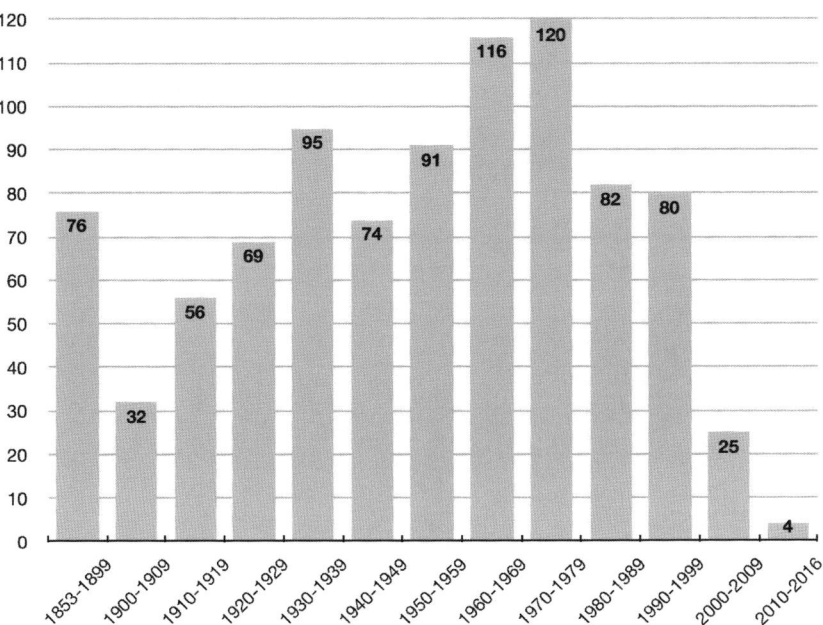

Figure 7.1 Articles featured in 2016 tweets by @NYTArchives
account divided per decade

Figure 7.1 shows more clearly the polarisation which, due to the issues regarding the 'TimesMachine', clearly favours content produced in the past decades if compared to more recent content. However, Figure 7.1 also demonstrates the variety of the time periods from which *The New York Times* Archive on Twitter has sourced its article references in 2016. The two decades from 1960 to 1980 represent the core of all references, which in some cases feature the front page of the newspaper. While the overall 920 tweets that have a direct reference to an article do achieve variety as they are selected from different time periods, it appears distant from the aggregation and curation activity proposed by Longform.org. Moreover, it is important to underline that this aggregation and curation process is not operated in an environment part of *The New York Times* and rather takes place on a social network such as Twitter, which is based on a 'feed fruition' dynamic.

However, the data we scraped from Longform.org's 2016 activity and the dataset we obtained by downloading all the 2016 tweets by *The New York Times* Archive account on Twitter, are comparable in size, as Longform.org published 1,074 single-story entries in 2016 we were able to manually identify approximately 920 tweets from *The New York Times* Archive Twitter account as containing a direct article reference.

In Figure 7.2, the different selection approach between Longform. org and *The New York Times* Archive account on Twitter is highly evident. While the latter concentrates its activity on older content, Longform.org's activity begins to be sizable in the decade between 2000 and 2009. The most evident difference between the two datasets regards the last two time periods, 2010–2015, and 2016. As we have seen above in this section, such a difference is probably due to the different nature of the two datasets, as Longform.org mainly mines archives which house more recent content and uses content from other time periods to achieve variety. *The New York Times* Archive Twitter account, on the other hand, is focused on content sourced from the 'TimesMachine', mainly focusing its activity towards older content, as not all newspaper editions are available in the news media outlet rendering and archive curation service. However, as we have seen in Figure 6.7, legacy outlet archives have the potential to be mined, combining time periods in a different fashion according to the mining activity performed by Longform.org.

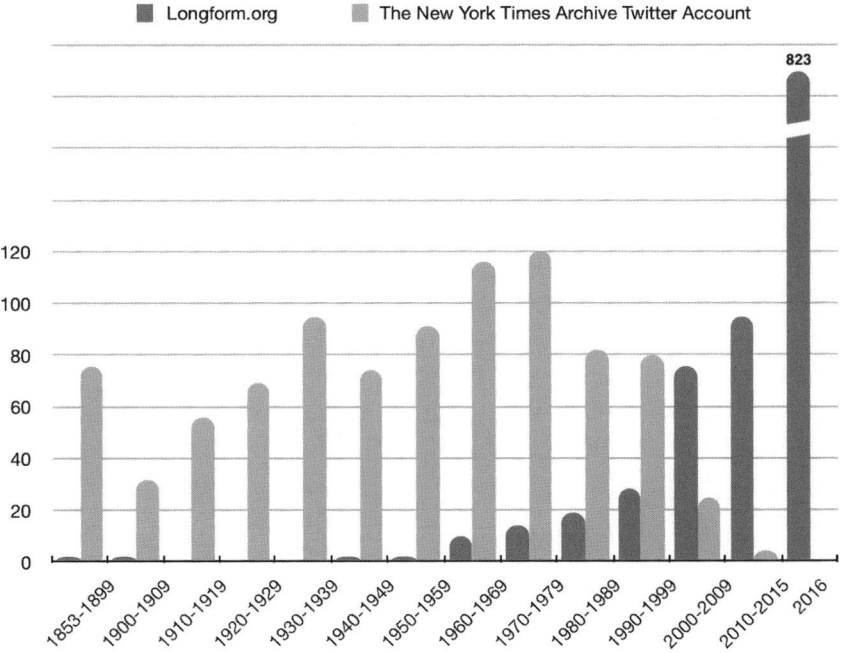

Figure 7.2 A comparison between Longform.org's 2016 single-story entries
and @NYTArchives tweets with a direct article reference

Hence, the difference between the two datasets is also probably due
to the underlining philosophy of the two curation and aggregation feeds,
as Longform.org's is driven by a thorough selection process, as underlined
by founder Max Linsky:

> there was all this great writing all over the Web; so much of it, in fact, that it was
> kind of hard to find the best of it. So, the idea of the site has always been the same
> thing; which is, we want to go and find the best stuff, and make it super easy to read
> not just on the Web but on your phone or your Kindle or your iPad. (Cornish, 2013)

The New York Times Archive feed's activity on Twitter is probably more
influenced by the drive to display 'TimesMachine' as a service available
to readers, hence its activity focuses more on events such as anniversaries
rather than freely curating content from *The New York Times* Archive.
Thus, Longform.org content aggregation and curation activity seem to be

more adherent to the intermediary role as theorised by Anderson (2009b) as its focus regards the efficiency of the distribution process, rather than the ownership of a specific product, in this case, long-form journalism. Incumbent entities usually outperform traditional industries by using new production distribution practices at scale as in the case of platform services such as social networks which – among other activities – perform an intermediary function between producers and crowds. Longform. org's case, in this sense, is highly relevant as it did not begin as a scale operation and, as the two founders remarked, 'the audience that came just kept getting bigger and bigger without us doing much' (McQuade, 2015). Hence, we can assume that, within the digital landscape, aggregation and curation are decisive factors in the growth of intermediaries, whereas production and ownership's role is diminishing in importance. However, the success of Longform.org as a long-form journalism aggregator and the observations around the difficulties in sourcing older content described in *The New York Times* 'Innovation Report' (*The New York Times*, 2014a) demonstrate that news media outlets have struggled to develop effective intermediation practices.

Digitisation, Datafication and Curation

As we have seen in the previous chapter, there are multiple directions that aggregation and curation activities could take, especially if the datafication process of news media outlets digital archives will progress in the future. We analysed studies based on person-centric mining (Coll Ardanuy et al., 2016) and based on geospatial data extraction (Yzaguirre, Smit and Warren, 2016) and these two examples indicate that there seems to be a fertile space for new types of user-centric aggregation and curation services originating from news media outlets' digital archives, once they are datafied. These new types of curation and aggregation seem to be tailored for news media outlets looking to develop aggregation and curation services among their archived production.

It is possible to imagine that new forms curation will hybrid datafication and aggregator selection, producing new narratives resulting from the combination of multiple long-form journalism stories. For example, once a news media outlets' digital archive is fully datafied, it will be possible to organise selections of different long-form journalism stories based on geographical and person-centric information, which seems to be particularly fit for narrative suites based on complex historical events which span across a significant amount of time.

This type of aggregation and curation activity is not entirely new in its underlining structure. A page collecting of Ernest Hemingway's dispatches from the Spanish Civil War was developed by *The New York Times* in 1999 and is now hosted on the news media outlet's digital archive (*The New York Times*, 1999). However, the difference between this type of static aggregation and curation activity and the possibilities opened up by a process such as datafication in the digital landscape, indicate that there is ample space for a radical re-imagination of this type of activity.

Moreover, it is possible that different long-form journalism stories will be combined not just as a source for aggregation and curation services, but as narratives, generating new long-form stories which result from the combination of archived content. These aggregation, curation and creation possibilities are particularly relevant for news media outlets, as their digitalised archives are not always openly available on the World Wide Web, limiting the possibility for third-party aggregators to develop a competitive alternative in this field. As more news media outlets focus only on digital production, they tend to archive their content on the World Wide Web without developing aggregation and curation services, as we have seen in Chapter 5. Such a stance is likely to favour third-party entities, as their sole focus is to curate and aggregate content, rather than be tasked with production and archiving.

We can assume that in the digital landscape, production of a good such as content does not necessarily imply that the producer will fully benefit from its distribution. Long-form journalism and archives are influenced by the main features of the contemporary digital landscape, which we identified in Chapter 1, such as the notion of flux and disruption. As we have seen, rather than being strictly limited to producers, value extraction in the contemporary digital landscape is leaning towards distributors, such as platforms or, in our example concerning to the news media industry, aggregators.

Yet, news media outlets do have a possibility to transform their information-rich content which is in the major currently digitised but not yet datafied, into possible new forms of aggregated content. As we have seen in the case of the creation of Google Books, Mayer-Schönberger and Cukier indicated it as a successful datafication process (Mayer-Schönberger and Cukier, 2013). The outcome, as underlined by Pybus, Coté and Blanke, was the creation of value for Google as it was fundamental for the creation of Google Translate 'realising the relational potential within those datasets to create what is now the most used translation platform in the world' (Pybus, Coté and Blanke, 2015: 3). Long-form journalism and digital news archives, as we have seen, are both information-rich entities which are digitised but not yet datafied. Moreover, they share relevance over time as a common aspect within the digital landscape. Alongside the datafication process that these entities can be subjected to, is the possibility of creating new aggregation and fruition practices. These practices, if directly performed by news media outlets themselves, could lead to potential new sources of revenue and modify the relationship between news media outlets and platforms within the digital landscape.

The result of this digitisation, datafication and curation process could lead to new forms of aggregation that explore – to the full extent – all the data points which are present in a long-form journalism story and within a news media outlet archive. Moreover, by focusing on the connection between data points across entities which are traditionally separated, it is possible to envision aggregation practices which could associate content which has been published using different journalistic formats and across different timeframes. Thus, it is possible to envision new forms of combination, aggregation and curation which will organise the relation between data points within long-form journalism and news media archives into new forms of narration which could be developed across multiple dimensions, such as time and space. This would potentially open up a number of unexplored relations and fully exploit and aggregate data points across traditionally separated entities.

The outcome of this datafication process will be conditioned by which entities will perform it. On the one hand, it implies the development of in-house tools by news media outlets, which might not be in the condition to sustain the economic and technological burden of their creation. On the other hand, platforms possess both the resources and know-how to create datafication and curation tools. Thus, whereas this is an open and yet unexplored field, the dynamic that shape it could well follow the current path in the relationship between news media outlets and platforms.

However, we can also envision this process as a possibility of radical transformation in the principle of ownership in the digital landscape. Ownership and distribution are not neutral practices: they define the interaction that clusters of individuals, such as crowds, experience in platforms in the digital landscape. If we focus on the examples we provided in previous chapter, we have seen how news media production is experiencing a transformation which increasingly leads to intermediaries such as platforms and aggregators gaining traction over traditional producers, such as news media outlets. If the production of a good in the digital landscape does not automatically translate in it being a source of revenue for the producer but rather a source of revenue for the more efficient distributor, we could also envision intermediaries which operate efficiently but are not driven by revenue but rather by other factors. For example, it is possible that non-profit distributors will establish themselves as relevant entities, transforming articles currently stagnating in news media archives with novel curation and aggregation practices into information as flow resource (Hess and Ostrom, 2003). If we envision new types of distributors, which are not driven by revenue, we can also envision potential new activities that could be performed.

As we have seen, one the common traits between long-form journalism and archives is that they are both resources which are currently digitised but not datafied and would need to undergo a datafication process, which transforms information in a quantifiable format (Mayer-Schönberger and Cukier, 2013). Once this process is complete, data can be harvested. However, it seems clear that this process is far from neutral, as Mayer-Schönberger and Cukier define it as capable of changing 'markets, organisations, the relationship between citizens and governments, and more' (Mayer-Schönberger and Cukier, 2013: 6). However, the current leading conception of data and datafication which opens numerous possibilities for platforms and raises many issues regarding individual data protection, could be modified or re-imagined, 'beyond programmes to make data public or keep data private through various attendant technical, policy and legal systems that facilitate or inhibit the flows of data in society' (Gray, 2016: 199). This 'more ambitious politics of data', as Gray defines it,

> would have to cultivate the political imagination and practical capacities to recalibrate digital information systems to be attuned to a broader set of societal interests […] opening up spaces for democratic deliberation and social participation around the creation of data and around processes of datafication. (2016: 199)

An example of a 'politics of data' that would entail 'opening up spaces for democratic deliberation and social participation' (Gray, 2016: 199) could be represented by framing data and the process of datafication within the notion of 'common' (Hardt and Negri, 2009). For these two authors, the 'common' comprises 'those results of social production that are necessary for social interaction and further production, such as knowledges, languages, codes, information, affects, and so forth' (Hardt and Negri, 2009: viii). However, Hardt and Negri underline how

> the content of what is produced – including ideas, images, and affects – is easily reproduced and thus tends toward being common, strongly resisting all legal and economic efforts to privatize it or bring it under public control. The transition is already in process: contemporary capitalist production by addressing its own needs is opening up the possibility of and creating the bases for a social and economic order grounded in the common. (2009: x)

Hence, we can imagine the birth of intermediaries which are not driven by revenue extraction, contrarily to what Anderson (2009b) theorised in his long-tail model, and are not performing datafication as framed by Mayer-Schönberger and Cukier (2013), but instead envision their activity as a practice of the common (Hardt and Negri, 2009). It is possible to assume that such operations, performed by new types of actors, will be finalised to complete the transformation of information into a true flow resource (Hess and Ostrom, 2003).

References

Adornato, A. (2017). *Mobile and Social Media Journalism: A Practical Guide.* Thousand Oaks: SAGE Publications.

Albalad Aiguabella, J. M. (2015). 'Slow journalism para una nueva audiencia digital. El caso de Longform. org (2010–2015)', *Revista de Comunicación*, 14, pp. 7–25.

Alexa (2020). 'Alexa - Top sites'. *Alexa* <https://www.alexa.com/topsites>, accessed 13 September 2020.

Alpert, L. I. (2016). 'Washington Post Looks to Publishing Platform as Growing Revenue Stream', *The Wall Street Journal*, <https://www.wsj.com/articles/washington-post-looks-to-publishing-platform-as-growing-revenue-stream-1465383602>, accessed 3 September 2020.

Anderson, C. (2009a). *Free : the future of a radical price.* London: Random House Business.

Anderson, C. (2009b). *The longer long tail : how endless choice is creating unlimited demand.* London: Random House Business.

Anderson, C. and Wolff, M. (2010). 'The Web is Dead. Long Live the Internet', *WIRED.* <https://www.wired.com/2010/08/ff_webrip/all/>, accessed 15 August 2020.

Apache Kafka (2016). 'Introduction to Apache Kafka', *Apache Kafka*, <https://kafka.apache.org/intro>, accessed 10 August 2020.

Apfelbaum, S. and Cezzar, J. (2014). *Designing the Editorial Experience: A Primer for Print, Web, and Mobile,* Beverly: Rockport Publishers.

Apple (2015). 'Apple Watch Overview', <https://www.apple.com/watch/overview/>, accessed 18 June 2020.

Armstrong T. Christian, K. M. (2015). 'How We Reported 'An Unbelievable Story of Rape', *The Marshall Project*, <https://www.themarshallproject.org/2015/12/16/how-we-reported-an-unbelievable-story-of-rape>, accessed 3 September 2020.

Assmann, A. (2011). *Cultural memory and Western civilization : functions, media, archives.* New York: Cambridge University Press.

Bailey, D. (2014). 'Like Explorer', <https://web.archive.org/web/20160201122452/http://www.likeexplorer.com/>, accessed 23 September 2020.

Bakshy, E., Messing, S. and Adamic, L. A. (2015). 'Exposure to ideologically diverse news and opinion on Facebook', *Science*, 348 (6239), pp. 1130–1132.

Barker, D. (2016) *Web Content Management: Systems, Features, and Best Practices.* Sebastopol: O'Reilly Media.

Bell, E. (2016). 'The End of the News as We Know It: How Facebook Swallowed Journalism', *Tow Center for Digital Journalism*, <https://medium.com/tow-center/the-end-of-the-news-as-we-know-it-how-facebook-swallowed-journalism-60344fa50962#.l4d6c51nb>, accessed 19 June 2020.

Belt, D. and South, J. (2016). 'Slow Journalism and the Out of Eden Walk', *Digital Journalism*, 4 (4), pp. 547–562.

Benedikt, M. (1991). *Cyberspace: first steps*. Cambridge, Massachusetts: MIT Press.

Benton, J. (2015). 'Get AMP'd: Here's what publishers need to know about Google's new plan to speed up your website', *Nieman Lab*, <http://www.niemanlab.org/2015/10/get-ampd-heres-what-publishers-need-to-know-about-googles-new-plan-to-speed-up-your-website>, accessed 11 June 2020.

Berardi, F. (2011). *After the future*. Oakland, California ; Edinburgh: AK Press.

Berardi, F. (2012). 'Cognitarian Subjectivation', *e-flux*, (20), <http://www.e-flux.com/journal/20/67633/cognitarian-subjectivation>, accessed 24 June 2020.

Bercovici, J. (2014). 'Longform's New App: More Great Journalism Without The Filter', *Forbes*, <https://www.forbes.com/sites/jeffbercovici/2014/09/17/longforms-new-app-more-great-journalism-without-the-filter/#552df27b42f6>, accessed 8 August 2020.

Berners-Lee, T. (1989). 'Information Management: A proposal', *CERN*, <https://www.w3.org/History/1989/proposal.html>, accessed 14 August 2020.

Berners-Lee, T. (1997). 'Universal Resource identifiers in WWW', *World Wide Web Consortium*, <https://www.w3.org/Addressing/URL/uri-spec.html>, accessed 5 September 2020.

Berners-Lee, T. (2010). 'Long Live the Web: A Call for Continued Open Standards and Neutrality', *Scientific* American, <https://www.scientificamerican.com/article/long-live-the-web/>, accessed 14 August 2020.

Berning, N. (2011). 'Narrative Journalism in the Age of the Internet', *Textpraxis*, (3), pp. 1–15.

Bharat, K. (2006). 'And now, News', *Google Official Blog*, <https://googleblog.blogspot.it/2006/01/and-now-news.html>, accessed 14 January 2020.

Bingham, A. (2010). 'The digitization of newspaper archives: Opportunities and challenges for historians', *Twentieth Century British History*, 21(2), pp. 225–231.

Blanke, T. (2014). *Digital asset ecosystems : rethinking crowds and clouds*, Chandos Information Professional Series, Amsterdam; Boston: Elsevier.

Blanke, T., Prescott, A. (2016). 'Dealing with Big Data'. In G. Griffin, and M. Hayler (ed.), *Research Methods for Reading Digital Data in the Digital Humanities*, Edinburgh: Edinburgh University Press.

Bockarova, M. (2013). 'Podcast' in M. Danesi (ed.), *Encyclopaedia of Media and Communication*, Toronto: University of Toronto Press.

Bohn, D. (2018). 'Inside Google's plan to make the whole web as fast as AMP', *The Verge*, <https://www.theverge.com/2018/3/8/17095078/google-amp-accelerated-mobile-page-announcement-standard-web-packaging-urls>, first accessed 9 July 2020.

Boiko, B. (2005). *Content management bible*. Hoboken, New Jersey: John Wiley & Sons Publications.

boyd, danah m. and Ellison, N. B. (2007) 'Social Network Sites: Definition, History, and Scholarship', *Journal of Computer-Mediated Communication*, 13 (1), pp. 210–230.

Boynton, R. (2013). 'Notes toward a Supreme Nonfiction: Teaching Literary Reportage in the Twenty-first Century', *Literary Journalism Studies*, 5 (2), pp. 125–131.

Braghieri, M. (2019). 'Longform.org Scraped data (2016)', <https://osf.io/8myj5/>, accessed 22 June 2020.

Branch, J. (2012). 'Snow Fall: The Avalanche at Tunnel Creek', *The New York Times*, <http://www.nytimes.com/projects/2012/snow-fall/index.html>, accessed 11 July 2020.

Branch, J. (2014). *Snow Fall: The Avalanche at Tunnel Creek*, ebook, Byliner, The New York Times.

Brock, G. (2013). *Out of print: journalism and the business of news in the digital age*. London; Philadelphia: Kogan Page Limited.

Brown, C. (2013). 'The New York Times told me to take this down', *Cody Brown, Medium*, <https://medium.com/meta/the-new-york-times-told-me-to-take-this-down-503b9c22080b>, accessed 4 March 2020

Brown, P. (2018). 'More than half of Facebook Instant Articles partners may have abandoned it', *Columbia Journalism Review*, <https://www.cjr.org/tow_center/are-facebook-instant-articles-worth-it.php>, accessed 23 August 2020.

Brown, C., Sarantakos M. (2019). 'Introducing Facebook News', *Facebook*, <https://about.fb.com/news/2019/10/introducing-facebook-news/>, accessed 5 January 2021.

Bruns, A. (2008) *Blogs, Wikipedia, Second life, and Beyond : from production to produsage (Digital formations)*, New York: Peter Lang.

Bruns, A. and Highfield, T (2012). 'Blogs, Twitter, and breaking news: The produsage of citizen journalism'. In R.A. Lind (ed.), *Produsing theory in a digital world: The intersection of audiences and production in contemporary theory*, 80, pp. 15–32 New York: Peter Lang.

Brynjolfsson, E. and McAfee, A. (2014). *The Second Machine Age: Work, Progress, and Prosperity in a Time of Brilliant Technologies*, New York: W. W. Norton & Company.

Burdick, A., Drucker, J., Lunenfed, P., Presner, T. and Schnapp, J. (2012). *Digital_ Humanities*, Cambridge, Massachusetts: MIT Press

Burel, F. and Baudry, J. (2003). *Landscape ecology : concepts, methods, and applications*. Enfield, New Hampshire: Science Publishers, Inc.

Burnett, R., Brunstrom, A. and Nilsson, A. G. (2005). *Perspectives on Multimedia: Communication, Media and Information Technology*, Hoboken, New Jersey: John Wiley & Sons Publications.

Busby, T. and Hamilton, J. A. (1840). *A Dictionary of Three Thousand Musical Terms, etc. (Third edition, revised by J. A. Hamilton.)*. London: D'Almaine & Co.

Bustillos, M. (2018). 'Erasing History', *Columbia Journalism Review*, <https://www.cjr.org/special_report/microfilm-newspapers-media-digital.php>, accessed 25 August 2020.

Carr, D. (2014). 'Facebook Offers Life Raft, but Publishers Are Wary', *The New York Times*. <https://www.nytimes.com/2014/10/27/business/media/facebook-offers-life-raft-but-publishers-are-wary.html>, accessed 4 August 2020.

Castells, M. (2010). *The rise of the network society*. Oxford: Wiley-Blackwell.

CERN (2012). *The Birth of the World Wide Web*, *CERN*, <https://timeline.web.cern.ch/timeline-header/90/export>, accessed 10 July 2020.

Chee, F. Y. (2020). 'Google to pay publishers $1 billion over three years for their news', *Reuters*. <https://www.reuters.com/article/us-alphabet-publishing-eu/google-to-pay-publishers-1-billion-over-three-years-for-their-news-idUSKBN26M5P7>, accessed 1 January 2021.

Christensen, C. M. (1997). *The innovator's dilemma : when new technologies cause great firms to fail*. Boston, Massachusetts: Harvard Business School Press.

Coll Ardanuy M., Knauth J., Beliankou A., van den Bos M., Sporleder C. (2016). 'Person-Centric Mining of Historical Newspaper Collections'. In: Fuhr N., Kovács L., Risse T., Nejdl W. (eds.) Research and Advanced Technology for Digital Libraries. TPDL 2016, Lecture Notes in Computer Science, vol. 9819. London: Springer.

Comscore (2019). *Global State of Mobile*, <https://www.comscore.com/Insights/Presentations-and-Whitepapers/2019/Global-State-of-Mobile>, accessed 12 September 2020.

Concoran, L. (2015). 'The Best Publishers on Social Media in 2015: The Whippies', *NewsWhip*, <https://www.newswhip.com/2015/12/2015s-best-publishers-on-social-media-the-whippies>, accessed 2 June 2020.

Concoran, L. (2016). 'What the New York Times' Most Shared Stories of 2015 Tell Us', *NewsWhip*, <https://www.newswhip.com/2016/02/new-york-times-shared-stories-2015-tell-us/>, accessed 3 August 2020.

Cook, C. and Sirkkunen, E. (2013) 'What's in a niche? Exploring the business model of online journalism', *Journal of Media Business Studies*, 10 (4), pp. 63–82.

Cornish, A. (2013). 'Website Longform Starts To Find Its Footing Online, All Things Considered', *NPR,* <https://www.npr.org/2013/04/12/177067530/longform-journalism-starts-to-find-its-footing-online>, accessed 26 September 2020.

Coté, M. and Pybus, J. (2007). 'Learning to Immaterial Labour 2.0: MySpace and Social Networks', *Ephemera,* 7 (1), pp. 88–106.

Cotler, J. and Sandhaus, E. (2016). 'How to build a TimesMachine', *The New York Times.* <https://open.blogs.nytimes.com/2016/02/01/how-to-build-a-timesmachine/>, accessed 5 June 2020.

Data Miner (2016) 'How Data Miner Works', *Data Miner,* <https://data-miner.io/how-it-works>, accessed 30 July 2020.

Deacon, D. (2007). 'Yesterday's Papers and Today's Technology: Digital Newspaper Archives and "Push Button" Content Analysis', *European Journal of Communication,* 22 (1), pp. 5–25.

Deleuze, G. (1992). 'Postscript on the Societies of Control', *October,* 59, pp. 3–7.

Derrida, J. (1996). *Archive fever : a Freudian impression, Religion and postmodernism.* Chicago; London: University of Chicago Press.

Derrida, J. (2005). *Paper machine.* Stanford, California: Stanford University Press.

van Dijck, J. (2014) 'Datafication, dataism and dataveillance: Big Data between scientific paradigm and ideolog', *Surveillance & Society,* 12 (2), pp. 197–208.

Domingo, D. (2008). 'Inventing Online Journalism: A Constructivist Approach to the Development of Online News', *Making Online News: The Ethnography of New Media Production,* New York: Peter Lang, pp. 16–28.

Döpfner, M. (2016). 'Mark Zuckerberg talks about the future of Facebook, virtual reality and artificial intelligence', *Business Insider.* <http://www.businessinsider.com/mark-zuckerberg-interview-with-axel-springer-ceo-mathias-doepfner-2016-2?IR=T>, accessed 13 September 2020.

Doub, J. (2020). 'Stepping Up Our Investment in News in the UK', *Facebook.* < https://about.fb.com/news/2020/11/launching-facebook-news-in-the-uk/>, accessed 3 January 2020.

Dowling, D. and Vogan, T. (2015). 'Can We "Snowfall" This?', *Digital Journalism,* 3 (2), pp. 209–224.

Doyle, G., Oakley, K. and O'Connor, J. (2015). *The Routledge Companion to the Cultural Industries.* London: Routledge.

Duenes, S. et al. (2013). 'How We Made Snow Fall - A Q&A with the New York Times team', *Source,* <https://source.opennews.org/articles/how-we-made-snow-fall/>, accessed 28 September 2020.

Dwyer, T. (2010). *Media convergence, Issues in cultural and media studies.* New York, New York: McGraw Hill / Open University Press.

ECMA (2017). 'Standard ECMA-404, The JSON Data Interchange Syntax', *Ecma International,* <https://www.ecma-international.org/publications/standards/Ecma-404.htm>, accessed 18 July 2020.

Ellingwood, B. (2012). 'Snow Fall Breakdown: How The New York Times Built a Multimedia Story', *Blue Collar Rocket Science*, <http://rocketscience. brookellingwood.com/2012/12/31/snow-fall-breakdown-how-the-new-york-times-built-a-multimedia-story/>, accessed 23 June 2020.

Elliott, C. (2012). 'The readers' editor on… the richness of digital archives bringing problems for readers and journalists', *The Guardian*, <https://www. theguardian.com/commentisfree/2012/oct/21/digital-archives-problems-readers-journalists>, accessed 14 July 2020.

Engelberg, S. (2015). 'About That Unbelievable Story', *ProPublica*, <https:// www.propublica.org/article/about-propublica-marshall-project-rape-story-collaboration>, accessed 3 August 2019.

Ernst, W. (2013). *Digital memory and the archive*. Minneapolis, Minnesota: University of Minnesota Press.

Ettema, J. S. and Glasser, T. L. (1988). 'Narrative form and moral force: The realization of innocence and guilt through investigative journalism', *Journal of Communication*, 38 (3), pp. 8–26.

Facebook (2012). 'How News Feed Works', *Facebook*, <https://www.facebook.com/ help/1155510281178725>, accessed 7 August 2020.

Facebook (2015). 'Graph API Overview', *Facebook*, <https://developers.facebook. com/docs/graph-api/overview/>, accessed 7 August 2020.

Facebook (2016). 'Graph API Reference', *Facebook*, <https://developers.facebook. com/docs/graph-api/reference/v2.5/url>, accessed 7 August 2020.

Facebook (2017). 'Facebook Mission Statement', *Facebook*, <https://investor. fb.com/resources/default.aspx>, accessed 7 August 2020.

Fairclough, N. (2001). *Language and Power*. Harlow: Pearson Professional Education.

Feagin, J. R., Orum, A. M. and Sjoberg, G. (1991). *A Case for the Case Study*. Chapel Hill, North Carolina: University of North Carolina Press.

Fisher, E. (2010). *Media and new capitalism in the digital age : the spirit of networks*. Basingstoke: Palgrave Macmillan.

Fisher, M. (2009). *Capitalist realism : is there no alternative?* Winchester: O Books.

Fisher, M. (2012). 'What Is Hauntology?', *Film Quarterly*, 66 (1), pp. 16–24.

Fitzgerald, M. (2016). 'Notable Narrative: Ken Armstrong, T. Christian Miller and "An Unbelievable Story of Rape"', *Nieman Storyboard*, <http:// niemanstoryboard.org/stories/notable-narrative-ken-armstrong-t-christian-miller-and-an-unbelievable-story-of-rape/>, accessed 22 August 2020.

Foer, F. (2018). 'Facebooks Finally Blinks', *The Atlantic*, <https://www.theatlantic. com/technology/archive/2018/01/facebook/550376/?utm_source=atlfb>, accessed 12 August 2020.

Forestal, J. (2020). 'Beyond Gatekeeping: Propaganda, Democracy, and the Organization of Digital Publics', *The Journal of Politics*, Ahead of Print.

Forman, R. T. T. and Godron, M. (1986). *Landscape ecology*. New York; Chichester: Wiley.

Foucault, M. (2012). *Discipline and Punish: The Birth of the Prison*. New York, New York: Knopf Doubleday Publishing Group.

Franck, G. (1998). *The Economy of Attention,* excerpts from *Oekonomie der Aufmerksamkeit*. Munich: Carl Hanser Verlag.

Franck, G. (2016). 'The Economy of Attention in the Age of Neoliberalism'. In Waddick, D. and Roda C. (eds.) *Communication in the Era of Attention Scarcity*. Heidelberg: Springer.

Franck, G. (2019). 'The Economy of Attention in the Age of Neoliberalism'. In Doyle, W., & Roda, C. (eds.), *Communication in the Era of Attention Scarcity*. London: Palgrave MacMillan.

Friedman, M. (2006). 'Free Markets and the End of History', *New Perspectives Quarterly*, 23, pp. 37–43.

Fuchs, C. (2010). 'Labor in Informational Capitalism and on the Internet', *The Information society*, 26, pp. 179–196.

Fürsich, E. (2009). 'In defense of textual analysis: Restoring a challenged method for journalism and media studies', *Journalism Studies*, 10 (2), pp. 238–252.

Galletta, A. (2013) *Mastering the Semi-Structured Interview and Beyond: From Research Design to Analysis and Publication*. New York: NYU Press.

Gandert, S. (2011). 'Gawker', *Columbia Journalism Review*, <https://www.cjr.org/news_startups_guide/2011/01/gawker.php>, accessed 4 July 2020.

Gardner, B. S. (2011). 'Responsive web design: Enriching the user Experience', *Sigma Journal: Inside the Digital Ecosystem*, 11(1), pp. 13–19.

Garrison, B. (1997). 'Online Newsgathering Trends 1994–96', in *Proceedings of the Annual Meeting of the Association for Education in Journalism and Mass Communication*, pp. 72–89

Genette, G. (1980). *Narrative discourse : an essay in method*. Ithaca, New York: Cornell University Press.

Gerlitz, C. and Helmond, A. (2013). 'The like economy: Social buttons and the data-intensive web', *New Media & Society*, 15 (8), pp. 1348–1365.

Gibbs Dominic, S. R. (2015). 'Apple takes on Facebook with revamped news app', *The Guardian*, <https://www.theguardian.com/technology/2015/jun/08/apple-wwdc-newsstand-flipboard-news-app>, accessed 20 June 2020.

Gibson, W. (2000). *Neuromancer*. New York: Ace Books.

Gibson, W. (2012). *Distrust that Particular Flavor*. London: Penguin Books Limited.

Gillespie, T. (2010). 'The politics of "platforms"', *New Media & Society*, 12 (3), pp. 347–364.

Giner, J. (2014). 'Why Scoop, The New York Times own CMS is so Important?', *Medium @Giner*, <https://medium.com/@GINER/why-scoop-the-new-york-times-own-cms-is-so-important-b9c3a4dceeb>, accessed 4 August 2020.

Golding, B. (2015) 'Tools we use 1: Publishing print newspapers online: CMSs', *Donald W. Reynolds Journalism Institute*, <https://www.rjionline.org/stories/tools-we-use-1-publishing-print-newspapers-online-cmss#methodology>, accessed 25 July 2020.

Google (2003). 'Q&A; with Krishna Bharat of Google News'. *The Internet Archive Wayback Machine: Google Friends Newsletter Page Two - July 2003*. <https://web.archive.org/web/20031008072016/http://www.google.com/googlefriends/morejul03.html>, accessed 8 June 2020.

Google (2011). 'Google Analytics Help Center', *Google*, <https://support.google.com/analytics?hl=en#topic=3544906>, accessed 12 August 2020.

Google (2015). 'AMP Project', Google. <http://apm.dev>, accessed 12 August 2020.

Google (2017). 'Google Mission Statement', *Google*, <https://about.google/>, accessed 2 September 2020.

Google (2020). 'Google Trends', *Google Trends*. <https://trends.google.com/trends/explore?date=2015-12-16%202020-08-31&q=unbelievable%20story%20of%20rape,%22Unbelievable%20netflix%22>, accessed 17 September 2020.

Gordy, C. (2015). 'How Almost Getting Scooped Brought Two Competing Reporters Together', *ProPublica*, <https://www.propublica.org/podcast/how-almost-getting-scooped-brought-two-competing-reporters-together>, accessed 28 August 2020.

Gottfrid, D. (2008). 'The New York Times Archives + Amazon Web Services = TimesMachine', *The New York Times*, <https://open.blogs.nytimes.com/2008/05/21/the-new-york-times-archives-amazon-web-services-timesmachine/>, accessed 20 September 2020.

Grabowicz, P., Hernandez, R. and Rue, J. (2014). 'Tutorial: Taxonomy Of Digital Story Packages', *UC Berkeley Graduate School of Journalism Advanced Media Institute*, <https://multimedia.journalism.berkeley.edu/tutorials/taxonomy-digital-story-packages/>, accessed 10 September 2020.

Gray, J. (2016) 'Datafication and democracy: Recalibrating digital information systems to address broader societal interests', *Juncture*, 23 (3), pp. 197–201

Greenberg, S. (2012). 'Slow journalism in the digital fast lane', in Keeble. R. L. and Tullouch J. (eds.) *Global Literary Journalism: Exploring the Journalistic Imagination*. New York: Peter Lang, pp. 381–393.

Greenfield, R. (2012). 'What the New York Times's "Snow Fall" Means to Online Journalism's Future', *The Atlantic*, <https://www.theatlantic.com/technology/archive/2012/12/new-york-times-snow-fall-feature/320253/>, accessed 13 September 2020.

Gripsrud, J. and Moe, H. (2010). *The digital public sphere : challenges for media policy.* Göteborg: Nordicom.

Grueskin, B., Seave, A. and Graves, L. (2011). *The Story So Far: What We Know About the Business of Digital Journalism'.* New York, New York: Columbia University Press

Hachten, W. A. and Scotton, J. F. (2016). *The world news prism : digital, social and interactive.* Chichester,; Malden, Massachusetts: Wiley-Blackwell.

Hansen, K. A. and Paul, N. (2015) 'Newspaper archives reveal major gaps in digital age', *Newspaper Research Journal*, 36 (3), pp. 290–298.

Hardt, M. and Negri, A. (2009). *Commonwealth.* Cambridge, Massachusetts: Harvard University Press.

Hedgecock, S. (2014). 'This Is the 161-Year-Old New York Times Article About 12 Years a Slave', *Gawker*, <http://gawker.com/this-is-the-161-year-old-new-york-times-article-about-1-1535199589>, accessed 9 August 2020.

Hermida, A. (2010). 'Twittering the news: The emergence of ambient journalism', *Journalism practice*, 4 (3), 297–308.

Hernandez, R. K. and Rue, J. (2016). *The principles of multimedia journalism : packaging digital news.* New York, New York: Routledge.

Hess, C. and Ostrom, E. (2003). 'Ideas, artifacts, and facilities: information as a common-pool resource', *Law and contemporary problems*, 66 (1/2), pp. 111–145.

Heyman, S. (2015). 'Google Books: A Complex and Controversial Experiment', *The New York Times*, <https://www.nytimes.com/2015/10/29/arts/international/google-books-a-complex-and-controversial-experiment.html?_r=0>, accessed 2 September 2020.

Higgins, P. (2018). 'Archiving the alternative press threatened by wealthy buyers', *Freedom of the Press Foundation*, <https://freedom.press/news/archiving-alternative-press-threatened-wealthy-buyers/> accessed 21 September 2020.

Hiippala, T. (2017). 'The Multimodality of Digital Longform Journalism', *Digital Journalism*, 5 (4), pp. 420–442.

Huang, J. S. and Wang, W.C. (2014) 'Application of the long tail economy to the online news market: Examining predictors of market performance', *Journal of Media Economics*, 27 (3), pp. 158–176.

Ingram, M. (2017). 'How the Washington Post Makes Money From Its Competitors', *Fortune*, <http://fortune.com/2017/03/13/washington-post-arc/>, accessed 24 September 2020.

Ingram, M. (2018). *Facebook changes could help the media kick its algorithm addiction.* Columbia Journalism Review. Available at: https://www.cjr.org/innovations/facebook-changes-news-feed.php.

International Communications Union (2019). 'Measuring digital development Facts and figures 2019', *International Communications Union*, <https://www.itu.int/en/ITU-D/Statistics/Documents/facts/FactsFigures2019.pdf>, accessed 12 September 2020.

Isbell, K. (2010). 'The Rise of the News Aggregator: Legal Implications and Best Practices', *Berkman Center Research Publication* 2010 (10).

Jackson, A. (2015). 'Ten Years of the UK Web Archive: What have we saved?', *British Library*, <http://britishlibrary.typepad.co.uk/webarchive/2015/09/ten-years-of-the-uk-web-archive-what-have-we-saved.html>, accessed 20 September 2020.

Jameson, F. (2002). *A Singular Modernity: Essay on the Ontology of the Present*. London; New York, New York: Verso.

Johnson, B. (2013). 'Snowfallen', *Bobbie Johnson Medium*, <https://medium.com/@bobbie/snowfallen-66b9060333ad#.07h3f7pac>, accessed 19 September 2020.

Jordan, T. (1999). *Cyberpower : the culture and politics of cyberspace and the Internet*. London: Routledge.

Jordan, T. (2015). *Information politics : liberation and exploitation in the digital society, Digital barricades: interventions in digital culture and politics*. London: Pluto Press.

Kachka, B. (2014). 'The Future of Reading According to Longform', *New York Magazine*, <http://nymag.com/daily/intelligencer/2014/09/future-of-reading-according-to-longform.html>, accessed 16 September 2020.

Kaplan, D. E. (2013). 'Global investigative journalism: Strategies for support', *Center for International Media Assistance*, < https://www.cima.ned.org/wp-content/uploads/2015/01/CIMA-Investigative-Journalism-Dave-Kaplan.pdf>, accessed 14 September 2020.

Kawamoto, K. (2003). 'Digital Journalism: Emerging Media and the Changing Horizons of Journalism'. In Kawamoto K. (ed.) *Digital Journalism: Emerging Media and the Changing Horizons of Journalism*, pp. 1–30. Lanham, Maryland: Rowman & Littlefield.

Kelly, K. (1994). *Out of control : the new biology of machines*. London: Fourth Estate.

Kim, T. (2015). 'Introduction to PageBuilder, Our Rendering Engine', *The Washington Post*, <https://web.archive.org/web/20151113150605/https://developer.washingtonpost.com/pb/blog/post/2015/11/12/introduction-to-pagebuilder-our-rendering-engine/>, accessed 3 September 2020.

Klinenberg, E. (2005). 'Convergence: News Production in a Digital Age', *The Annals of the American Academy of Political and Social Science*, 597 (1), pp. 48–64.

Koblin, J. (2019). 'Netflix's Top 10 Original Movies and TV Shows, According to Netflix', *The New York Times*, <https://www.nytimes.com/2019/10/17/business/media/netflix-top-ten-movies-tv-shows.html>, accessed 17 September 2020.

Kovach, B. and Rosenstiel, T. (2003). *The elements of journalism*. London: Atlantic Books.

Kramer, M. (2015). 'Does the rise of ephemeral content spell the death of archives?', *Poynter*, <https://www.poynter.org/news/does-rise-ephemeral-content-spell-death-archives>, accessed 16 June 2020.

Ku, R. S. R. (2001). 'The Creative Destruction of Copyright: Napster and the New Economics of Digital Technology', *The University of Chicago Law Review*, 69 (1), pp. 263–324.

Küng, L. (2015). *Innovators in Digital News*. London and New York: Reuters Institute for the Study of Journalism, IB Tauris & Co. Ltd.

Kwak, H. et al. (2010). 'What is Twitter, a social network or a news media?', *Proceedings of the 19th international conference on World Wide Web*, 591–600. Raleigh, North Carolina: ACM.

Lacy, S. (2012). 'Snow Fall: Finally an articulation for the digerati of what a big, expensive newsroom can do', *Pando*, <https://pando.com/2012/12/21/snow-fall-finally-an-articulation-for-the-digerati-of-what-a-big-expensive-newsroom-can-do/>, accessed 1 September 2020.

Lafrance, A. (2015). 'Raiders of the Lost Web', *The Atlantic*, <https://www.theatlantic.com/technology/archive/2015/10/raiders-of-the-lost-web/409210/>, accessed 4 September 2020.

Lanier, J. (2011) *You are not a gadget : a manifesto*. London: Penguin.

Lasorsa, D. L., Lewis, S. C. and Holton, A. E. (2012) 'Normalizing Twitter: Journalism practice in an emerging communication space', *Journalism studies*, 13 (1), pp. 19–36.

Latour, B. (2005). *Reassembling the social : an introduction to actor-network-theory*. Oxford: Oxford University Press.

Le Masurier, M. (2015). What is slow journalism?. *Journalism practice*, 9 (2), 138–152.

Le Masurier, M. (2016) 'Slow Journalism: An introduction to a new research paradigm', *Journalism Practice*, 10 (4), pp. 439–447.

Lepore, J. (2015) 'The Cobweb - Can the Internet be Archived?', *The New Yorker*, <https://www.newyorker.com/magazine/2015/01/26/cobweb>, accessed 15 September 2020.

Lessig, L. (2009). 'Against Transparency', *The New Republic*, <https://newrepublic.com/article/70097/against-transparency>, accessed 11 September 2020.

Lillie, B. (2013). 'Finding ways to let the story tell itself: Jacky Myint at TED2013', *TED Blog*, <https://blog.ted.com/finding-ways-to-let-the-story-tell-itself-jacky-myint-at-ted2013/>, accessed 26 September 2020.

Lipsky, D. (2010) *Although Of Course You End Up Becoming Yourself: A Road Trip with David Foster Wallace*. New York, New York: Crown / Archetype.

Liu, A. (2013). 'The Meaning of the Digital Humanities', *PMLA*, (128), pp. 409–423.

Longform.org (2010a). *Longform.org.* <www.longform.org>, accessed 1 September 2020.

Longform.org (2010b). 'Publications', *Longform.org,* <https://longform.org/archive/publications?from=1>, accessed 1 September 2020.

Longform.org (2017). 'Why We've Removed Longform from the App Store', *Longform Medium,* <https://medium.com/@longform/why-weve-removed-longform-from-the-app-store-823d599a34d4>, accessed 1 September 2020.

Lovink, G. (2011). *Networks without a cause : a critique of social media.* Cambridge: Polity.

MacCormack, A., Verganti, R. and Iansiti, M. (2001). 'Developing Products on "Internet Time": The Anatomy of a Flexible Development Process', *Management Science,* 47 (1), pp. 133–150.

Mackenzie, A. (1997). 'The Mortality of the Virtual: Real-time, Archive and Dead-time in Information Networks', *Convergence,* 3 (2), pp. 59–71.

MacKinnon, R. (2012). *Consent of the networked : the worldwide struggle for Internet freedom.* New York, New York: Basic Books.

Maguire, M. (2014). *Advanced Reporting: Essential Skills for 21st Century Journalism.* New York, New York: Taylor & Francis.

Maier, S. R. (2000). 'Digital diffusion in newsrooms: The uneven advance of computer-assisted reporting', *Newspaper Research Journal,* 21 (2), pp. 95–110.

Manoff, M. (2004). 'Theories of the Archive from Across the Disciplines', *portal: Libraries and the Academy,* 4 (1), pp. 9–25.

Marcuse, H. (2013). *One-Dimensional Man: Studies in the Ideology of Advanced Industrial Society.* London: Routledge.

Martínez, A. (2013). 'New York Times' Jill Abramson @ ISOJ: "To Snow Fall" now means to tell a great multimedia story', *Knight Center for Journalism in the Americas,* <https://web.archive.org/web/20130514160452/https://knightcenter.utexas.edu/blog/00-13616-new-york-times%E2%80%99-jill-abramson-isoj-snow-fall-now-means-tell-great-multimedia-story>, accessed 4 September 2020.

Maurantonio, N. (2014). 'Archiving the visual: the promises and pitfalls of digital newspapers', *Media History,* 20 (1), pp. 88–102.

Mayer-Schönberger, V. and Cukier, K. (2013). *Big data : a revolution that will transform how we live, work and think.* London: John Murray.

McCain, E. (2015). 'Plans to save born-digital news content examined', *Newspaper Research Journal,* 36 (3), pp. 337–347.

McChesney, R. W. (1996). 'The Internet and U. S. Communication Policy-Making in Historical and Critical Perspective: McChesney', *Journal of Computer-Mediated Communication,* 1 (4).

McKenzie, H. (2013). 'Sorry, "Snow Fall" isn't going to save the New York Times', *Pando*, <https://pando.com/2013/05/13/sorry-snow-fall-isnt-going-to-save-the-new-york-times/>, accessed 24 September 2020.

McLuhan, M. (1994). *Understanding media : the extensions of man*. Cambridge, Massachusetts: MIT Press.

McQuade, E. (2015). 'Aaron Lammer, The Art of Podcasting', *The Timbre*, <https://web.archive.org/web/20150906075223/http://thetimbre.com/aaron-lammer-art-podcasting-no-5/>, accessed 11 August 2020.

Miller, T. C. (2015a). 'A Brutal Crime, Often Terribly Investigated', *ProPublica*, <https://www.propublica.org/article/a-brutal-crime-often-terribly-investigated>, accessed 4 August 2020.

Miller, T. C. (2015b). 'Rape is Rape, Isn't It?', *ProPublica*, <https://www.propublica.org/article/flawed-rape-statistics-hamper-understanding-and-preventing-the-crime>, accessed 4 August 2020.

Miller, T. C. and Armstrong K. (2019). *Unbelievable: The shocking truth behind the hit Netflix series*. New York, New York: Random House.

Miller, T. C. and Armstrong, K. (2015). 'An Unbelievable Story of Rape', *ProPublica* and *The Marshall Project*, <https://www.propublica.org/article/false-rape-accusations-an-unbelievable-story>, accessed 4 August 2020.

Miller, T. C. and Armstrong, K. (2018). *A False Report: A True Story of Rape in America*. New York, New York: Crown.

Mitchell, R. (2015). *Web Scraping with Python: Collecting Data from the Modern Web*. Sebastopol, California: O'Reilly Media.

Moore, J. E. and Bonnet, J. L. (2015). 'Survey finds differences on preserving born-digital news', *Newspaper Research Journal*, 36 (3), pp. 348–362.

Morozov, E. (2013). *To save everything, click here : technology, solutionism and the urge to fix problems that don't exist*. London: Penguin.

Mullin, B. (2014) 'New app from Longform allows freelancers to cultivate audiences', *Poynter*, <https://www.poynter.org/news/new-app-longform-allows-freelancers-cultivate-audiences>, accessed 20 June 2020.

Murphy, J. E. (1974) 'The new journalism: a critical perspective', *Journalism and Communication Monographs*, 34.

Mussell, J. (2012). *The nineteenth-century press in the digital age*. Basingstoke: Palgrave Macmillan.

Nicholson, B. (2013). 'The Digital Turn: Exploring the methodological possibilities of digital newspaper archives', *Media History*, 19 (1), pp. 59–73.

Norris, P. and Inglehart, R. (2009). 'Max Weber and the Protestant Work Ethic'. In Peil J. and van Staveren I. (eds.), *Handbook of Economics and Ethics*. Cheltenham: Edward Elgar Publishing.

Olfati-Saber, R. (2006). 'Flocking for multi-agent dynamic systems: algorithms and theory', *IEEE Transactions on Automatic Control*, 51 (3), pp. 401–420.

Olson, J. E. (2003). *Data Quality: The Accuracy Dimension*. San Francisco, California: Morgan Kaufmann Publishers.

Olson, L. C., Finnegan, C. A. and Hope, D. S. (2008). *Visual Rhetoric: A Reader in Communication and American Culture*. Newbury Park, California: SAGE Publications.

O'Nolan, K. (1969). 'Homer, Virgil and oral tradition', *Béaloideas*, 1051, pp. 123–130.

Papacharissi, Z. (2002). 'The virtual sphere: The internet as a public sphere', *New Media & Society*, 4 (1), pp. 9–27.

Papacharissi, Z. (2009). 'The virtual geographies of social networks: a comparative analysis of Facebook, LinkedIn and ASmallWorld', *New Media & Society*, 11 (1–2), pp. 199–220

Pariser, E. (2012). *The filter bubble: what the Internet is hiding from you.* London: Penguin.

Patel, C., Patel, A. and Patel, D. (2012). 'Optical character recognition by open source OCR tool tesseract: A case study', *International Journal of Computer Applications*, 55(10), pp. 50–56.

Pavlik, J. V. (2001). *Journalism and New Media*. New York, New York: Columbia University Press.

Peabody Awards (2013). *Peabody Awards - Snow Fall: The Avalanche at Tunnel Creek* <http://www.peabodyawards.com/award-profile/snow-fall-the-avalanche-at-tunnel-creek>, accessed 20 September 2020.

de la Peña, N. et al. (2010). 'Immersive Journalism: Immersive Virtual Reality for the First-Person Experience of News', *Presence: Teleoperators and Virtual Environments*, 19 (4), pp. 291–301.

Pew Research Center (2016a). 'Long-Form Reading Shows Signs of Life in Our Mobile News World', *Pew Research Center*, <http://www.journalism.org/2016/05/05/long-form-reading-shows-signs-of-life-in-our-mobile-news-world/>, accessed 22 September 2020.

Pew Research Center (2016b). 'State of the News Media 2016', *Pew Research Center*, <https://assets.pewresearch.org/wp-content/uploads/sites/13/2016/06/30143308/state-of-the-news-media-report-2016-final.pdf>, accessed 22 September 2020.

Pew Research Center (2019). 'Trends and Facts on Newspapers, State of the News Media', *Pew Research Center*, <https://www.journalism.org/fact-sheet/newspapers>, accessed 22 September 2020.

Philo, G. (2007). 'Can Discourse Analysis successfully explain the content of media and journalistic practice?', *Journalism studies*, 8 (2), pp. 175–196.

Picard, R. G. (2011). 'Charitable Ownership and Trusts in News Organisations'. In Levy D. A. L. and Picard R. G. (eds.) *Is There a Better Structure for News Providers?*, 17–30. Oxford: Reuters Institute for the Study of Journalism.

Potter, A. (2015). 'Dodge that Memory Hole: Saving Digital News', *Library of Congress, The Signal Blog*, <https://blogs.loc.gov/thesignal/2015/06/dodge-that-memory-hole-saving-digital-news/>, accessed 18 September 2020.

Prensky, M. (2001). 'Digital Natives, Digital Immigrants Part 1'. *On the Horizon*, (9), pp. 1–6.

ProPublica (2009a). 'About Us', *ProPublica*, <https://www.propublica.org/about/>, accessed 20 September 2020.

ProPublica (2009b). 'Awards', *ProPublica*, <https://www.propublica.org/awards>, accessed 20 September 2020.

ProPublica (2009c). 'Series', *ProPublica*, <https://www.propublica.org/series/>, accessed 20 September 2020.

Pulitzer Prizes (2013). 'The 2013 Pulitzer Prize Winner in Feature Writing', *The Pulitzer Prizes*, <https://www.pulitzer.org/prize-winners-by-year/2013>, accessed 25 September 2020.

Pulitzer Prizes (2016). 'The 2016 Pulitzer Prize Winner in Explanatory Reporting', *The Pulitzer Prize*, <http://www.pulitzer.org/winners/t-christian-miller-propublica-and-ken-armstrong-marshall-project>, accessed 25 September 2020.

Pybus, J., Coté, M. and Blanke, T. (2015). 'Hacking the social life of Big Data', *Big Data & Society*, 2 (2).

Rawassizadeh P.; Price B. A., Petre, M. (2015) 'Wearables: Has the Age of Smartwatches Finally Arrived?', *Communications of the ACM*, 58, pp. 45–47.

Remington, A. (2016). 'How The Washington Post built a publishing platform accidentally on purpose', *Donald W. Reynolds Journalism Institute*, <https://www.rjionline.org/stories/how-the-washington-post-built-a-publishing-platform-accidentally-on-purpose>, accessed 27 September 2020.

Rey, P. J. (2012). 'Alienation, Exploitation, and Social Media', *American Behavioral Scientist*, 56 (4), 399–420.

Reynolds, C. W. (1987) 'Flocks, herds and schools: A distributed behavioral model', *Proceedings of the 14th annual conference on Computer graphics and interactive techniques*, pp. 25–34.

Robischon, N. (2016). 'How BuzzFeed's Jonah Peretti Is Building A 100-Year Media Company', *Fast Company*, <https://www.fastcompany.com/3056057/how-buzzfeeds-jonah-peretti-is-building-a-100-year-media-company>, accessed 24 September 2020.

Rockley, A., Cooper, C. and Abel, S. (2015). *Intelligent Content: A Primer*. Laguna Hills, California: XML Press.

Rogers, R. (2013). *Digital Methods*. Cambridge, Massachusetts: MIT Press.

Romenesko, J. (2012) 'More than 3.5 Million Page Views for New York Times' "Snow Fall" Feature', *JimRomenesko*, <https://web.archive.org/web/20121227205233/jimromenesko.com/2012/12/27/more-than-3-5-million-page-views-for-nyts-snow-fall/ >, accessed 23 September 2020.

Rowthorn R., Ramaswamy R. (1997). *Deindustrialization - Its Causes and Implications, Economic Issues*. International Monetary Fund, <https://www.imf.org/EXTERNAL/PUBS/FT/ISSUES10/INDEX.HTM>, accessed 24 September 2020.

Rue, J. (2013). 'The "Snow Fall" Effect and Dissecting the Multimedia Longform Narrative', *Multimedia Shooter*, <https://web.archive.org/web/20130422205021/http://multimediashooter.com/wp/2013/04/21/the-snow-fall-effect-and-dissecting-the-multimedia-longform-narrative/>, accessed 21 September 2020.

Sandhaus, E. (2013). 'Introducing the New TimesMachine', *The New York Times*, <https://open.blogs.nytimes.com/2013/07/11/introducing-the-new-timesmachine/>, accessed 24 September 2020.

Sanghvi, R. (2006). 'Facebook Gets a Facelift', *Facebook*, <https://www.facebook.com/notes/facebook/facebook-gets-a-facelift/2207967130>, accessed 19 September 2020.

Schumpeter, J. A. (2010). *Capitalism, socialism and democracy*. London: Routledge.

Shapiro, M., Hiatt, A. and Hoyt, M. (2015). *Tales From the Great Disruption - Insights and Lessons From Journalism's Technological Transformation*. Big Roundtable Books.

Silver, N. (2013). *The signal and the noise [electronic resource] : the art and science of prediction*. London: Penguin Books.

Smith, V., Connor, M. and Stanton, I. (2015). 'Going In-Depth: Finding Longform on the Web', *Proceedings of the 21th ACM SIGKDD International Conference on Knowledge Discovery and Data Mining*, pp. 2109–2118.

Smyrnaios, N., Marty, E. and Rebillard, F. (2010). 'Does the Long Tail apply to online news? A quantitative study of French-speaking news websites', *New Media & Society*, 12 (8), pp. 1244–1261.

Steensen, S. and Ahva, L. (2015) 'Theories of journalism in a digital age: An exploration and introduction', *Digital Journalism*, 9 (1), pp. 1–18.

Svingen, B. (2017) *Publishing with Apache Kafka at The New York Times*. Confluent. Available at: https://www.confluent.io/blog/publishing-apache-kafka-new-york-times/.

Tanzer, M. (2014). 'Exclusive: New York Times Internal Report Painted Dire Digital Picture', *BuzzFeed*, < https://www.buzzfeed.com/mylestanzer/exclusive-times-internal-report-painted-dire-digital-picture>, accessed 19 September 2020.

The Guardian (2017). 'Burst your Bubble' <https://www.theguardian.com/us-news/series/burst-your-bubble>, accessed 24 September 2020.

The Marshall Project (2014). 'About Us', <https://www.themarshallproject.org/about>, accessed 24 September 2020.

The Marshall Project (2019). 'An Unbelievable Story of Rape | The Record', *The Marshall Project*, <https://www.themarshallproject.org/records/2276-an-unbelievable-story-of-rape>, accessed 24 September 2020.

The New York Times (1999). 'Hemingway's Dispatches From Spain', *The New York Times*, <https://archive.nytimes.com/www.nytimes.com/books/99/07/04/specials/hemingway-dispatches.html>, accessed 22 September 2020.

The New York Times (2008). 'TimesMachine', *The New York Times*, <https://timesmachine.nytimes.com/browser>, accessed 22 September 2020.

The New York Times (2012) 'Q. and A.: The Avalanche at Tunnel Creek', *The New York Times*. <http://www.nytimes.com/2012/12/22/sports/q-a-the-avalanche-at-tunnel-creek.html?_r=0>, accessed 22 September 2020.

The New York Times (2014a). 'Innovation Report', *The New York Times*, <https://mashable.com/2014/05/16/full-new-york-times-innovation-report/?europe=true>, accessed 22 September 2020.

The New York Times (2014b). '@NYT Archives', *Twitter*, <https://twitter.com/NYTArchives>, accessed 22 September 2020.

The New York Times (2017). 'Journalism That Stands Apart, The Report of the 2020 Group'. *The New York Times*, <https://www.nytimes.com/projects/2020-report/index.html>, accessed 22 September 2020.

This American Life (2016). 'Anatomy of Doubt'. <https://www.thisamericanlife.org/581/anatomy-of-doubt>, accessed 17 September 2020.

Thompson, N. and Vogelstein, F. (2018). 'Inside the two Years that Shook Facebook - and the World', *WIRED*, <https://www.wired.com/story/inside-facebook-mark-zuckerberg-2-years-of-hell/>, accessed 24 September 2020.

Timm, T. (2015). 'The Most Concerning Element of Facebook's New Power', *Columbia Journalism Review*, <https://www.cjr.org/criticism/facebook_news_censorship.php>, accessed 24 September 2020.

Trachtenberg, J. A. (2020) 'Coming Soon to a Screen Near You: Shows Inspired by a Magazine Story', *The Wall Street Journal*, <https://search.proquest.com/docview/2353543564?accountid=11862>, accessed 17 September 2020.

Treanor, P. (1996). *Internet as hyper-liberalism*. <http://web.inter.nl.net/users/Paul.Treanor/net.hyperliberal.html>, accessed 24 September 2020.

Tulloch, C. and Ramon, X. (2017). 'Take Five: How Sports Illustrated and L'Équipe redefine the long-form sports journalism genre', *Digital Journalism*, 5 (5), pp. 652–672.

Turner, M., Budgen, D. and Brereton, P. (2003). 'Turning software into a service', *Computer*, 36 (10), pp. 38–44.

Twitter (2016). 'The Times was highly skeptical of the first Labor Day in 1887. <http://nyti.ms/2b2ps7w>'. <https://twitter.com/NYTArchives/status/772781402903445504>, accessed 17 September 2020.

Twitter (2017). 'Twitter New User FAQ', *Twitter*, <https://help.twitter.com/en/new-user-faq> accessed 23 September 2020.

UKOM (2020). 'Digital Market Overview'. *UKOM*, <https://ukom.uk.net/digital-market-overview.php>, accessed 20 September 2020.

Ubl, M. (2018). 'Standardizing lessons learned from AMP', <https://blog.amp.dev/2018/03/08/standardizing-lessons-learned-from-amp/>, accessed 24 September 2020.

Usher, N. (2016). *Interactive journalism: Hackers, data, and code*. Champaign, Illinois: University of Illinois Press.

Vamvacas, C. J. (2009). *The founders of Western thought : the Presocratics*. Dordrecht: Springer Netherlands.

Van Valkenburg, S. and Sandhaus, E. (2016). 'The Future of the Past: Modernizing the New York Times Archive', *The New York Times*, <https://open.blogs.nytimes.com/2016/07/26/the-future-of-the-past-modernizing-the-new-york-times-archive/>, accessed 23 September 2020.

Vehkoo, J. (2010). *What is Quality Journalism and how can it be saved*. Oxford: Reuters Institute for the Study of Journalism.

Venturini, T., Bounegru, L. Gray, J., Rogers, R. (2018). 'A reality check(list) for digital methods', *New Media and Society*, 20 (11), pp. 4195–4217.

Verborgh, R. and De Wilde, M. (2013) *Using OpenRefine*. Birmingham: Packt Publishing.

Vigneaux, S. (1996). 'The integration of a newsroom computer system with a server-centred news production system', *International Broadcasting Convention (Conf. Publ. No. 428)*, pp. 512–518.

Vnenchak, L. (2014). 'Scoop: A Glimpse Into the NYTimes CMS', *The New York Times*, <https://open.blogs.nytimes.com/2014/06/17/scoop-a-glimpse-into-the-nytimes-cms>, accessed 22 September 2020.

Wang, S. (2018). 'Here's how Arc's cautious quest to become the go-to publishing system for news organizations is going', *Nieman Lab*, <https://www.niemanlab.org/2018/02/heres-how-arcs-cautious-quest-to-become-the-go-to-publishing-system-for-news-organizations-is-going/>, accessed 24 September 2020.

Webby Awards (2013). 'Webby Awards - Online Film & Video - Best Use of Interactive Video', *The Webby Awards*, <http://webbyawards.com/winners/2013/online-film-video/performance-craft/best-use-of-interactive-video/snow-fall-the-avalanche-at-tunnel-creek/>, accessed 24 September 2020.

Weber, M., Parsons, T. and Giddens, A. (2001). *The Protestant ethic and the spirit of capitalism*. London; New York: Routledge.

Wolfe, T. (1973). *The New Journalism*, New York, New York: Harper & Row.

Wrobel, Tim. (2015). 'Nest's Tony Fadell Now in Charge of Google Glass, Separates Into Independent Division (Updated)', *DroidLife*, <https://www.droid-life.com/2015/01/15/nests-tony-fadell-now-in-charge-of-google-glass-separates-into-independent-division/>, accessed 23 September 2020.

Yzaguirre, A., Smit, M. and Warren, R. (2016). 'Newspaper archives+ text mining= rich sources of historical geo-spatial data', *IOP Conference Series: Earth and Environmental Science*, 34 (1).

Zuckerberg, M. (2018a). 'One of our big focus areas for 2018 is making sure the time we all spend on Facebook is time well spent', *Facebook*. <https://www.facebook.com/zuck/posts/10104413015393571>, accessed 24 September 2020.

Zuckerberg, M. (2018b). 'Continuing our focus for 2018 to make sure the time we all spend on Facebook is time well spent', *Facebook*, <https://www.facebook.com/zuck/posts/10104445245963251>, accessed 24 September 2020.

Zuckerberg, M. (2018c). 'Our next update on our 2018 focus to make sure Facebook isn't just fun but also good for your well-being and for society', *Facebook*, <https://www.facebook.com/zuck/posts/10104493997365051>, accessed 24 September 2020.

Appendices

Appendix A

Interview with Joe Sexton, senior editor at *ProPublica*

Joe Sexton is senior editor at *ProPublica*. Before joining *ProPublica* and working on 'An Unbelievable Story of Rape', which we analysed in Chapter 4, he worked for twenty-five years at *The New York Times*. During his time at *The New York Times* his staff won two Pulitzer prizes and as sports editor, he was directly involved in the creation and editing of *The New York Times* story 'Snow Fall', which we analysed in depth in Chapter 3. The following interview was performed via email, and what follows is the complete transcript.

Q: 'An Unbelievable Story of Rape' was not developed as a conventional partnership story for *ProPublica*, as narrated on the outlet's website by Engelberg (2015). Was the decision to collaborate after finding out that *The Marshall Project* was working on the same story influenced by the fact that you are both non-profit news outlets?

R: I think the answer is yes. Not because non-profits are more virtuous. They just have developed fewer habits in their young lives. If I'd have been at *The New York Times*, my reflexive idea would have been to race the competitor to publish or bail entirely on the story. [And] the reasons for that, if they sound ignoble, are pretty reasonable in the end. Newspapers are businesses. Competitive business, fighting for readers and economic models and survival. Of course, non-profits compete for things – attention, awards, funding, brand extension. But the imperatives aren't as hard and fast. It also helped that I'd worked with Bill Keller for twenty-five years. There was trust, affinity, a shared sense of adventure, and a reasonably pure determination to do right by our subjects.

Q: T. Christian Miller and Ken Armstrong produced a first draft of the story which was then submitted to editing. Was editing likewise a collaborative effort between *ProPublica* and *The Marshall Project*?

R: It was a full collaboration. We agreed on an outline for the story before anyone started writing. We talked as a group after each draft. We jointly solicited outside feedback when we were close and uncertain about some things.

Q: In a podcast hosted on *ProPublica* by Cynthia Gordy (2015), you describe, along with Bill Keller from *The Marshall Project*, how both writers and editors were male and was the story was shared with women in the editing process. How was the editing process articulated in this case?

R: Not articulated at all. Some women were naturally part of the process – Robin Fields, our managing editor; Kirsten Danis, the mp's ME; Amanda Zamora, our audience czar; Amy Zebra, the copy editor. But we widened the circle of women, gave them the story cold and invited feedback. Nothing more pre-arranged or articulated.

Q: You are credited in an interview with both writers by Michael Fitzgerald (2016), as the one who came up with the structure of the story. How did you come up with the structure?

R: Both writers are overly generous. No structure can be conceived or executed without a rich supply of foundational reporting and individual artistry. But it seems like the requirement that new approaches be considered at every stage of reporting and writing has never been more urgent or necessary. There were two great, propulsive narratives. The idea to braid them was hardly rocket science. For me, the daring part was to save the brutal rape scene for the end. And to begin with a scene of muted modesty and mystery. Seems like it worked.

Q: An 'Unbelievable Story of Rape' is a 12,000-word, ten-chapter read. Did you feel it was the right length regardless of the medium or did publishing it on the Web influence structure and editing as opposed to what would happen in a traditional medium?

R: Story length discussions I no longer have patience for. I wearied of them at *The New York Times*. And I weary of them since I left. The story justifies its length, in print or online. People will read stuff that engages them, if they have to turn the page or swipe right. Newspapers have long kidded themselves they make a meaningful dent with readers if they cut stories from 1,200 words to 700. Or 5,000 words to 2,500. Few readers finish stories of any length. So why not dream big.

Q: Who came up with the idea of having an illustrator work at the story?

R: Gabe Dance and David Sleight and Lisa Iaboni all shared the impulse. For all its gripping narrative, it was a historical piece on a brutal and nuanced topic, and not, actually, all that photographically vital. Illustrations allow readers to use their imaginations more, I think. And they can, oddly, make the story more human, more universal.

Q: *ProPublica* long-form journalism is developed around 'Series' on your website. For 'An Unbelievable Story of Rape' the web page features multiple articles from different writers. What is the idea behind developing an environment of different articles?

R: The subject matters, not the names on the bylines. Our reporting on rape happened accidentally, organically, with a powerful kind of momentum. Offering readers as much of it as possible seems the obvious and right thing.

Q: How many readers has the story had on *ProPublica*? What is the average reading time?

R: It's closing in on a million page views. If you count the mp's traffic, it's the most trafficked story in *ProPublica*'s history. And engagement if off the charts.

Appendix B

Interview with Andy Rossback, former editorial designer at *The Marshall Project*

Andy Rossback is the former editorial designer at *The Marshall Project* and now works at *The New York Times*. The following interview was performed via email and what follows is the complete transcript.

Q: An 'Unbelievable Story of Rape' was published in partnership with *ProPublica*. The story has two layouts, one in each website. Did you develop yours independently?

R: We worked with *ProPublica* from the early stages of design to create something that could work on either site and that we agreed upon conceptually. There are slight variations in the two layouts but mainly this reflects the different styles of each site. Our version maintains the same typographic palette we use across our site but uses it in a markedly different way, as do many of our major projects. It introduces new colours, as well, and removes the standard navigation, allowing us to start the project with an essentially blank slate.

Q: An 'Unbelievable Story of Rape' is 12,000 words long. At *The Marshall Project*, you often vary in font style and size within the same story. To what end is that done?

R: There are various levels of typographic hierarchy within this piece. The headline, byline, and deck [set in italics] are meant to read as a group. Then you introduce to a system, a simple 'x' marking a section break, a timestamp, a location and then an enlarged lead paragraph. This configuration is meant to signal to the reader that they are entering a new chapter in the story. The design backs up this signal by shifting storylines taking place in Colorado to the right side of the page and storylines taking place in Washington to the right. The introduction and epilogue of the story are centred.

For photo captions, I wanted the images to feel more like evidence so I gave each a 'title' which is set in all capital letters above the caption. The idea is that these little kickers are clever, like the name of a piece of art or evidence. Under the image of the two detectives together: 'A partnership forms.'

There's also some recirculation devices, linking users to other items from the package.

Finally, there's an audio player containing the victims' recount of her rape toward the end of the piece which is labelled directly with a note saying that she wanted her story to be heard. It was important to me that this type was not played up or meant to feel like it paid any disrespect to her story or her request that people hear it.

Q: Being the story divided in ten chapters did you think about splitting it up into different pages?

R: The length of the piece did raise some important challenges for me as a designer. Slicing into a paginated layout was not one of them for a couple of reasons: Asking the user to click the next button to move to the next chapter would introduce nine more mouse clicks into the project. A general principle of my job is to reduce the friction between the user and the content, removing pain points, like the need to click, which would likely get annoying after a chapter or two. It's also of benefit to users who arrive from search engines. They are invited to read the story from the start instead of becoming confused when they have arrived on a specific chapter in the middle of the story, from their search query.

Q: Whose decision was it to use illustrations for 'An Unbelievable Story of Rape'? They are the same, as images are the same for both *The Marshall Project* and Republican versions, yet the layout and order differs. Did you choose each element in collaboration with *ProPublica* while designing the story?

R: Former *The Marshall Project* art director Lisa Iaboni worked with an illustrator from early on, because we knew since the main character is anonymous source – it would be difficult to find a photograph to lead the piece. We worked together with the *ProPublica* team to select the illustrator, photographer for secondary images and design the piece and ultimately used the same assets for final publication, as well.

Some of the assets moved around at the discretion of each publication. We've done dozens of partnerships at *The Marshall Project*. Sometimes partners request the exact same layout, sometimes there is editorial discretion because different publications have different voices and that affects how the art is played.

Q: As a designer and developer what does your work involve? How many projects do you work on at the same time? How many people are involved in working on a feature story like this at *The Marshall Project*?

R: For this particular project, my role was to design and build the story. That means to work with editors and reporters to understand what the story is about, use that information to inform an artistic concept of the story. Those then inform the creation of static designs. I use Adobe Illustrator to do this. In this case, I created several based on several different concepts.

I then worked with my editors at *The Marshall Project*, mainly a wonderful editor and mentor of mine named Gabriel Dance, as well as editors at *ProPublica*, including David Sleight, to 'edit' the design. Around this same time, I was working with Iaboni, who was beginning to commission the illustrations so we worked together to see that her concept and my concept ultimately were in-sync.

Once we were in agreement about a concept, I went to work to translate the static mock-up of the project into code [HTML, CSS, JS] stored in a Git repository shared between the two organisations. Along the way, sharing previews of my work with the editors who suggested improvements. Toward the end of the project, *ProPublica* reskinned the design to match the typographic, colour and spatial sensibilities of their site.

Generally, I am working on between one and three of these types of projects at any given time. Although, our team (six people) works on many more as a group, often all throwing in together on a given project as it gets closer to publication.

Index

Printed by
CPI books GmbH, Leck